AF593958

THE DRINKERS' GUIDE TO WALKING

THE SOUTH-WEST

PROTEUS

PROTEUS BOOKS in an imprint of
The Proteus Publishing Group

United States
PROTEUS PUBLISHING CO., INC.
733 Third Avenue
New York, N.Y. 10017
distributed by:
THE SCRIBNER BOOK COMPANIES, INC.
597, Fifth Avenue
New York, N.Y. 10017

United Kingdom
PROTEUS (PUBLISHING) LIMITED
Bremar House,
Sale Place,
London, W2 1PT.

ISBN 0 906071 75 5 (p/b)
0 906071 76 3 (h/b)

First published in UK 1981

Printed and bound in Great Britain by
The Anchor Press Ltd., Tiptree, Essex.

Acknowledgements

Researched, walked, photographed, compiled and written by
Nigel Matheson and Peter Gerard-Pearse

Maps, illustrations, layout and paste-up
Bill Goodson

Cartoons
Peta Maughan

Travel research
Martin Hitchcock

Editor
Nicola Hodge

Introduction

THE DRINKERS' GUIDE TO WALKING: SOUTH-WEST is a complementary edition to our nationwide book, THE DRINKERS' GUIDE TO WALKING, and is a lively and essential travelling companion for anyone in the South-West of England. We shall shortly be bringing out some more regional guides and an updated edition of the first book.

Once again we hope that we have taken into account a wide range of interests as this is not a book purely for the hardened drinker nor the hardy hiker – it's crammed with anecdotes, ghostly tales and informative snippets of natural history.

It is important to read through the talk-round before starting out, by this I don't mean to suggest that you won't be in a fit state to do so 'en route', but that it's sensible to get an idea of the mileage involved, the public transport available and the overall difficulty of the walk. Although we have started nearly all the talk-rounds at the pubs, the walks are all circular and therefore it is possible to begin at any point and even to treat the pub as a well-deserved reward after a hard day's foot-slog. The maps should be seen as a supplement to the detailed talk-round, which is designed to direct you, right down to the last hedge.

Our researchers have asked me to stress the advisability of warm and protective clothing, namely wellingtons and kagoules, along with a few points of protocol on arriving at the pub; please don't eat your own sandwiches in the pub, and take off your muddy boots outside. As we stated in the first edition, we have tried, wherever possible, to make these walks suitable for young children and/or grannies and, as a result, the average walk in this book is between three and four miles. As far as the pubs are concerned, children and dogs are probably less trouble in the summer months, as most of our featured pubs have gardens.

As the words in this guide are not timeless, the countryside and its landmarks, both man-made and natural, being subject to change, we would like to ask for a certain amount of common sense and cooperation from our readers. Don't write and tell us if Mrs Brown of Rose Cottage has painted her door yellow, but do write and tell us if you find that footpaths have been closed or if cliff edges have crumbled into the sea.

Finally I'd like to draw your attention to The Drinkers' Guide Country Code.

1. Guard against all risk of fire, especially in, or near, woodland.
2. Fasten all gates that you open securely and, if you climb a gate, climb at the hinged end, not the latched.

3. Keep dogs under control. Farmers have been known to shoot even friendly ones.
4. Keep to the path when crossing farmland.
5. Respect other people's property and privacy.
6. Litter is matter in the wrong place; keep yours with you.
7. Avoid damaging hedges, fences and walls.
8. Don't contaminate streams, rivers, ponds or lakes.
9. Protect wildlife, plants and trees.
10. Please walk and drive with special care on narrow country roads. *Never* drink and drive.

Nicola Hodge
January 1981

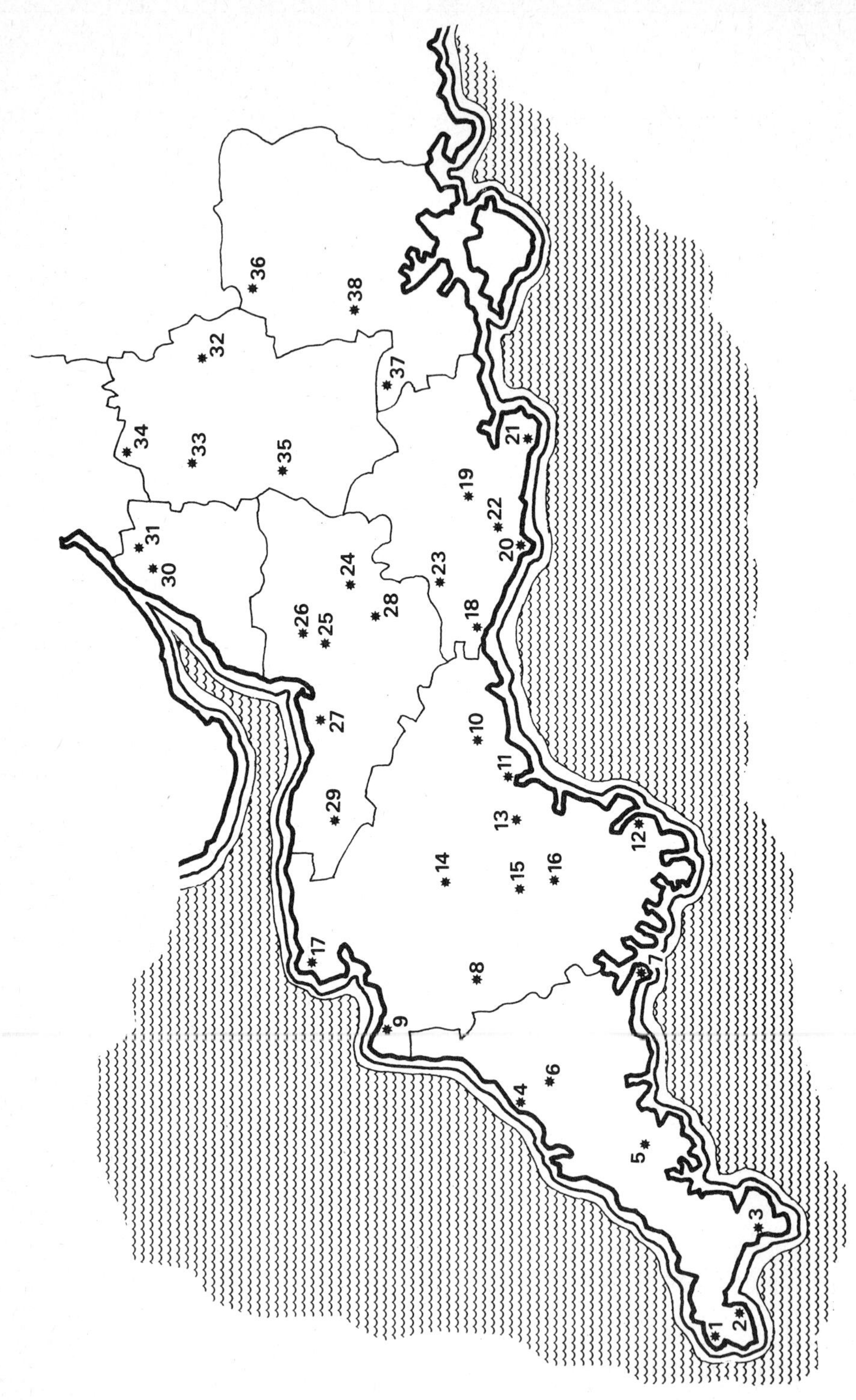

The Index to the Walks

Titles in the series

The 'National' Drinkers Guide to Walking
(80 walks) £6.50 (h/b)

The 'National' Drinkers Guide to Walking
(80 walks) £3.95 (p/b)

London and The South-East
(34 new walks) £3.50

The South-West
(38 new walks) £3.50

Key for the Maps

THE ROUTE:

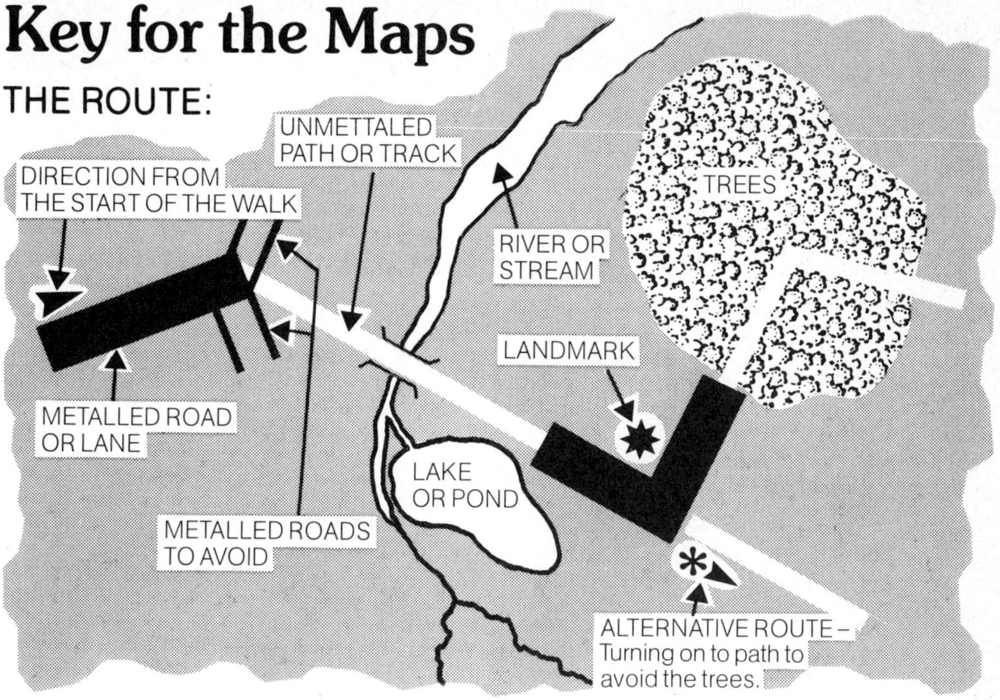

UNMETTALED PATH OR TRACK

DIRECTION FROM THE START OF THE WALK

TREES

RIVER OR STREAM

LANDMARK

METALLED ROAD OR LANE

LAKE OR POND

METALLED ROADS TO AVOID

ALTERNATIVE ROUTE – Turning on to path to avoid the trees.

THE SYMBOLS:

	INN, PUBLIC HOUSE		SCENERY
	FARM		HOSPITAL
	HOTEL, HOUSE, COTTAGE, ETC.		CASTLE, FORT
	LARGE HOUSE, MANSION	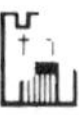	RUINS OF CASTLE
	WATERMILL		RUINS OF CHURCH
	CHURCH, ABBEY, ETC.	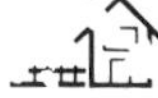	RUINS OF FARM

 — — — — — — — — RAILWAY STILL USED

—·—·—·—·—·—·—·— DISUSED RAILWAY

MAPS NOT IN PROPORTION – BUT COMPASS DIRECTION CORRECT.

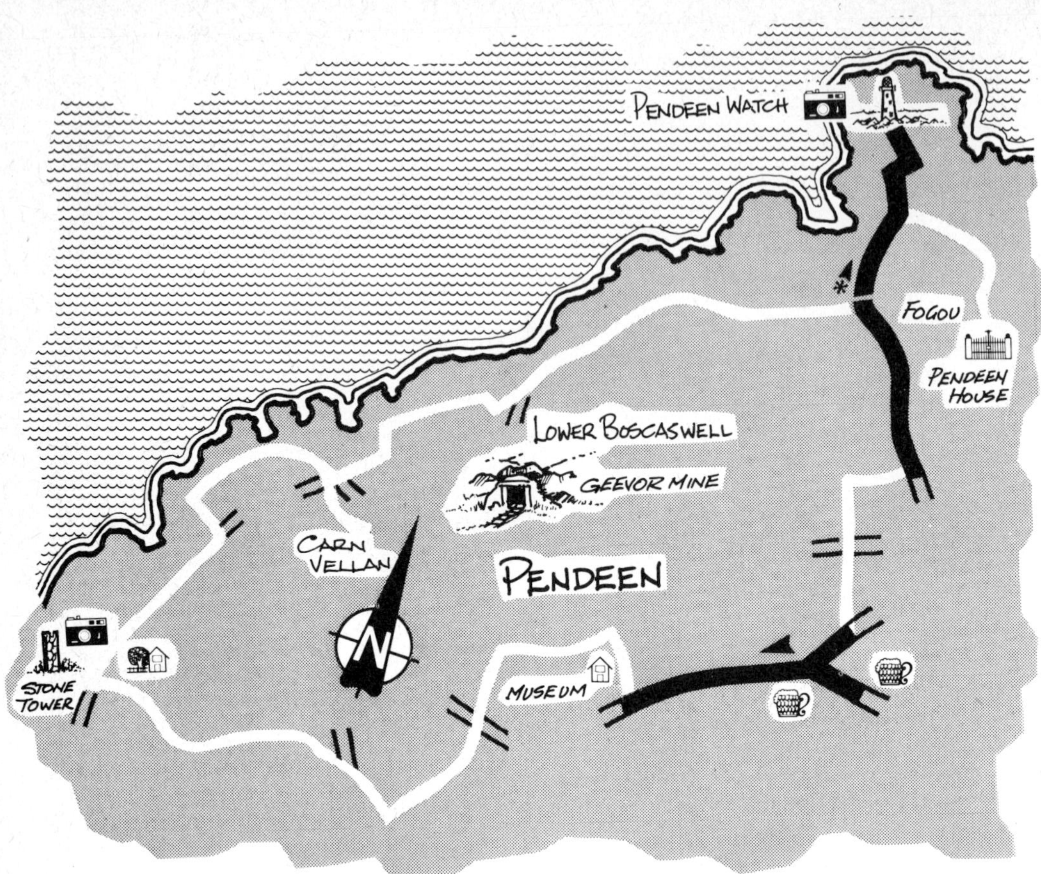

1 Pendeen

APPROXIMATELY 5½ Miles

The District

Dramatic. Stunning. Spectacular. Yet, it is a gaunt landscape to the north of Cape Cornwall, England's only cape. This is an area which has been hollowed out by the tin and copper workings and which was undermined by the mines' near collapse at the end of the 19th century. Geevor, which the walk takes you past, is the last active mine in West Penwith, it was visited by the Queen and Prince Philip in 1980 and the walls were white-washed for the occasion!

Penwith is the most westerly block of land in Britain and has stood its ground unflinching against the full power of the Atlantic breakers for eons. Here in the Pendeen district, the battle with water has been constant – the cliffs against the sea and the miners against leaks which have caused continual flooding of the mines.

The ground around here has been worked since prehistoric times for its tin and, since the 18th century, for copper. By 1800 Cornwall was the world's greatest supplier of copper but discoveries of the ore elsewhere precipitated a slump.

On the subject of ups and downs, the miners led a relentlessly harsh life which necessitated travelling half a mile down (and later up) vertical ladders from the surface to the pit face. They were paid for productivity but shareholders were the only real winners from this deal which resulted in dividends of £1,000 on a £2 10s share (in one local mine at the height of the boom) and an average life expectancy for miners of 27. Over this cruelly short span of time they were nourished at work by the original Cornish pasties, spicy at one end and sweet at the other, a pocket-sized meal with a seam you could grip in filthy hands. The mines themselves go out under the sea, as far as half a mile in some cases, and miners used to hear the pebbles on the sea bed above their heads, rolling and tumbling with the ocean swell.

How to Get There

By road take the A30 west out of Penzance, then right onto the A3071 and right again onto the B3318. Pendeen is at the intersection of the B3318 and the B3306 (approx $7\frac{1}{2}$ miles from Penzance). Alternatively, take the B3306 from St Ives, Pendeen is approx 10 miles away. *By rail* there is a regular 125 service to Penzance and St Ives. *By bus* on weekdays the 510 bus runs between Penzance and St Ives (limited service on Sundays). The 515, an open top bus, operates in the summer.

This cliffside walk takes you along a desolate and beautiful stretch of coastline to Pendeen Point Lighthouse. Before it was built in 1900, wrecks regularly created jagged and forlorn new outcrops along the jagged and forlorn rocks by the sea.

The Pendeen Walk

In bad weather this exhilarating and inspiring walk can be a rough and strenuous battle against the elements. Though the going is never very steep, the wind and the sea air ensure that you finish healthily weary and in the mood for a reviving pint. The tracks and paths can be muddy in all but the finest conditions, so gumboots are advisable as well as warm and waterproof clothing.

The Radjel, Pendeen

Pendeen wouldn't be Pendeen without a pub like The Radjel and people like Mr Warren, the proprietor of this traditional local. In Cornish, 'Radjel' means home of the fox and this pub has its own hunt meet which takes place once a year on Mr Warren's birthday. How many people can claim to have their birthday celebrated in this way?

Born in the house itself, Mr Warren is 80 years old and has held the license for 60 years (it's been in the family for 100) – it's thought that this is the record for an English pub. He is ably assisted behind the curved bar by Mrs Clara Strick, no novice she, with 38 years of service behind her.

The pub has a delightful old fashioned interior with scrubbed tables and fine old plain wooden panelling. The atmosphere is peaceful, friendly and quiet and this must be respected. There is also a room for children.

The beers are all gravity fed St Austells and quite excellent. Snacks are limited to peanuts and crisps.

The North Inn, Pendeen is our starting point. Leaving it, turn right along the pavement and walk several hundred yards to a large turning on the right leading to Geevor Mine and its museum where you'll learn something of the processes of tin mining. Of particular interest are the photographs; they show how hard mining life really was.

Continue past the museum, the weighbridge nearby and down the concrete road. Just after the first 'Geevor Mine Plant' sign, turn left through a gate and walk 20 yards to the visible gap in the wall which is half right. Cross the field bearing left to the sunken (and muddy!) gateway.

Once through, walk straight across the field to the far corner in the direction of the old ruined engine house and chimney. Collectively they pumped water out of, pumped air into and drove the machinery of the tin and copper mines. Climb over the stone wall, turn left along the grassy track and head towards the farm. Pass through a metal gate and, at the blue storage tank, swing left onto a muddy stone track. Those with delicate nostrils would do well to hold their breath as the air here is fresh, yet pungent. Leaving the farm behind to the left, walk along the metalled lane. At a house called Trevaylar, fork left.

Follow the lane to a junction and take the track practically opposite to the right of the stern granite house. Walk along the track which gets muddier and puddlier as you go. If you're a bit peckish and it's the right time of the year, go on, be a devil and have a blackberry or twenty.

Follow the winding track and watch out for the line of ventilation chimneys to your left. At a fork, turn left towards the cluster of old buildings. Keep to the track through the buildings past the stable on your left and aim for the metal gate slightly to the left. On a miserable autumn day, your researcher met a bedraggled pony sheltering in the lea of a stone wall here. If he's still there, blow up his nostrils and he will be an instant friend.

Hug the wall to your left and follow through the gap into the next field. In this second field walk diagonally right, to and through the gap in the wall. Turn left just after this and climb down from the wall – easy does it here.

Cross to the far right-hand corner of this field and then to the far right-hand corner of the next one, aiming roughly for the clifftop farmhouse. Take the path leftish between two stone walls and out on to the track near the cliffs and the farmhouse.

You can detour here to the stone tower for your first breathtaking close-up of the Atlantic spume and surf. Watch out for the sea thrift here and the derelict tin workings; watch out, too, for vertigo, it's a long way down.

From your original direction, turn right along the track and past the clifftop farmhouse and a triangulation point on your left. Continue, ignoring the fork to the right, and follow the dip in the track, down and up, then left along the grassy track towards the sea.

At the outcrop of rock, bear right and follow the coast as the path descends. Just before the fenced mineshaft, where you must be very careful with dogs and children, there's a large moss ball two feet in diameter on a rock to your right . . . which just goes to show that, conversely, a static stone does gather moss.

From now on when you see what seems like a giant rabbit-hole, under no circumstances go chasing white rabbits, for these are almost certainly disused mineshafts and highly dangerous. Your researcher lost his hat in a gust of wind and, believe it or not it flew irretrievably down a hole, leaving him colder and wiser.

Below, you can see a lower path and as you round the corner Pendeen Watch Lighthouse comes into view. Press on to the old Levant mine (a striking number 9 is painted on the wall). Due to a land slide you must follow the fence steeply upwards, then round, taking special care until you get back on to the metalled track. Where this track hairpins, stride straight on round following the coast, past a pile of earth and debris. You may spy hunting kestrels near the cliff edge.

Go on past two chimneys on your right and one on the left, then down through the derelict buildings below Geevor mine, which is still in operation. Take care as you proceed – ankles can be twisted on this loose masonry. As you make for the little concrete bridge over the vivid clay coloured stream, pause, turn back and survey the neo-Roman ruins. The red stream is not coloured by clay but by iron oxide waste from the bowels of Geevor. Interesting to note that it tints the sea for miles around and I was astonished to discover that eight metals come out of the mine, as well as fifty separate minerals.

Keep going along the path by the coast and, before you turn a corner, glance back at the ruins and the green (copper) streaked rock below. Where the path forks, go right and up a steepish hill. Pass the wooden bench and over the top of the rise to the stile. Follow the gentle path down and, at the wall, turn half left and continue down into the gully. Cross another stile. At the junction of paths as you come out of the gully, turn right up the hill – this path exits onto a road by the old and white coastguard cottages.

If you've still got the puff and the interest, it's well worth turning left and walking down to visit the lighthouse, whose beam is visible for 20 miles – but only at night. At the lighthouse there are steps down to the rocks and if you're still feeling Olympian after this, you can turn left along the drive with a cattle grid to Pendeen House, which has a 'fougou' in the back garden. This is a prehistoric burial chamber and, on request, at the house, you are sometimes allowed to see it. In dismal weather, this house could come straight out of *Wuthering Heights*.

Retrace your steps to and past the coastguards' cottages. Walk along the road to just beyond a white house on your left, turn right through a hitherto concealed gate. Go to the nearest telegraph pole and cross the stream. Cross the field between the grassy mounds and then climb through the gap in the wall to the right of a long metal trough. Walk along the path through the gorse and bracken roughly following the line of the telegraph poles. Turn left when you meet a muddy track and follow through the gate to the road. Take the gate opposite and cross the field leaving the mine and Lower Boscawell to the right. Go through the right-hand gap in the wall and turn left immediately. Follow the path towards Pendeen and just before you get to the houses bear left to bound over the wall after 30 yards and right along the road back to civilisation. At the main road drag your weary limbs left and 40 yards to **The Radjel** and refreshment.

The North Inn, Pendeen

Situated off the road in its own little square, this attractive stone-walled pub is more than 200 years old. It has one spacious bar which, in bygone days, was six little rooms and so although there is only one fire there are many fireplaces. The bearded publican, Mr Richard Quick, has a collection of old watercolours (by a famous St Ives painter Arthur White) on the walls. In the BBC series *The Golden Soak,* Ray Barrett downed his last whisky at the bar here before driving his car off the quay à la John Stonehouse and was a regular customer during filming. He would, however, have had trouble talking to 'stone-deaf Joe' a 72 year old local who is notorious for passing off the effects of drinking binges as indigestion.

In warm weather, children (and everyone else) are welcome to use the square and the two fields outside – indeed there are free donkey rides. Ladies, however, are warned against the vicissitudes of the geese which guard the toilets.

There are two draught and two keg beers available – all from St Austells and there's the possibility of (gravity drawn) Hicks Special Draught soon. In winter, pasties are the only items on the menu but, in summer, a wide range of snacks of the sausage and chips variety are available.

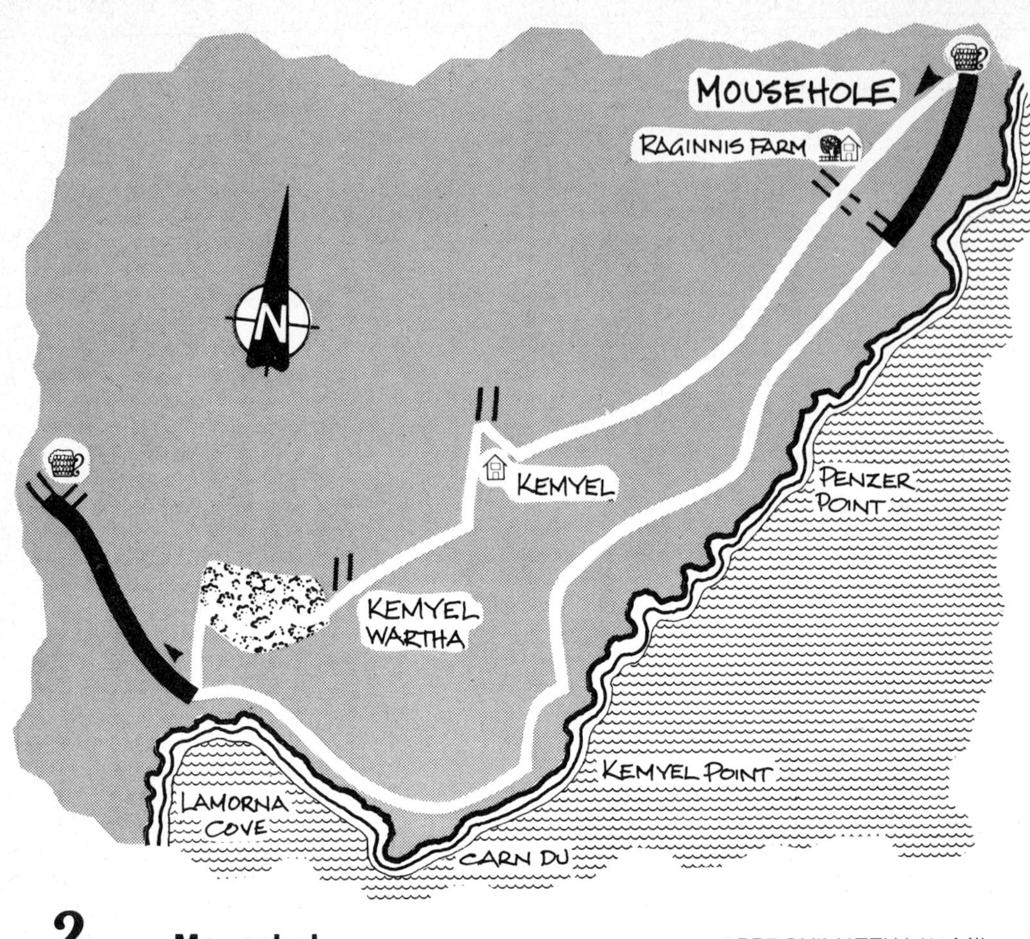

2 Mousehole

APPROXIMATELY 4¾ Miles

The District

Tom Bowcock's Eve: 23rd December
A merry place, you may believe
Was Mouzel 'pon Tom Bawcock's Eve.
To be there then who wudn' wish
To sup o' sibm soorts o' fesh!
When morgy brath had cleared the path,
Comed lances for a fry,
And then us had a bit o' scad,
An starry gazy pie.

The intriguingly named yet unphonetic village of Mousehole (pronounced Mowzel) has a recorded history dating as far back as the Phoenicians who came here to barter for Cornish tin. This history includes the devastating raid by Spaniards in 1595, in revenge for the failure of the Armada which left only one house standing, that of Jenkin Keigwin, who unfortunately bore the full brunt of a flying cannonball, thereby achieving immortality on the spot. His son, John Keigwin, became one of the famous scholars of the old Cornish language and it is heartening to see this once almost extinct tongue being revived today.

Mousehole's most famous legend relates to Tom Bowcock, a man who, at a time of near starvation in the village, set out to sea into the teeth of a gale and returned several days later with his boat full of fish, just two days before Christmas. The deed is commemorated in the song above and if you go to The Ship Inn on the 23rd December you could strike lucky and be handed a slice of the deliciously named 'Starry Gazy' pie (a fish pie made of the seven different kinds of fish brought back by brave Mr Bowcock).

The village itself is a labyrinth of steep and narrow alleyways which snuggle together for comfort above the harbour, with its hanging fishing nets and gently bobbing boats. Mousehole has a strong history of Methodism and this may be responsible for the unspoilt and unpretentious nature of its housing.

How to Get There

By road take the A30 west out of Penzance, turn onto the B3315 and then right onto an unclassified road after Newlyn and continue through Paul to Mousehole (approx 4 miles). *By rail* there is a regular 125 service to Penzance. *By bus* the 508 runs regularly from Penzance (open top service on Sundays in summer).

The walk takes you up quaint, cobbled streets to the hill above town, then across open fields by narrow woodland paths to Lamorna Cove. The final furlongs cover the coastal path by the growling Cornish sea back to Mousehole. You have a range of views along the way – window boxes, cabbage fields, a wooded valley and last but not least the sea.

The Mousehole Walk

Start, if you like, with a typical village view through one of **The Ship Inn's** upturned glasses. Proceed out of the door hard to port (left, landlubber). Walk the short distance to the War Memorial, with its fine view of the harbour – the rocks you can see beyond are called St Clement's Isle. Brace yourself for a stiff climb ahead.

Turn left by the War Memorial and take the small left-hand fork past 'The Mousehole Club'. You soon come to some steps, after which you turn left then first right by Cuckoo Cottage. Keep straight up this cosy street till you take the right-hand fork by the light blue railing to go past a tiny fountain on your left. Keep going uphill, ignoring the acute turn to your right where the handrail is, and then take the next right-hand fork leading to the set of stone steps beside which a gutter runs. At the top, your path meets at right angles with a track, which you cross to get to the break in the fence ahead, and into the field with telegraph poles.

You're heading for Raginnis Farm. In the field, go diagonally right to the far corner where you'll find a stile. Climb over and

►

The Ship Inn, Mousehole

The tide of events in the history of Mousehole has always ebbed and flowed through its harbour mouth and, keeping a custodial eye on things since the early 17th century, The Ship Inn occupies a point of vantage over this fateful entrance and thus the important business of most of the village.

The Ship Inn really is the centre of the community with people coming in early of an evening for a chat in the warmth of the coal fires. The inn has been filmed for television's *Nationwide* and *Blue Peter* programmes and the interior is quietly elegant and spacious, with nautical decorations everywhere, as you might expect. Of particular interest is a copy of 'Close's Fishing Map', a rarity now; and you can even buy a 'Ship's Inn' sweatshirt of the kind sported by many of the pub's 'bohemian' fringe.

Much money is raised by Mr Greenhaugh, the publican, with charity evenings held on the premises, often in aid of the local lifeboat service, a praiseworthy necessity around the wild Cornish coast.

The keg beers here are St Austell (pronounced 'snozzle') Ale and Mild, there's draught Guinness, too, a choice of lagers and cider. A good range of snacks is available and there's a seasonal à la carte menu

►

keep beside the wall to your left till you come to a gate (with a track to its left). Go through the gate and carry on beside the nearby wall, pausing briefly to glance backwards at the perpendicular church of Sheffield. In the far left-hand corner of the field, there's another stile beside a fine old iron gate. The grassy path from here will lead you into Raginnis farmyard, passing a thatched cottage on the way. After this cottage take the track which leads off to the right and to the main road.

Cross the road; just to the right and almost opposite, is a gate and a stone stile. Hurdle the stile and go across the field to the next one roughly in a straight line. Step gingerly here as there are numerous large cowpats. Leap the stile and make for stile number three (in this section of the walk). Scale number three and you find yourself in a vast cabbage field. Take the cart track to your right till you reach number four. Take note of the standing stone lording it over the vegetables and the bushy growths, sprouting on top of the stonewalls like the work of some demented topiarist.

You are now approaching Kemyel Farm which you should see ahead of you. Pass through a gate and down the middle of the farm buildings till you fork left at the end of the yard and then right at the public footpath sign, to follow the grassy track in the direction of Kemyel Crease Farm. The track/path winds over stone steps and past a disused windpump to reach stile number five. Leap it, cross the field to the far right-hand corner and number six. Hop, skip and jump it and you're on a metalled road again.

Here you have to avoid the farm buildings, so turn right at the road and take the first left past the house on the corner. Soon you come to a junction with a track and a sign for Kemyel Crease Farm. Climb over the stile by the sign for the farm and, ignoring all cows, ruminating or otherwise, stride across the field to the stile opposite. The farm will be on your left now and you have circumnavigated it.

After the stile, continue alongside the wall to the right of the field. Nod a brisk 'good day' to the standing stone on your left as you plump for the gate which leads to Kemyel Wartha Farm straight ahead. After the gate there's one more stile before you come out into the yard.

Make your way through the farm buildings and, on your way, look out for the public footpath signs which you should find on the track which forks left out of the farmyard. It's likely you may have to fight off barking dogs here, remember the old saying about barks and bites. The public footpath sign points in three directions, you should go down left along a winding path. This is an old smuggler's path to Lamorna valley and it takes you firstly to a pile of granite boulders with a view of the sea, where you branch off downhill left and then, some minutes later, to a magnificent disused quarry which has the serene quality of a temple. Continue downwards till you come out into the open by Lamorna village, a spot often featured in the paintings of Sir Alfred Munnings.

To help you unwind after this twisting, tortuous path, it may be best to head for **The Lamorna Wink**, which is ½ mile up the metalled road from the centre of the village. As the road is steep, this detour is only advised for the energetic. The name 'Lamorna' means 'valley by the sea' in Cornish.

The coastal path to Mousehole exits left from the village as you look out to sea, and weaves ingeniously and unstoppably past all the obstacles that nature has strewn in its way. Soon you are cruising past gravestone-sized slabs of granite and up to the summit above Carn Du, a reluctant sounding rock.

Keep to the upper path and you will be rewarded by a sweeping view of the ocean. Soon you see St Michael's Mount, a monastery on the far side of the bay, which looks like a castle. Mousehole itself peeps briefly round at you but disappears as you vanish into a wood before climbing towards the Coast Guards' look-out post at Penzer Point. Look out here and see the vast ocean with its army of white horses stretching to the horizon and meeting the sky. Enough of infinity, walk on ... up a sheltered path which becomes a track before you reach the road. At the road, turn right and walk down into Mousehole passing the Wildbird Sanctuary on the left, dependent, incidentally, on generous donations. In the village, your unerring instinct should enable you to rediscover The Ship Inn.

in the restaurant. Of course you have to be punctual to get to the most seasonal dish of all, 'Starry Gazy' pie, which can only be obtained on December 23rd. All in all, The Ship Inn is a pub which epitomises the unassuming charm of Mousehole and you should not dream of missing it.

The Lamorna Wink Inn, Lamorna

The mind boggles at the vast range of 'nautical artefacts' which cover the walls of The Lamorna Wink Inn. The publican, Mr Drennan, is most specific about the term 'nautical artefacts' and they include divers' helmets, ships' propellers, model ships, battleships' nameplates, Saccone and Speed naval cartoons, paintings of ships and also a very fine collection of hats! That is to mention but a few of my favourite things. However, Mr Drennan warns the public that he has a lot more objects in store and that he is still getting round to putting them out on display. What further treasures you will eventually see I can hardly guess at ... but the Wink should rival Aladdin's cave.

The inn has a relaxed atmosphere, with a large cross-section of holidaymakers in the summer and a smaller coalfire heated clientele, mainly locals, in the colder months. The snacks are excellent with lobster and crab the specialities when available. The beers on draught are Devenish and Cornish best bitter. In summer you can park the kids on benches outside the pub in its wooded valley setting and then go in to enjoy a game of pool, a game of euchre or just a nice quiet drink.

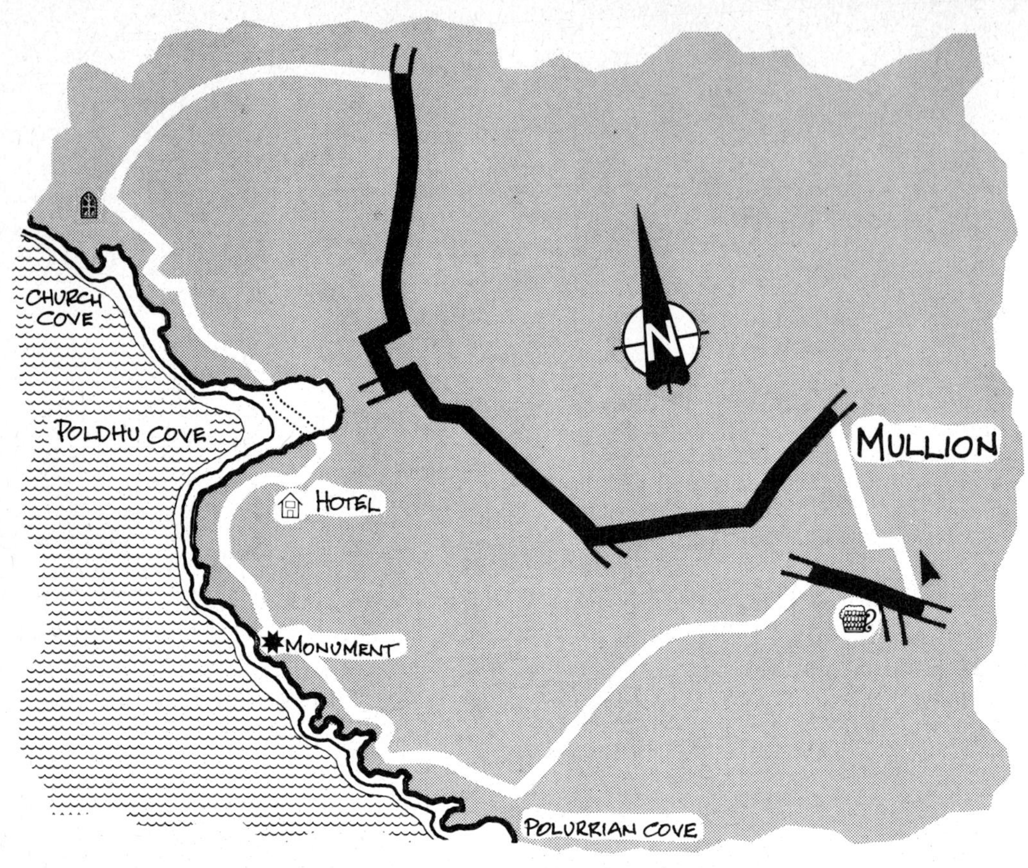

3 Mullion

APPROXIMATELY 4¾ Miles

The District

'Hoary, lichen-covered cliffs, rocks piled on rocks, vaulted, tunnelled, ribbed and groined' – so Mullion Cove and the coastline to the north and south have been described. In fact the writer continues to wax poetic about the Cove's 'cathedral-like' qualities, and the multi-coloured serpentine (stone) cliffs are indeed impressive, if not exactly like 'cathedrals'. The whole stretch of coast here is part of an Area of Outstanding Natural Beauty.

Mullion's small church contains some of the best carved oak bench-ends in the West Country and, at one time, the local congregation were under the wing of one, Rev. Thomas Flavel, who was by chance an exorcist and practitioner of the black arts. His serving-girl once opened one of his necromantic books and was instantly covered with bruises inflicted by invisible, pinching and punching demons which she had inadvertently released. Flavel broke off the service he was conducting at church to come to her aid; he read the magical words backwards (exercising an exorcism) and swung his walking-stick, cudgelling the spirits away.

He wasn't the only man with paranormal powers, for Marconi was more than a dabbler in magic. He managed to communicate, through the invisible medium of radio, with kindred spirits across the vast black surface of the Atlantic. Mullion's coast can still cast magic spells as a million Mullion admirers have discovered.

How to Get There

By road take the A30 east out of Penzance, go right onto the A394, right again onto the A3083 at Helston and then right again onto the B3296 for Mullion (approx 20 miles). Alternatively, take the A39 from Falmouth, turn left onto the B3291, right onto the A3083 and right again onto the B3296 (approx 19 miles). *By rail* there is a regular 125 service to Penzance. *By bus* from Penzance to Helston the 502 and 503 services operate regularly on weekdays. Take the 537 from Helston to Mullion.

The walk crosses fields to a lane, which it then follows to a road which leads down to Poldhu Cove and up to Mullion Golf Club House. You walk across the golf course to St Winwalloe Church and then a dramatic stretch of cliff path takes you via Poldhu Cove to Polurrian Cove, where you follow the valley up into Mullion.

The Mullion Walk

The walk starts, depending on your preference, either from **The Old Inn** or from the car park opposite. So, when you have downed your drinks, leave the pub and turn right up the road, or when you have bought your 'Pay and Display' ticket, turn left up the road. You walk up as far as Colroger Creamery and Bistro. Just opposite this (you can stock up on sweets for the walk here), you turn left on to the marked Public Footpath and walk down past the building on your right, over the stile and into a field. Walk along the edge, keeping the line of brambles and trees on your left. Where this hedge-line turns left, continue to the telegraph pole ahead and then turn half left towards the gap in the trees with two gates. Go through the right-hand gate and walk diagonally across the field to the top right-hand corner. Here you'll see a gap in the wall with a peculiar stile-cum-trough – clever people the Cornish. Carefully negotiate this minor obstacle and turn left along the lane.

You now walk along the lane, stopping, whether you bought sweets or not, for seasonal refreshment at the many wayside blackberry bushes – rural take-aways – and, ignoring a turning to the left continue to the junction with the larger road (B3296). Having put children and pets on their leads, turn right here and follow the road as it winds down to Poldhu Cove. The road ➤

The Old Inn, Mullion

The thatched part of the pub is 16th century though additions were built at the turn of this century. The wood-panelled main bar has an open fire and most of the furniture therein was made from driftwood collected from the nearby coves at Polurrian, Poldhu and Mullion. I'm sure Mr Marconi was pleased to get back here to the comfort of the bar and his room, from his experiments and research into wireless communication up on Poldhu's windy cliffs.

Prior to coming to Mullion, Jack Gayton, the landlord, had been a diver and had spent seven years diving in the Scillies to the wreck of Dutch East Indiaman 'Hollandia', which sank in 1742 with a cargo of silver bullion. Some photos and artefacts are on display in the bar and, no doubt, some of the silver bullion is in his bank account!

There's Devenish Bitter and Best Bitter from beer engines and Tankard, Heineken, and Guinness and Mild on draught, and to go with your drink, there are, in winter, hot bar snacks at lunchtime and, in summer, a cold buffet with many salads. In the evenings there's an à la carte menu.

crosses a bridge over a stream and it's interesting to wonder why the GPO has seen fit to position a post box slap-bang in the middle of the little bridge. No real reason seems apparent, but answers on a postcard (posted here, naturally), please, to...

Any stops at the beach should be kept shortish, as we reappear here later. So continue uphill along the road through beautiful cedar trees and then, flatter now, along the edge of Mullion's justifiably famous coastal golf course. You'll have noticed by now the many helicopters that seem to continually buzz across the sky, but noisy though they are, the flyers and their machines from nearby Culdrose do admirable rescue work in all weathers all round the treacherous Cornish coastline whenever ships, yachts, climbers, and even walkers(!) get into difficulty.

When you reach the Club House, turn left into its car park and take the track out the far side. Make sure you stick to the track and keep an eye open for the flying golf balls of golfers on the 18th, desperate to reach the 19th. Follow the track right across the course and then cross the little stone bridge over the reedy stream. You can now see delightful St Winwalloe Church. Positioned in splendid isolation and sprayed by the surf in rough weather, it nestles behind a great bluff of cliff and was reputedly built in the 13th century by a thankful survivor of a shipwreck off Gunwalloe. Its squat tower, separate from the church, has been built over a cave; it's a man-made extension to a natural sounding chamber and houses a bell cast in 1480.

To continue the walk, cross Church Cove beach where, in 1770, a certain John Knill wasted a lot of his time and presumably money, searching for treasure chests that were supposedly buried in the sand by a pirate. Also, it's said, that in 1785 a ship carrying $2\frac{1}{2}$ tons of money was wrecked here and 100 years later locals tried to salvage the money by building a dam across the cove on the seaward side of the wreck. However, strong winds destroyed the dam and consequently nothing was recovered. So, eyes down for doubloons or sovereigns – you never know your luck.

On the far side of the beach, take the cliff footpath, keeping an eye on children and pets as parts of the cliff edge can be dangerous. Where the path meets a metalled lane, turn seaward and follow the footpath over very springy, mossy turf. From here, there's a good view across to imposing Poldhu Hotel, which you'll get a closer look at later. Descend to Poldhu Cove's beach. On the far side, there are some steps to the right of the wall; climb these and then go on up the path until it meets the Hotel drive. Turn right here, towards the Hotel, but before you reach it, turn right again on to the marked coastal footpath. This dips down below the Hotel and then climbs, skirting its well-kept lawns and garden. You now pass a National Trust sign and if any member of the party is showing signs of breathlessness, there are regular benches for taking the weight off aching feet and, of course, for admiring the wonderful views of the sea and the scarred coastline.

As you continue, you pass the Marconi Monument, erected to commemorate the existence of the Marconi Telegraphy Station and more importantly the first transoceanic wireless signals, sent from here and received in Canada. The monument plaques are well worth reading for fuller information, but they omit to mention that the first news of the sinking of the Titanic was received at the now disappeared wireless station here – a foretaste of how bad news can now flash across the world in seconds.

Immediately after the broken kissing-gate, fork right onto the lower path and at the National Trust sign, fork right again towards the white house. Leaving the house on your left, fork left down towards Polurrian Cove and at the T-junction turn left again. You now descend to the beach.

After a quick dip or perhaps just a sandcastle, take the path inland up the left-hand side of the valley. Follow this public footpath up to a crossing at a cluster of houses and continue along a stony track in the same direction. At the next crossing head on, leaving the postbox on your right and just after the track becomes metalled, take the footpath marked 'Mullion' up to the right. At the road, continue straight on, aiming for the 'No Cycling' sign and here again go straight on along the path towards Mullion's church. Pass through the gap in the wall to your left and then walk diagonally right, across the recreation ground and back to the car park, but more importantly, The Old Inn.

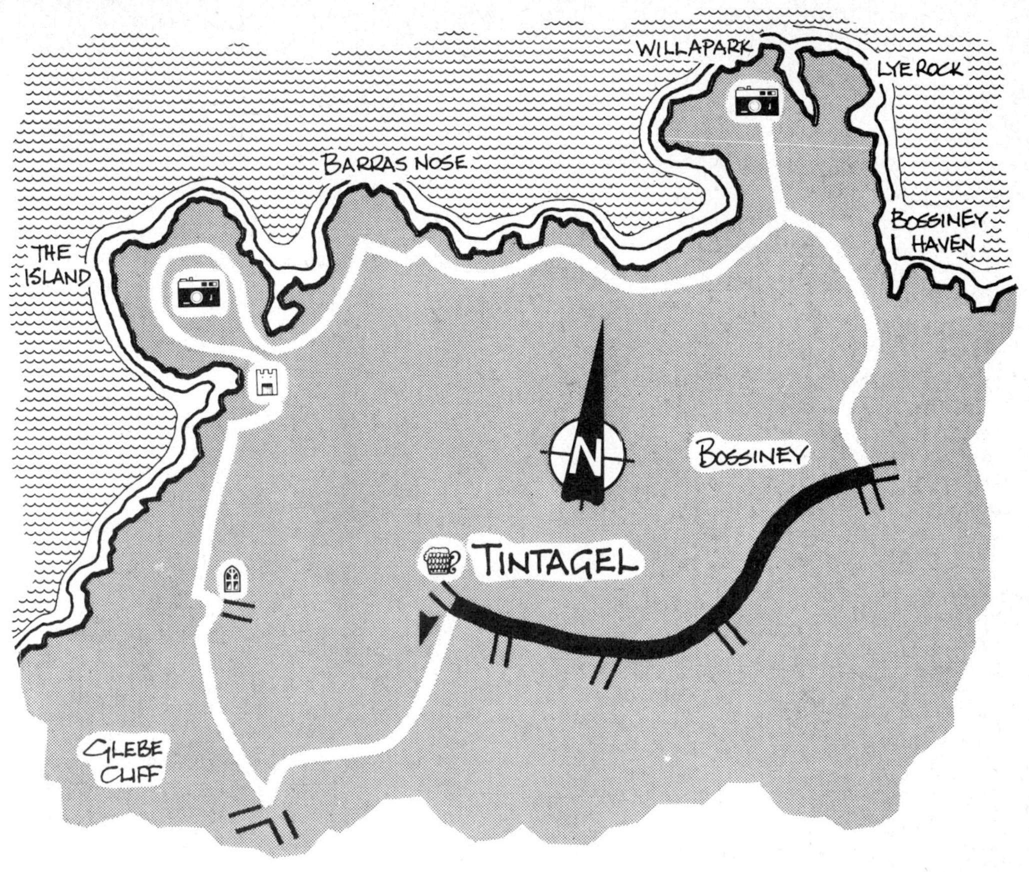

4 Tintagel

APPROXIMATELY 4½ Miles

The District

If you think Skegness is bracing – try Tintagel. No, seriously, most of the walk is truly exhilarating with stiff sea breezes, magnificent views, majestic scenery and a very real sense of the past. While the village of Tintagel has been rather spoiled by tacky 'gifte shoppes', coach tours and other tourist ugliness, the conflict only half a mile away between cliff and breaker remains as potent as it has ever been. Add a large dose of legend, and castle ruins precariously perched on soaring cliffs, and you have an unbeatable mixture.

How to Get There

By road from the A39 between Newquay and Barnstaple take the B3266 at Camelford, go left onto the B3314 and right onto the B3263 through Trewarmett to Tintagel. *By rail* to Plymouth or Barnstaple. *By bus* the 301 runs regularly between Barnstaple and Bideford and then bus from Bideford to Launceston, where you have to catch the local service to Tintagel. A bus also runs from Plymouth to Tintagel at 4.30 (not Wed, or Sun).

This is a walk for strong legs as well as stout hearts and in order to derive maximum pleasure from it, it's best to follow the advised digressions, though these, especially the first, make the walk fairly strenuous in parts. You should take some money for

admission to the castle – it will be money well spent. (It's open during the week 9.30-17.30 in March, April and October; 9.30-16.00 November to February; 9.30-19.00 May to September and on Sundays, October to March, it opens at 14.00.).

The Tintagel Walk

The walk starts at the car park next to **The King Arthur's Arms,** ideally located for an invigorating quaff before you get underway. Thus fortified, step across the street to the old Post Office. A 14th century minor manor, used for 50 years as a Letter Receiving Office, it's now preserved by the National Trust. Marvel a moment at its eccentric contours – perhaps the architect had one too many in the King Arthur's Arms. Walk up the road and turn left into the car park just before the Tintagel Hotel. Climb the stile directly ahead of you and then turn left on to a track, marked as a Public Footpath. Follow this round and down to another sign, which points you along a path, through a copse of small trees – over a wooden bridge – to a stone stile. Climb this and take the path signposted Trebarwith Strand. This path runs along the edge of field, over a wooden stile and into another field, where you aim for a stone stile. Once over this, follow the path between fence and wall to another stone stile and a small wooden gate. All this mention of stiles as if they were going out of style – groan!

Now aim across the field for the pink house, which you will discover is called Trevillick Cottage, and go through the broken gate to its left. Turn left up the track to a crossing of tracks, where you turn right along a stony track in the direction of the church. Walk just past the 'National Trust – Glebe Cliff' sign, over the cattle grid and fork right, still heading for the church. As you face out to sea, there is a fine view to your left past Trebarwith Strand to Dennis Head and beyond.

The old stone cattle grid at the gate is only one interesting feature of the parish church of St Materiana, perhaps another name for St Mabyn, but these Cornish saints get a trifle confusing, there being no lack of them, to put it mildly. She was a princess from Gwent who, reputedly, converted the local people to Christianity way back around 500 AD. Of interest inside are the many little chapels incorporated in the church's cruciform shape and the ubiquitous Mr Norman Font with his five legs and his crudely hinged lid.

On leaving, skirt round the seaward side of the serene and spacious churchyard, forking left on to a wide grassy path and follow this to meet the coast path. Continue in this direction, i.e. between the four-square hotel and the Island, now coming into view. Ignoring turns to left and right, you begin to descend more steeply and after climbing a stone stile over a wall, you follow the path down the side of another wall to a large bluff of rock, crowned by ruined walls.

You are now at your first digression and even if you don't do the others, this one is essential. Sometimes the ticket attendant is not in his little booth, in which case you'll find him on the Island or, in rain, down in the café. After exploring the mainland section of the castle, you go down innumerable steps, over a newish wooden bridge and then up innumerable steps, to the heights of the

The Old Post Office, Tintagel.

Island. When you stop halfway up for a breather, turn and look just how high the opposite cliff is and how close the walls are to the edge – being a Norman building contractor was no joke. Perhaps this is the time for an obvious warning about the perils of going too close to any edge, and to keep a tight rein on children and dogs. Go through the gate at the top and you are now in what must have been one of the most naturally impregnable castles, in our galaxy at least. The castle dates from the 12th century, but before that there was a Celtic monastic settlement here.

Instructions here become redundant, so wander at will all over the Island – a peninsula slowly becoming a real island as its isthmus (try and say it fast without lisping) is worn away and weather and pounding sea are its only aggressors now. Things to look out for are the various sites of the Celtic settlement, the two wells (just where does the fresh water come from?), the small bridge over a natural tunnel and the chapel of St Julitta. The views stretch from beyond Dennis Head to the south (if one of your party is called Dennis, this could be extremely confusing), Lundy Island to the north and round past Bude to Hartland Point to the north-east. When you've had enough of this awesome chunk of wild geography, dark-age history and inspiring legend, put one foot in front of the other and go down the steps back to reality, turning left after the bridge along the path and continue down yet more steps to the small grey beach.

If you haven't visited the castle (mad fools – you don't know what you've missed), turn right at the large bluff of rock with ruins atop and then left down as the path zigzags its way to the bottom of the valley. Walk between the café and the row of cottages and descend to the beach by going to the left and then down the steps. It's well worth a ►

King Arthur's Arms, Tintagel

Partly 14th century, this is the oldest pub in Tintagel. No more touristy than the rest of the village, this modernized holiday pub has a genial atmosphere with its stone walls, mostly original beams, open fire and friendly bar staff. Also, and perhaps more to the point, it serves good drink and food.

Hand-pumped Ushers and Whitbread Best head the list, closely followed by Devon Scrumpy from the wood. Lager, Whitbread and Watney keg bitters provide good back up, along with a wide selection of liqueurs. An extensive range of hot and cold food, from meals (steaks etc) through to sandwiches which should satisfy any Desperate Dan and kids are amply catered for either in the electronic game-filled children's room, or outside.

quick look with its three waterfalls and, best of all, Merlin's Cave which shows just how nearly the Island is an island. Being careful about the tide – Merlin's magic will be of no help if you get stranded – you can walk through to see the sea coming in the far end. One tale tells how the baby Arthur was washed ashore here, a snippet adding to the charm of this little cove, though it's probably too dangerous for bathing.

Now begins a climb as steep as, but a little shorter than, the north face of the Matterhorn. Go up the steps and cross the concrete bridge over the stream. Just round the corner, take the steps which are part of an old wall, up to the right and then go on up again round the old building to a level area. You can have a quick breather here, but be strict with yourself and remembering how much good this is doing you, turn hard left and climb – well, struggle – up the steep path to some wooden railings, where you turn left on to the coast path. Here you can begin to count the number of leg-muscles you never knew you had.

Walk past the carved stone National Trust sign and bench and on through gorse and heather. You can now see a large cave down to your left. Just after the stream, fork left and follow the path out to the point for more excellent views of the coastline. Walk back along the ridge, aiming slightly left and keeping to the seaward side of the small gorse-covered hill. Follow the well-defined path up and along the edge of the wall, over a stile and carry on with the wall still at your side.

Now the way is simplicity itself as you continue along the path, keeping the rocks and surf below in view. Pass a beach and go through a kissing-gate. Try not to look too often over the beautifully built 'herringbone' walls as you will see a disgraceful eyesore – a caravan park laid out with absolutely no imagination and with as many caravans squeezed in as possible, with the mind firmly fixed on the ringing cash register. Ugh! But to your left the pale mass of a different kind of park rises sheer from the sea. At the wall and 'National Trust – Willa Park' sign you can turn left for a five minute stroll to the end of this majestic but crumbling promontory. Otherwise, turn right after the wall and follow it and, when the ground slopes downhill, strike out diagonally left across the field and follow the coast footpath as it winds very steeply down. Cross the stile and bridge and make for the steps uphill. After about twenty steps, walk the five yards to the fence for a glimpse of charming Bossiney Haven with its natural arch and sandy beach – then on up the steps. Climb the stile at the top and walk on up the path in the gully. Before emerging from this gully, put your dog on the lead – there are sheep in the field above and you see the shepherd's warning somewhat late, in fact as you leave the field through the gate in the top corner. Turn right along the road through Bossiney, once one of the rottenest of the rotten boroughs. There was a period when it boasted one solitary voter, who returned two MPs to Parliament. At one time, that singer of royal Spanish beards, Sir Francis Drake was one of Bossiney's two MPs. You now have an easy saunter back along the road to Tintagel and the range of potions and elixirs at the pub, which the mighty Merlin would have been pleased to concoct.

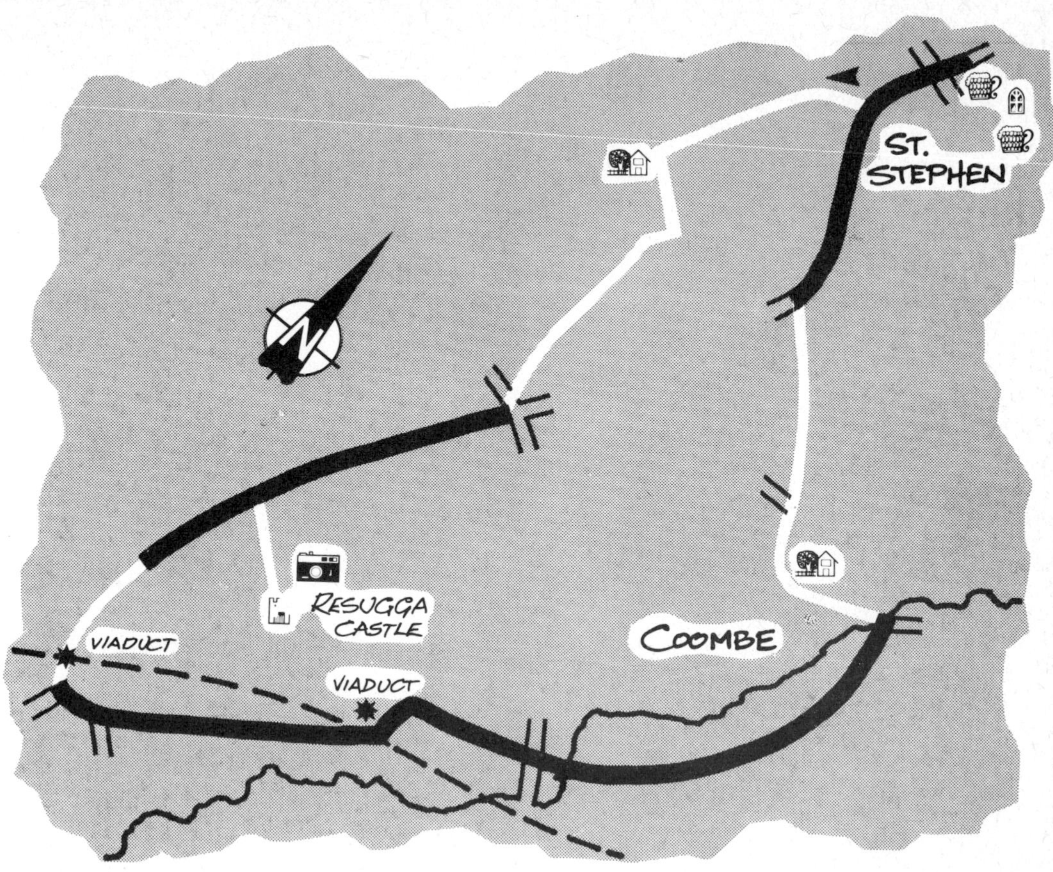

5 St Stephen in Brannel

APPROXIMATELY 4¾ Miles

The District

The inland parts of Cornwall have always seemed to be the poor cousins of their more glamorous coastal relatives. Don't worry, though, about reputations, for here at St Stephen you will find pleasant relief from the bluster and bravado of the cliff walks. This is another side of Cornwall, an area of calm and tranquillity, of sheltered valleys and well-kept fields, enough indeed to still the raging passions in your breast and bring you to a state of peace with the world – if a little poetic exaggeration may be used. Let's hope the rain holds off for you, after such a claim.

St Stephen is in China clay country. China clay, which is also called kaolin from the Chinese for 'high hill', came into existence through the age-long action of heat, pressure, gases and water on granite, which decomposed as a result and is now extracted by high-pressure hosing. Demand far outstrips production and Cornwall is extremely fortunate in possessing such a valuable resource. Kaolin is used not only for pottery but also in the manufacture of paper and textiles and as a constituent of lino shaving soap, cosmetics and medicines. For every ton of pure China clay you also get five tons of waste to be used for concrete and breeze blocks.

The 15th century church has an oval churchyard, probably inherited from earlier Pagan worshippers, and it's possible you'll

spot an albino sparrow batting around the belfry here. It may or may not interest you to know that Silas and Joseph Hocking grew up and preached in St Stephen. Silas was the more prolific author and was the first man to clock up sales of a million books in his lifetime . . . but would you want to read one?

How to Get There

By road take the A3058 west from St Austell, St Stephen is approx 5 miles along the road. *By rail* there is a regular 125 service to St Austell. *By bus* on weekdays the 522 runs from St Austell to St Stephen.

The walk takes you from The Kings Arms in St Stephen up to the old hill fort of Resugga and then back through Coombe to The Queen's Head. On the way you'll be taken past a graceful viaduct or two, a lush pasture or twenty and, er, a sewage works – ah well, you can't win 'em all. Seriously, it's a pleasant and easy walk through typical English countryside.

The St Stephen in Brannel Walk

The walk begins at **The King's Arms** which is roughly in the centre of the village. As you leave you should turn left down the road which leads past the village notice board to the main road. At the junction, head straight across and up Rectory Road. Take the first turning on the right opposite a house called Saltram and here you find yourself on a short old cart track.

At the end of the track, 40 yards in, there is a kissing-gate on your left. Go through and follow the diagonal path across the field. To your right, as you go, you can see the 'snow-capped' peaks above the China Clay deposits, which William Cookworthy first discovered in 1755. Soon you arrive at another kissing-gate – don't miss this opportunity to have a wish, you are allowed one each.

Pass through, onto a track and in the direction of distant hills. Follow the track as it winds gently downhill till you see another kissing-gate on the right, just before the track bends into Resugga farmyard. The view into the valley from this point can be used as an excuse for further brief dalliance but on no account should you go through the kissing-gate as you might really be led astray and off the path.

Carry on through the farmyard with its fine old ivy-covered farmhouse almost hidden from view. Take the fork to the right past the large stone buildings on your left and an artificial reservoir on the right, then on to a brief stretch of concrete road. In a minute, you come to a crossing of tracks – go straight over and carry on up a leafy, tree-lined track. Keep a weather eye open for buzzards and other birds of prey remorselessly hovering in search of the next meal. Birds abound roundabout here and you may spot larks among other common species.

Keep heading along the track till you come to a metal gate. Go through this and walk up to the junction of the track and four country lanes. This junction could be described as 'unsymmetrical' – take the second road on your right, marked Tremouth and Grampound, and head uphill along the lane. Watch out for rare sightings of traffic here, for, when I was walking here, not a car passed by.

At the crest of the hill (actually, just over it) after a steady climb you will find a wooden gate to the left. Pass through and inspect the site of the ancient Bronze Age fort. It's a shame that there is little left of Resugga Castle save the outlines of the ramparts which are now marked by grassy mounds and gorse bushes. Savour the view all around and imagine how people used to gather together up here at nights for protection against a hostile universe of animal and human predators, scratching a meagre living by day from the surrounding slopes.

Back at the road, through the same wooden gate, turn left for a swift descent under a canopy of trees – through which the sunlight filters magically if you're lucky with the weather. Follow the road under the arches of the railway viaduct glancing upwards at the pubescent grey stalactites clinging beneath. Walk down to the road junction and take the Coombe road to your left. But first make sure you've had a good look at the viaduct which spans the valley. It was built in the heyday of the railways and now carries the 125s from city to city.

Follow the road into Coombe itself, after branching left where the sign says Coombe one mile. You will be in the company of some fine old oaks along this stretch, as well as beech trees and silver birch along with the aforementioned sewage works to your left. Soon you come to another viaduct with its little brother beside it, the old railway bridge covered by a profuse confusion of parasytical greenery and a fetching outfit it is too. Pass under it and look around. This is idyllic English countryside.

Move on straight through Coombe – don't take the turning to the left marked St Stephen. Keep on to the left and downhill out of Coombe, past a sign for a playground and some council houses. Soon you're heading past 'flashy' modern houses including the fancifully named 'Laredo'. Follow the stream on your left till it leaves the road and at this point fork up left towards a farmhouse – you will cross over the stream as you go.

Go up the track, passing the farmhouse on your right. Sweep round the outhouses in a large arc curving to the right. You'll come to three tracks just past the buildings – take the one to the right and follow it till you come to a gate. Fork right here down a natural tunnel formed by bushes which protects a muddy path. Carry on till you reach the road and turn right towards St Stephen (not signposted). Soon you pass the local school and then you find yourself back on Rectory Road. At the end of Rectory Road, turn right and take the first left past the telephone box. Thus you arrive at **The Queen's Head,** drag yourself to the bar and order.

The King's Arms Inn, St Stephen in Brannel

By the church in the middle of the village, the inn has a typically Cornish granite exterior. Inside there are two spacious rooms where the regulars include clay miners from the local pits.

The pub used to be a shop and even used to own many of the meadows around here; well, that is to say the brewery did.

The beers are St Austell keg and draught from the nearby brewery and there's also draught Guinness. Snacks include pasties, sandwiches and ploughman's lunch. This is a plain but friendly pub.

The Queen's Head, St Stephen in Brannel

The Queen's Head was once a coaching inn in the days when a journey to Newquay took four hours to cover the 12 miles. The coaches used to stop at every inn on the way.

Bow-tied Frank Morgan has been the publican here for quite a few years and recalls the old village postman who used to give advance information on the contents of the letters he was delivering. There are pictures of Cornish wrestlers on the walls and a large old photo of the inn which shows the village water pump, which is still there today.

Inside, there are stone walls, new fittings and an open fire in a bar which is comfortable and spacious.

There are St Austell keg and draught bitters, snacks and hot meals (only to order). Children can be accommodated 'seen but not heard' in the garden in summer, while parents can enjoy a game of euchre, darts, dominoes or ringboard inside. This is a pub I recommend . . .

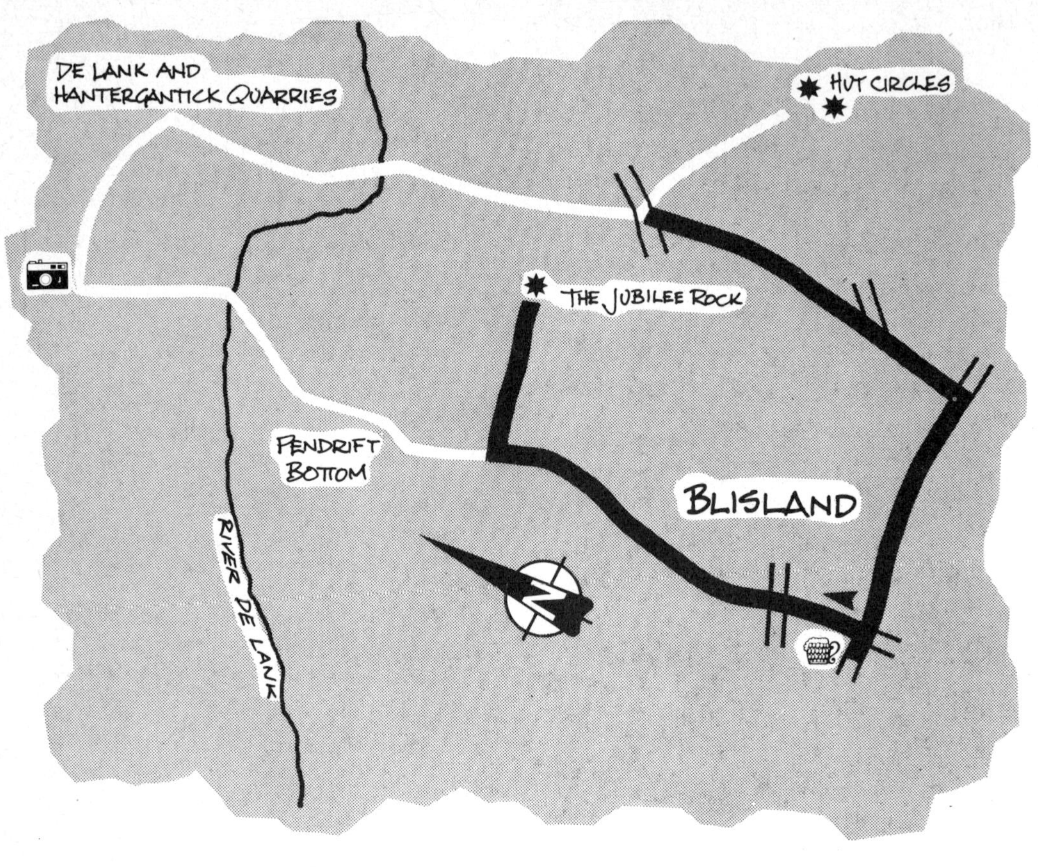

6 Blisland

APPROXIMATELY 3¾ Miles

The District

Centre of an old moorland parish, Blisland is a peculiarity amongst Cornish villages in that it is the possessor of a village green, a rarity in a country with such a strong dose of Celtic culture in its past. Tall elms, ash and sycamore ring this grassy forum, as do Georgian houses of architectural distinction. At one end of the green stands the church of SS Protus and Hyacinth (or St Pratt's), one of Sir John Betjeman's favourites, with its colourful rood screen and well-preserved wagon roof; at the other, the village smithy still operates next door to The Royal Oak Inn, formerly a coaching inn. People can nip in for a drink while their horses are being shod . . . and, apparently, do.

The feast of St Pratt is marked each year by a patronal procession on the 22nd of September which takes place some way down the road from the church. On the next day there is the annual sheep fair . . . as things go from verse to baa-aa-aad. (This 'joke' takes some bleating).

The pretty village of St Tudy, nearby was the birthplace of Captain Bligh, who sailed on a boat named after a popular coconut chocolate bar, and also the site of the first successful blood transfusion – between two sheep. A certain Mr Richard Louser was the fearless innovator and his epitaph in the local churchyard commends him most heartily for the selfless way he was prepared to experiment on his wife and family in the interests of science (and fame?). This kind of praise could give Dracula a good name!

You should take time out to see the canal at St Breward, the china clay pits and the large 15th century church with its granite tower and Norman pillars. The hills around St Breward afford a tremendous panorama of the surrounding countryside with its magnificently bleak and rugged scenery. Menhirs, dolmens and hut circles pepper the brackened slopes, but are all too often enshrouded by Bodmin Moor's notoriously frequent mists. Watch out, therefore, that you make your visit on a day when you *can* watch out.

How to Get There

By road take the A389 east from Bodmin, turn on to the A30 and then left on to an unclassified road for Blisland (approx $5\frac{1}{2}$ miles). *By rail* to Bodmin Road station, bus into Bodmin. *By bus* there is no bus service to the starting point, Bodmin is the nearest you'll get by public transport.

This is a mildly strenuous ramble – aren't they all? – which takes you from the civilised centre of Blisland, over low lying Pendrift Bottoms and on up to the dramatic heights of the De Lank quarry – then back to Blisland over grazing land and along a country lane; all for the price of a few hours' effort. It should be said here that the second half of the walk requires a certain intuitive sense of direction on the part of the walker so, if it's getting dark or you're feeling less than intrepid, then return the way you came. (In this case, you would do well to make a note of landmarks on your way out).

The Blisland Walk

Turn left out of **The Royal Oak Inn** and walk past the Georgian houses on your left. Turn left where the signpost points to Pendrift and Launceston. As you walk up the road there are houses to your left of a later less graceful era – that is to say of 20th century design. Next you go past a roadside sign (to Pen Tor) and on up a steep-banked lane till you come to a cross-roads. Head straight across here (despite the 'dead end' sign) in the direction of Pendrift and past a house named 'Electra' and a cattle grid.

Soon you reach Trepolen Farm and here there is a compulsory excursion to Jubilee Rock. You turn right and go between the buildings and up a gloriously muddy track

The Royal Oak Inn, Blisland

Within earshot of the local blacksmith's ringing blows on the anvil, The Royal Oak Inn has strong connections with the equestrian world. For one thing it used to be a thatched coaching house, in fact, the one shown in the photograph in the lounge bar. However, that building burnt down in the 19th century. The present building replaced it and continues the 'horsey' tradition by supporting the local hunt which meets outside the pub on New Year's Day, prior to terrorising the local fox population. Another photograph, to look for, shows a woman (who looks remarkably like the queen) in a headscarf talking to a red-coated huntsman on a horse, the spitting image of Harvey Smith (not the horse). I was assured that neither was who they appeared to be. Was the horse, I wonder.

There are two pleasant bars and they cater mostly for local trade. It is reckoned that, at any one time in the bar 75% of the custom is likely to come from the Greenaway family. Before you begin to think that this village family are all very heavy drinkers, it should be said that the family members are numerous (positively epidemic) and cover several generations, ranging from grannies on the hard stuff to toddlers on Coke.

The Whitbread Best Bitter (hand-drawn) is just one of many things about the pub which help to put the 'bliss' in 'Blisland'. There's also Double Diamond, Tankard and Trophy on draught and chilled wine. The menu for snacks is good, children are welcomed and there's an assortment of games to play including euchre (A Cornish card game), dominoes, draughts, darts and pool.

with a roof of trees. This track brings you out into a field where you'll find the Jubilee Rock lording it over a plethora of humbler stones. This ancient rock was first engraved with the figure of Britannia for the jubilee of George III. One thing led to another and now there is a full-sized tattoo of the Royal Insignia – 'Dieu et Mon Droit' – and a variety of other crests and configurations including such ambiguous mottoes as 'One for all' and 'Patience passes science'. Choose your slogan and cut back to the track, scanning the splendid rocky field on your way. At the farm buildings, where you turned right in the first place, turn right again and continue in your original direction. On your right, just after turning, there is an old stone house and, if you look closely at the wall by the track, there is a barely discernible date, 1781, cut into the stone.

Go straight ahead through a gate and follow the grassy muddy track into a field. Take the gate to the right on to a further track and follow down beside the wall to the far right-hand corner of the steep field where you will find a helpful stile with a handrail and stone steps below. Descend by the path and strike off half-right across the marshy area. As there are so many tracks here in Pendrift Bottoms, I suggest you follow the line of telegraph poles to the river. When you arrive at the river bank, turn right following the river upstream in search of the bridge over the River De Lank. The river here originates from Brown Willie, the highest point on Bodmin Moor and a big lad at 1,375 ft tall. Under the trees by the river is a vibrant world of rustling trees and noisily flowing water, white where it rushes over rocks. It is easy to be captivated by this airy underworld but keep going, soon you come to a small wooden bridge, which you cross and turn left past the hydro-electric sub plant which supplies electricity to the quarry. Ten yards after a stone stile by the sub plant, you turn right and go up the steps that some kind benefactor has provided.

A track crosses your path by a small square-set tower, turn left on to the track for a couple of strides, then sharp right before the cattle grid on to a path which follows the fence uphill and to the left of the farmhouse. When you come to the track leading to the farmhouse go straight across and through the wooden gate. Follow the wobbly path uphill till just after the point where a track has joined you (or vice versa) and hurdle the wooden stile to your right. Now stick to a right-hand path in the direction of the top of the quarry as it winds up to a smallish cairn. Hold on to dogs and kids and hats, the view is mesmerising, and the drop is bone-crunching. Keeping well clear of the edge, follow the paths round the quarry. From this point on it gets difficult, if you're going to re-trace your steps, now is the time to do so. If not, brave reader, read on step by careful step.

Skirt the quarry till you see a track going off to your left and through a gate. Once through the gate, you'll find an old tin hut lurking low to your right by the quarry's edge. From it a sunken old overgrown track moves off down between the De Lank quarry and the mellifluously named Hantergantick quarry, the border of which is marked by a pile of granite slabs which form an unsightly slope, to your left as you look towards the river. It is, I warn you, difficult to tell where one quarry stops and the other begins . . . you must aim to steer between the two. From the old track, find a path to the river and then some stones in the river slightly to your left as you approach. Once over these stones, the second stretch of water can be negotiated by an amazing man-made bridge of giant granite boulders which join together above and let the river flow underneath. You may have to look hard here since the bridge is virtually hidden till you cross the stones. It's an exciting spot but don't go into the quarry to your right.

After the bridge, scramble up the far bank and keep beside the fence. Following the path, which is not well-defined (something of an understatement) you will see the quarry to your right and the crows which fly across it in ominous black clouds. Eventually, as you follow the fence, you pass below a derelict farm with particularly small buildings. Just below this farm you climb a fence under the umbrella branches of a small gnarled old tree. Again follow the fence on your right towards the wood, which you penetrate along a muddy track with trees entwined overhead. Follow the main track till you come into the open and more isolated old farmland.

Here it becomes difficult to give directions. Move off diagonally left along a path (at about 45°) – the paths are quite confused here – but keep to this line and you'll meet up with a fence to your left. Keep along beside this till a group of trees looms and then cross over the fence to find a blocked up stile . . . and a gate to its left. Go through the gate and ford the stream just behind it – (the stream?) – then take the path opposite for a couple of yards before following the track you meet to your left. After 50 yards or so, strike off right following a track through the gorse bushes.

Soon you're on an openish plain and you must continue roughly along the line you're already following – bearing maybe a fraction right – to the road which is a fair distance away. Turn right at the road and continue till you come to a crossroads. (There's a path here bisecting the angle of the St Breward/Launceston road and the Carwen, Cassacawn and Treworder road – follow this round right to the Hut Circles, which turn out to be prehistoric mounds among the trees. Then return). Follow in the direction of the sign for Carwen, Cassacawn and Treworder – not for Blisland, till you get to the road junction where you turn right and walk back into the village. Make a beeline for The Royal Oak and a nectar tasting pint or two.

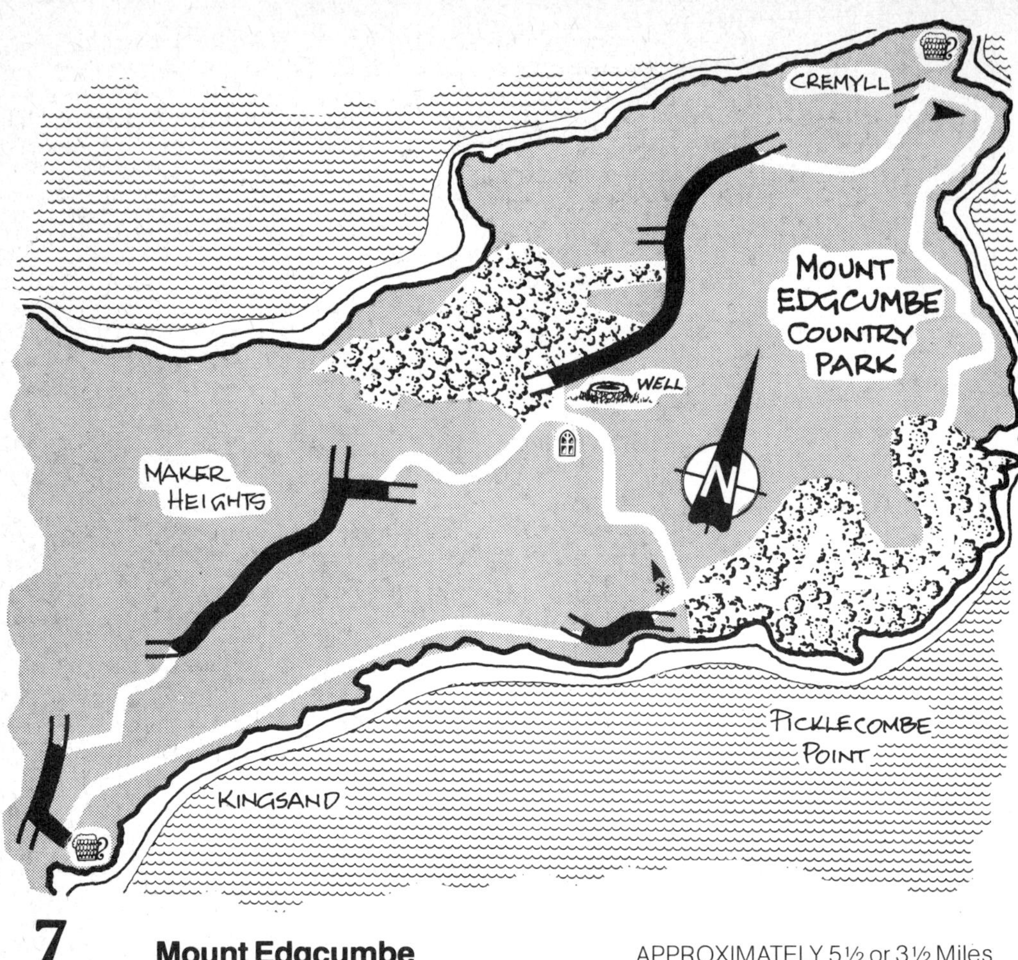

7 Mount Edgcumbe

APPROXIMATELY 5½ or 3½ Miles

The District

The Duke of Medina – Sidonia, High Admiral of the Spanish Armada – had reserved the Mount Edgcumbe estate for himself after his country's planned conquest of England, so much did he admire and covet it. However, this admiral's admirable (!) taste was never satisfied, due partly to his nautical and strategic incompetence, partly to wily Sir Francis Drake (former English bowling champion), but mostly to the unpredictability of the English coastal weather. Built in the 16th century by Richard Edgcumbe, the house was badly damaged by Nazi bombs in 1941 but was extensively restored in 1960. It's open May-Sept on Monday and Tuesday 14.00-18.00 and there's an admission charge. However the park and lower gardens are open daily all year round and are free.

The park, now jointly owned and run by Plymouth and Cornwall, is for many Plymouthians a quiet place away from the hustle and bustle of city life, reminding them of days when the pace was much slower as they amble through its tranquil 'sylvan' grounds. It is reached by the Cremyll passenger ferry from Stonehouse – this crossing was for 700 years the main route into Cornwall.

How to Get There

By road. From Plymouth you have to take a ferry to the A374 and then proceed left onto the B3247 after Antony. Mount Edgcumbe is just off the road (approx 8 miles). *By rail* to

Plymouth. *By bus* the 47 bus will take you to the ferry, from where there is a regular service to Mount Edgcumbe.

If you look at the map above, this walk is almost Devon-and-Cornwall-shaped. And, to horrendously mix my metaphors, it comes, dear customer, in two models – the family runabout (Devon) and the rather more sporty touring version (Devon and Cornwall) – got it?

The Mount Edgcumbe Walk

You'll be pleased to hear that the walk starts and finishes (in both versions) in **The Edgcumbe Arms,** just opposite the Cremyll Ferry landing stage. Turn right out of the pub and walk along the straight road leading to the park gates. Once through, turn left and, as you walk towards the Gatehouse, look to your right up the broad grassy avenue to the commanding house looking down at you. Go through the Gatehouse arch into the Formal Gardens. You pass the Orangery with its huge windows, where once oranges were grown, but now where orange pop and other consumables are merely sold. This is in the Italian Gardens and also within the area are French Gardens, English Gardens and a spot named Dingle Dell. You can get more information from the warden in the Gatehouse.

Having thrown a penny in the fountain, carry on along the track past Thomson's Seat. Just beyond are the old gun batteries – the newer to your left, where you get a real gunner's eye view of Plymouth Sound and the older on your right, which you can climb up inside onto the roof. Having successfully defended the straits against all enemies, you can smugly saunter along the parapet with its old cannons which defy any intruders between here and Devil's Point. Follow ➤

The Edgcumbe Arms, Cremyll

When the landing stage for Cremyll's 700 year old ferry was moved from Barnpool in 1720, the pub was built in 1730 as its Cornish passage house. The Earl and Countess used to wait here for their boatmen to collect them and ferry them upstream to Cotehele, their second house; indeed the bay window was added and kept specifically for them. Many an hour could have been spent waiting for tardy boatmen and many a goblet drained, as they watched the majestic sailing-ships and the attendant bobbing whalers and jollyboats ride the waters of the Sound.

Round to the side of the pub, there is an external stairway to the first floor, supporting the theory of 'Pat' Patterson, the landlord, that the building at one time served as an occasional courthouse – it being required by law that the magistrate, the Earl naturally, should have his own personal entrance.

This century, the pub has welcomed, among others, all of the Devonport Destroyer Squadron, who used it as an HQ in the war and in more recent times many notable singlehanded sailors – Sir Francis Chichester, Sir Alec Rose, Edwin Allcard and Anne Davison.

A pub with two bars and a family lounge, it is warm and snug with 18th century panelling, wood beams and collections of ships' ➤

the path across a lawn, between two astonishingly high hedges, to the gate out of the Formal Gardens.

Follow the curve of the small beach, where the aristocrats used to come to buy fish direct from the seine-boats. Watch out for the cormorants cruising just above the water, cutting out the need for middlemen. You join a metalled track as it runs uphill along the coast through a wood. You may be confused by the sight of ducks paddling about on the sea, but the mystery is revealed when you pass the small lake in the Ampitheatre and realize they've got their bearings a little wrong. From the concrete slab, there are good views past Drake's Island (an ex-prison, now an Adventure Centre) to Plymouth behind, but don't dally here – they get better. Continue past the little gazebo – Milton's Temple – and on up the path under spreading chestnut trees. At the right time of year, there's a feast to be had here, unless the squirrels beat you to it. Climb on up to and through the wooden gate and then up to the folly to your right. From here there are excellent views across all of the Sound (it's not often you can see sounds!) from right up the Tamar, over to Plymouth, across to Bovisand and beyond the breakwater out to sea. The folly was built as a ruin in the 18th century showing the less than practical preoccupations of the decadent aristocrats with more money than sense in an age of mass poverty.

To go on with the walk, descend the hill towards the sea and turn right onto a stony bridleway. Follow this through a lovely deciduous wood and soon you come to Lady Emma's Cottage – a black and white half-timbered house built in 1882. Fork left here diagonally across the stretch of grass and then swing right, round the bottom of the pinewood. Keeping to your right, stay above the rhododendrons at the red 'Dangerous Cliffs and Paths' sign – we want no accidents. Through the trees and bushes you may be lucky to see oystercatchers as they pipe and squeak their flitting way over the rocks below, while the pine wood above remains still, silent and spooky.

Because the lower path becomes dangerous, follow the acorn-marked coastpath sign up to your right through what is by now a beech wood and turning left, join the broad bridleway through the trees. Beware the woodpigeons here – your researcher was bombed by a rather startled one as he trudged along. Just past an area of bracken on your left, turn hard right uphill, almost back in the direction you've come and then hard left to resume your forward progress. This ascending path meets a bridleway and here you turn left through rhododendrons and soon pass under an old arch. Below you can see Picklecombe Point with its small jetty.

Stay on this bridleway as it turns inland and then passes a small, damp, shrine-like place – Picklecombe Seat – handy for the weary traveller, but a trap for the more bronchial members of the party. You continue under huge trees which darken the way, on past a spot the map calls The Earthquake, a gouge out of the side of the hill, to arrive at a fork, which poses you with a problem. For you must decide if you want to continue along the coast to Kingsand and the attractive possibility of a reviving pint or two in **The Devonport Inn** or whether you want to cut up to St Macra's Church and thence back to Cremyll and The Edgcumbe Arms.

If you want to take the shorter option and head for the church, then fork right along the track, which on leaving the wood, gives you great views across Kingsand and Cawsand to Penlee Point. Stay on the track up the side of Hooe Lake Valley to the top where it swings to the left and then to the right across a field towards the church in the trees. The path follows a fence to a gate, through which you go. As you reach the crest, you get views ahead of the Hamoaze and of the two Tamar-spanning bridges – Brunel's railway cantilever and the modern road suspension. Go through the gate next to Maker Lodge and after a quick visit to the church, take the footpath marked Empacombe 1, Cremyll Ferry 1¾ (funny scores they get in the local football matches, ho, ho). Now you must wait for five paragraphs while the more energetic walkers catch up with you.

If you want to continue to Kingsand, then fork left and go straight on down a wood-darkened path, through an old metal gate and on down, now surrounded by bracken and monstrous gorse bushes. At the bottom, cross a stile and turn right onto a lane. To your left is a white pyramid with its orange stripes and light to guide the toing and froing of ships. Just below Hooe Lake Cottage, turn left along the marked coast path that skirts the bottom of the wood. The path rises and falls and is easy and relaxing, so you have time to look out for the wild flowers in the bracken and, in summer, the many butterflies that flutter about doing whatever it is butterflies do. You pass below a fort-like building and then the path comes out into a lush field gently sloping down into Kingsand. Just before you enter the village, watch out for the house to your left with a peculiar second storey door. Leave by that door and you'd really know about it!

The twin fishing villages of Kingsand and Cawsand are off main tourist routes and their maze of narrow streets and tortuous alleys have consequently remained unspoilt and largely as the 19th century smugglers would have seen them. Before your triumphant arrival, other notable visitors have included Henry VII who landed here before the Battle of Bosworth and Napoleon who after his escape from Elba was a prisoner on HMS Bellerophon here, before being whisked away, for his own safety, to St Helena.

As you come into the village, turn left round a red stone house called Minnadhu and go down 'Unsuitable for motors' Heavitree Road (Road?!). Turn left down Market Street and at the sea go left to The Devonport Inn.

Suitably revived, for you will need to be, as you must now climb from a few feet above sea-level to approximately 400ft high Maker Heights, with hardly a level stretch between one and the other. Retrace your steps to where you entered Kingsand, but now continue up Devonport Hill, past all the houses, the last of which is the Glass

crests and prints.

'Pat' Patterson stocks a wide range of drinks, notably the gravity-tapped Courage Best and handpumped Directors and a good selection of whiskies (six malt, six grain, two bourbon and one Irish). Enough? The food is of the finger rather than knife and fork variety and can be taken out to the paved courtyard or the tables on the water's edge.

The Devonport Inn, Kingsand

On a good day, Cawsand Bay and Plymouth Sound fill the three downstairs windows of The Devonport Inn as you look out over the lip of your pint to the sea. On rough days, though, this view is cancelled out by the storm shutters across the windows which protect the glass from the endless lashing of the waves; it's impossible however, to cancel out the rumble and hiss of the raging seas no matter how loud you put up the juke box. Shiver a little for pity's sake, then resume the pleasant business in hand (in glass).

The Devonport Inn has been an alehouse since 1740 and grew up to be a three storey building in 1810. One of its best periods of prosperity came when Napoleon was being kept prisoner aboard the Bellerophon in Plymouth Sound – nowadays it's somewhat quieter. There used to be a drying cellar below the pub, for salting pilchards but that's now filled in; there used to be a fair sprinkling of smugglers amongst the customers but now they're no longer so prevalent; there used to be lots of fishermen in the bar and thankfully there still are, providing a thoroughly seagoing atmosphere – as long as you're not offended by their often too 'salty' talk.

Enjoy, too, The Devonport Inn's hand-drawn Best Bitter and the Ind Coope on draught which are ideal for washing down the pasties and sandwiches available in the plain and pleasant interior of this one-bar pub.

House. Round this, you'll see a footpath marked 'Maker Church $1\frac{1}{4}$'. Walk up this path, overhung with brambles and ivy and, at the crossing of paths, go right. The path follows a broken black fence, under the fort-like building, now derelict and left to the weeds and brambles. Here the path swings away from the coast. As you continue climbing, notice the covered, though unfortunately polluted, well. Just after it, you turn right onto a lane which you follow for a while down past a farm, after which you turn right towards Fort Picklecombe. Watch for the footpath marked 'Maker Church $\frac{1}{2}$' over a two metal bar stile to your left and here you know you've walked $\frac{3}{4}$ of a mile since the last sign. Easy, wasn't it?

The path follows a line of telegraph poles – so do you – and then you cross a second stile and go round the right-hand edge of a field to a third stile by the white house. Cross its drive and walk along the edge of the building to a fourth stile. The path sticks to the top edge of the field and cuts through a broken kissing-gate – (all those broken hearts – aaahh) into another field where you turn right and hug the wall to the sharp corner of the field for your fifth and final stile. A regular little steeplechase this walk is turning out to be. Aim for the church and after a quick visit, you take the footpath already mentioned with the silly joke about football scores.

And so now, if you've collected any members of the party who went the short way, proceed down the path indicated above and through the gate and out onto the road. Turn right, letting your legs appreciate the joys of easy, downhill walking. On your right is an interesting looking thing which, though it looks like a trough for thirsty horses (and no doubt is used as such) is, in fact, St Julian's Well. Well, well. Continue down the road watching both for traffic and for charming glimpses, through the trees, of Millbrook Lake, though at low-tide only a few little streams wearily wend their way across the mud to the Tamar.

After a while, you'll see Higher Lodge on your right, an arched entrance to Mount Edgcumbe Park. Go through this gateway and then fork left off the metalled roadway down along a bridleway. Follow this through a plantation of huge trees and where you can see the Earl's house up to your right, turn left down a metalled track, along the edge of the grassy avenue back to the park gates at Cremyll and a welcome tipple to wet your whistle at The Edgcumbe Arms. Cheers to the Earl.

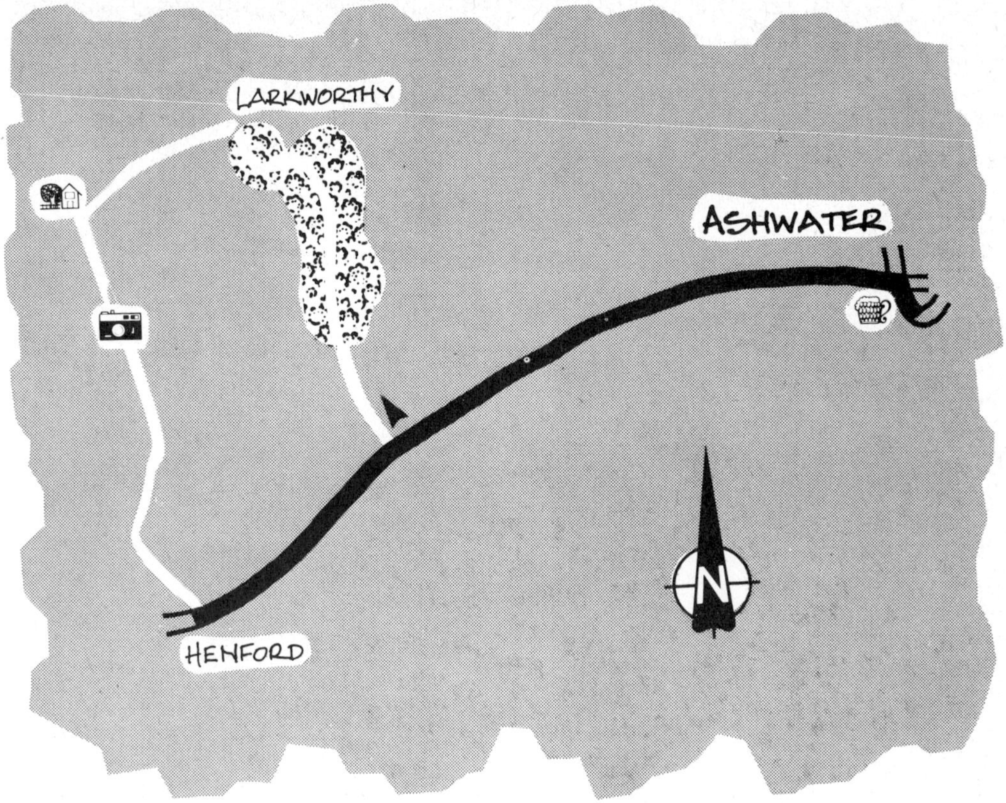

8 Ashwater

APPROXIMATELY 3½ Miles

The District

Ashwater is an attractive village which has seen better days. Remote and passed by now, Ashwater wears an air of slight melancholy which grows with each new event in the chain of its gradual decline. Since the closure of the railway forced it off the beaten track, the village has become a backwater with a high proportion of older people in its population. Its that same old story of the countryside as young people leave for the opportunity of the towns and cities and, in so doing, cut themselves off from their rural heritage. It can sometimes seem as if time here is marked by the intervals between the funerals which are held at St Peter's in Chains, the local church.

All this is not to say that Ashwater is without charm; far from it, there is life around the old village green yet. It's a sociable spot where the villagers greet strangers with a smile as they go about their business. A row of Victorian cottages looks out over the triangular green to St Peter's church, which in turn faces over to The Manor Inn, the nub of local life and your starting point.

How to Get There

By road take the A388 north from Launceston and turn right on to an unclassified road for Ashwater (approx 9 miles). Alternatively take the A388 south from Holsworthy and turn left on to the unclassified road (approx 6

miles). *By rail* there is a regular train service to Plymouth. *By bus* On weekdays you can catch the 637 to Ashwater.

The walk should be considered as an aperitif. It's an easy amble out of town to Larkworthy Farm, then across to Henford and back to base.

It's short and to the point and the point is what nicer way could there be of working up a thirst. Be warned – it is muddy in parts; it's also the easiest walk in the book and full of what gladdens the birdwatcher's heart – so don't leave your binoculars behind.

The Ashwater Walk

Begin at the bar of **The Manor Inn,** where you can afford to indulge yourselves a little since the walk will not be tough. The Ushers Ale is hand-drawn and should be washed down with cockels and mussels – or is it the other way round?

Turn left out of the inn and left again along the road in the direction marked Launceston. On your left you'll pass some stables and a row of houses on the right. Keep going for about 600 yards till you come to Kit Hill House which is on your right. Turn right down the muddy path beside the house and watch out for the family of cats in the farmyard who may or may not own the joint but certainly give the impression that they do.

This track used to be a vital local artery to Blagdon and Nethercroft before modern transport rendered it redundant for anyone but the local farmers and rabbits. Towering trees line the track – lofty oaks, ash and sycamores, with stunted hollies and hawthorns striving vainly to emulate their heights. In the neighbouring fields pheasants strut in season where warblers warble, chaffinches twitter and passing wood pigeons coo in an ornithological medley of sight and sound. Above them, the buzzards circle adding menace to the harmonious scene.

The track bends right, then left; a stream flows quietly by at your feet – the steep-banked lane abounds in foxgloves, dandelions, buttercups and shepherd's purse. As the line bends sharply right, proceed through the gate on the left, from which you can see Larkworthy Farm.

Head for the farm buildings across the field – go through a gate and turn sharp left after the cowshed. Leave the actual farmhouse behind and to your right as you head for your next gate – avoiding the first gate which is slightly to the right and before the one you want.

After the gate, turn off to the right and follow the public footpath-cum-track which curves left to the far corner of the field. In the corner there are two gates, take the right-hand one downhill into a large sloping field. Follow the hedge on your left and leave by the gate in the far left-hand corner. There's a hedge down the middle of the next field and you can walk on either side of it down to the stream below.

Turn left at the stream and go along the bank to the point where the power lines cross it. Now you have to wade across – piranhas are rare around here – or find your own stepping stones; there are some somewhere. This mild problem over, follow the power lines up the field – not the ones going left – and into the next field. When you reach the top of the second field, pass through the obvious gap between the two trees and then through the garden gate to the parish road.

At the road, turn left and follow into Ashwater. First the road goes down – what goes down must come up (in this book, anyway) – then up as the road swings left past peaceful meadows and spinnies over a narrow stone bridge. As the hill looms above, switch into lowest gear and ease up. You may see a pair of donkeys in a field here doing a Tweedledum, Tweedledee act. This reminds me of the need at this point to dangle a carrot in front of your noses – picture a brimming pint of Ushers real ale and surge up the hill and into Ashwater. You'll find the inn on your right and you'll arrive there with all the strength you could want in your right arm, the one you do the drinking with.

The Manor Inn, Ashwater

The Estate of Portsmouth used to own the inn and even stuck a large letter 'P' on the building to prove it. In fact, The Manor Inn used to be a shooting lodge with gun racks where the bar is and servant's quarters upstairs, now the haunt of an unhappy spirit who is sadly fated to emerge from time to time from the burning fireplace.

The inn is built of white painted Devon stone and in winter it is well heated by two coal fires. Hunting scenes line the wall and if you look out of the window at the right time of year, you can see the cherry blossom which decorates the village green.

Beers are hand-drawn Ushers and keg Ben Truman, Worthington E and Draught Devon Cider. Snacks are more than adequate too, including ploughman's lunches, pasties and sandwiches.

If you fancy your hand at darts, there's an entertaining old machine for sharpening the tips and, at the week-ends, there's live country and western music.

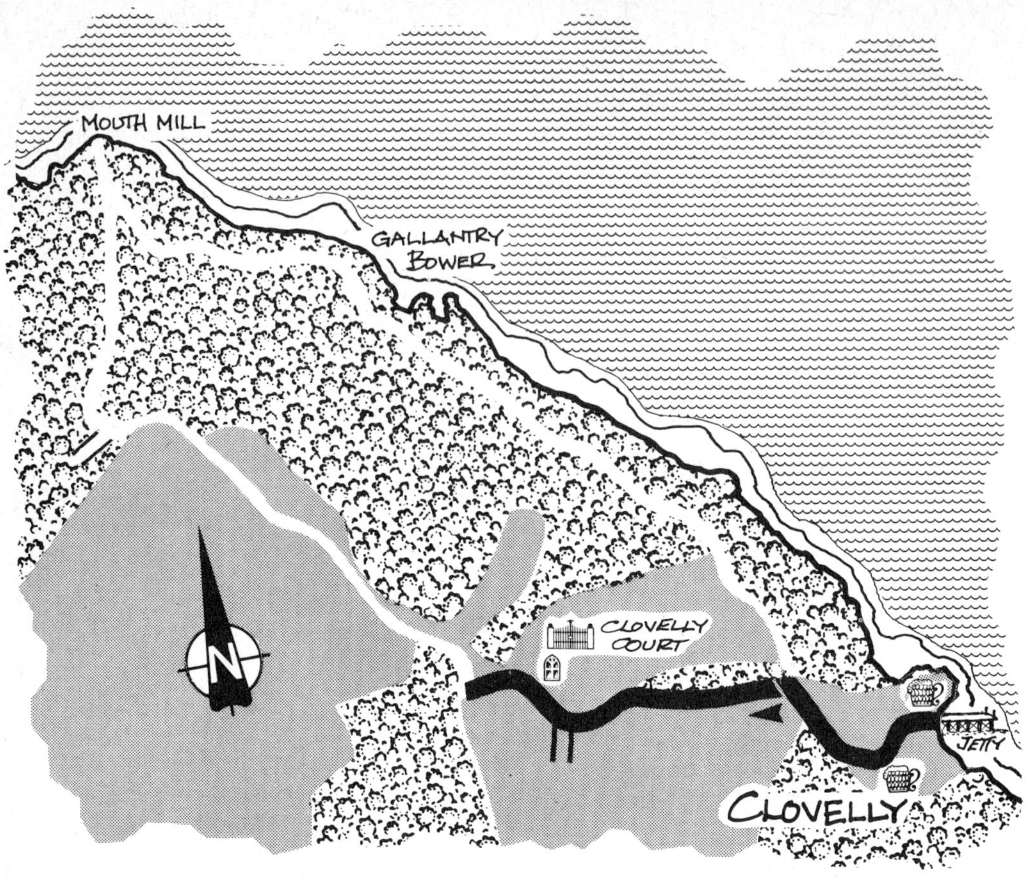

9 Clovelly

APPROXIMATELY 4 Miles

The District

'Britain in Bloom' winner in 1975 Clovelly has an unspoilt chocolate box prettiness. Its cottages cluster, 'perched on each others' shoulders', on either side of its one cobbled street. Much of the attractiveness of the village is due to Mrs Patricia Hamlyn and her daughter Christine, former local gentry from Clovelly Court, who philanthropically restored and embellished most of the cottages and planted many of the fuchsias, roses and honeysuckle in the handkerchief-sized gardens.

Flanked by richly wooded, soaring cliffs, Clovelly was painted by Whistler and Turner, was described by Charles Kingsley (whose father was rector) in *Westward Ho!* and was renamed 'Steepways' by Dickens in *A Message from the Sea.* It is a village of steps, donkeys, cats and cannibalism ... er, perhaps this needs a little explanation. There was once a Clovelly family called the Greggs who were cannibals and who reputedly murdered about 1,000 people. Unforgettably, pickled legs were their favourite snack – much in the way that the French eat frogs' legs. It certainly wasn't the Greggs who put the lovely in Clovelly.

How to Get There

By road take the A39 west from Bideford and turn right onto the B3237, passing through Dyke to Clovelly (approx 10 miles). *By rail* there is a regular 125 service to Barnstaple. *By bus* the 301 and 326 run between Barnstaple and Bideford regularly; then a 319 to Clovelly.

The walk takes you to the church near Clovelly Court and leads you on through peaceful English farmland, down a small stream to the pretty beach at Mount Mill, where you climb steeply up to the top of the astonishingly sheer and tall Gallantry Bower. You weave through serene and elegant woodland back to Clovelly. It's a walk of rich variety and not one to be hurried.

The Clovelly Walk

So, dear hedonistic walker, steel yourself for a surfeit of pleasure, put on your gumboots if it has recently rained, sling binoculars nonchalantly over your shoulder and set off out of Clovelly's upper car park, down the road where you came in. You pass a field on your left with a half-eaten sign, asking you not to feed the donkeys or the mule. I trust that in fact the sign is simply broken and that the animals are well-fed, because they are one of the methods by which everything is taken down to and up from the village. Consequently they are an important, indeed essential, part of village life. Turn left at the white lines and walk along the pavement until a sharp left-hand bend in the road, where you turn right through the white gates down the path to the church. The church, set snugly with its stately yews and well-kept churchyard in the lea of Clovelly Court, looks nothing if not a picture of tranquillity, until you enter and realise that the village is in fact a hotbed of campanolgists, desperately striving for the Torridge Inter-Parish Victor Ludorum. Put less pompously, the village can boast a lovely small church and expert and famed bellringers.

To continue the walk, go round the church tower (on the path, naturally) and out of the churchyard through the small metal gate that was presumably for the exclusive use of the squire and his family. Turn left ➤

The New Inn, Clovelly

Half-way down the street, the double-balconied New Inn is a lovely, if not very new, inn. It's 15th century. It's snug and cosy in the bar with mementoes from all over the world (including an antipodean Clovelly) and if you have children, there's a pretty, walled garden outside as well as a children's room (with pinball).

You may be called 'chap' or 'maid' by Wally Davey, the landlord, or indeed by any villager; this is due to the large number of visitors and the impossibility of remembering their names. One name not forgotten is Christine Hamlyn, whose 12ft x 6ft picture hangs in the dining room, and whose ghost has been seen in the hotel – but only by other women. ➤

immediately round the churchyard wall to a metalled drive. Here you follow the signs straight on to Court Farm, the Estate Sawmill and the public bridleway. Ignoring the sewage treatment plant down to your right (a small blemish on the otherwise pure complexion of the walk), follow the drive down to the wood and over a crossing, staying on the tarmac drive. You go over the bridge and up to the farm, where there are fine old mill-stones leaning against a wall. Walk past the farmhouse with its sundial and Latin inscription and past a beautiful old open barn and then pick your way daintily across the concrete yard to a wooden gate marked with blue and yellow arrows.

Go through the gate and straight on along a stony track across the field. Leave the field through another gate and then proceed along a track between brambles and woods below and the bank with its cropped hedge above. This part can be muddy, so don't be tempted to look up at a passing jet (from the Chiverton base) or you may come a cropper. Go through the gate at the end and look to your right at the beautiful woodland as you strike out on the track that goes right, diagonally across the field. The track leads you down to a gate, through which you go. From here you go straight ahead along the edge of the wood until you see a gate.

This leads you down a small path, lushly overhung with all manner of vegetation. After rain, stop at the bottom and sniff: the differing smells of stream, pine and other greenery are worth a few moments deep inhalation. Turn left along the track and then soon turn right down over the bridge with its babbling brook below (a spot of alliteration for you) and then turn right again along a path leading down through the pines. Unless it's the height of summer, this is where you'll curse if you're wearing anything less waterproof than gumboots, as this path can be extremely wet. You follow the path down as it follows the stream, past an old stone cottage on the far bank, and out to the sea by the derelict mill buildings. The stream disappears under a ridge of pebbles, providing you with a crossing point.

The beach here at Mouth Mill is enclosed by cliffs – their strata have been twisted and folded by great geological upheavals way back in the world's infancy. This dramatic sight is heightened both by a waterfall that tumbles from cliff top to sea to your left, and the natural arch of Blackchurch Rock jutting into the waves to your right.

Cross the stream over the pebble bridge and go round the wall and then left up to the grassy area above. From here take the marked coast path up the stony drive. Soon you see a path that doubles back up to the left and now begins *the* climb: so, girding up your loins, begin your ascent, following the grassy path as it doubles back again to the right. Then fork left up the really quite steep path along the edge of the cliff. At the top – well done – you are amply rewarded with a fantastic view from this almost 400ft and completely sheer cliff, though, of course *great* care should be taken.

The complete panorama stretches from the rolling and wooded hills and fields inland, past Blackchurch Rock, out to sea to Lundy Island, once the haunt of pirates, now mostly of sea birds, out to sea again and round to Morte Point in the east. As for the view downwards, it's enough to give a steeplejack vertigo and gives all two-up, two-down dwellers an exaggerated idea of what the 25th floor of a tower block must be like.

So, glutted with magnificence, follow the path on past holly trees, laden with berries in season, and gorse to where it rejoins the grassy track. You turn left here as marked by the coast path sign and soon you pass a beautifully carved wooden sheltered seat. As you walk, watch for woodpeckers, pigeons and the countless squirrels that peck, swoop and scurry about their various businesses. The grassy path continues through the trees until just after a minute quarry where it becomes stony and, when it begins to go downhill, fork left along the grassy coast path, again marked.

From under spreading oaks, you come to a kissing-gate (the first of many). Go through, wishing of course, and pass by the bench round the tree to another kissing-gate. Once through, go down the steps, along through rhododendrons and up the steps to another but plainer sheltered seat. Take the path behind, again through rhododendrons, up to a wooden kissing-gate this time. Negotiate this and turn left along the fence to yet another kissing-gate. Are you courting? If so, I hope you're capitalising on all these little aids to romance. That was your final kissing-gate and after it, keep on between the fence and the line of trees. When the path begins to descend, you reach a fork. Go right here and soon you meet a stony track above the trees where you turn left and walk to a green gate. Through this, go straight on to meet the road and continuing in the same direction, you arrive at the top of the steep descent to Clovelly, just above small Mount Pleasant Park, donated by the Hamlyn family to the village. Walk down into Clovelly, down its cobbled street between its white and colour-washed cottages, looking for the sledges that, along with the donkeys and mule and, it must be added, a Land Rover, are the means of carrying everything in and out of the village. You almost tumble into **The New Inn** and if this isn't enough, you can rush on down to **The Red Lion Hotel** on the 600 year old harbour wall. For those of you who might be wary of the stagger back up the hill, there is a Land Rover service, operating between 9.00 and 17.00, which can take you back up, though one of the nicest things about Clovelly is the absence of cars and the noise that goes with them. Talking of absences, there are no or, at least, very few dogs. Yet cats abound. An unwritten law that doesn't allow the owning of dogs recognises that while cats are known for their burying habits, dogs aren't and a cobbled street is difficult to wash.

There is hand-drawn Whitbread Bitter, local cider and two lagers for you to choose from along with a standard range of bottled beers and spirits. The list of bar meals is as extensive as it's tasty (both hot and cold) and there's an à la carte menu in the evenings.

The Red Lion, Clovelly

It's only natural that a village as charming and unique as Clovelly should also have The Red Lion. It's built on Clovelly's 600 year old pier, though the inland section of the building is even older, dating from the 13th century. No doubt it would have been a lively place on evenings after the village's fishermen had landed successful herring catches and perhaps even more lively when sailors brought Welsh coal here. In fact the coal cellars would have been filled and the cider houses emptied, though sadly these no longer exist.

The pub is suitably decked out with fishing and nautical decoration – nets, floats, lobster pots, naval hatbands etc – and the old beams, stone fireplace and original cobbles on the wall all add to its charm. It's a free house with Courage Best on handpump. A standard range of other beers, bottled beers are augmented by a good range of wines and some malt whiskies. The menu in the restaurant is a mixture of à la carte and table d'hôte and bar food, all home-made, ranges from cold snacks through pies and pasties to basket meals. Naturally, the Red Lion makes sea food a speciality.

PUB – 5 MILES

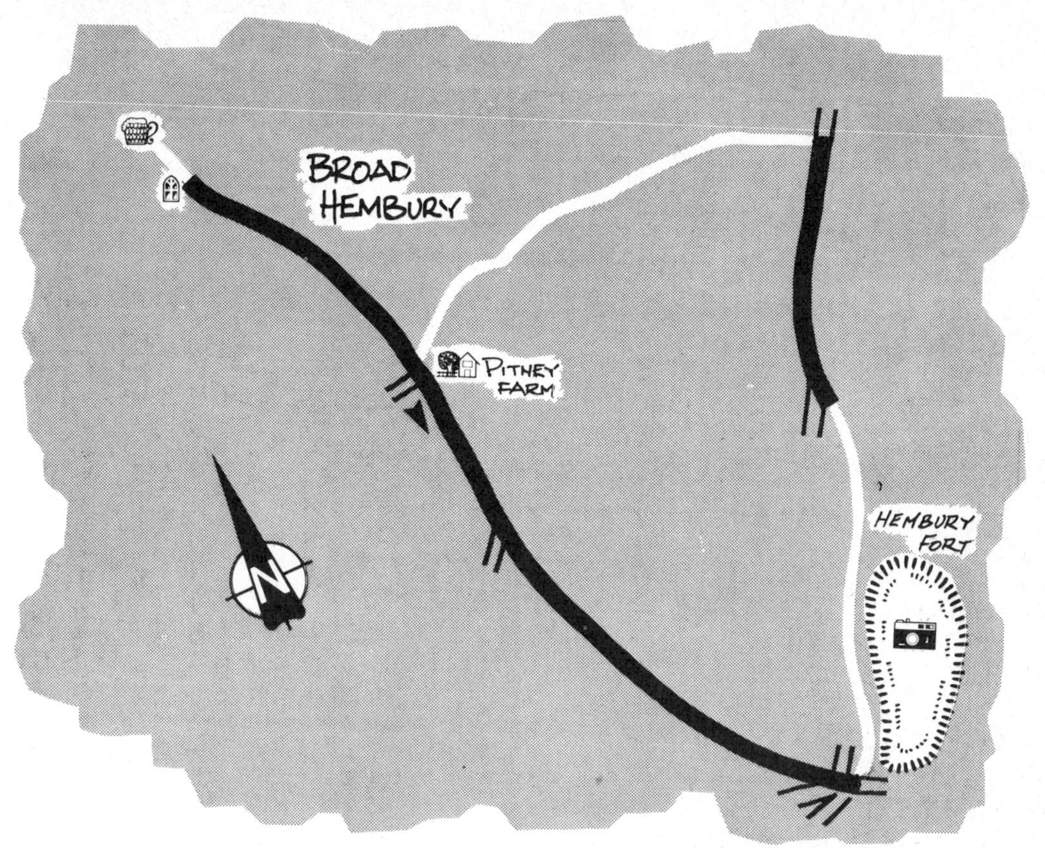

10 Broadhembury

APPROXIMATELY 3½ Miles

The District

The nearest town to Broadhembury is Honiton which is the proud possessor of a long straight Roman main street, part of the Fosse way. Honiton is a town of antique shops and Georgian architecture which will repay the price of a morning or afternoon's visit with interest; the interest, largely being provided by St Margaret's Hospital's 16th century thatched cottages, the mammoth bones uncovered by the by-pass builders which you can discover in the local museum, and Allhallows Museum which will put you in the picture about Honiton lace-making, which arrived with Flemish refugees in the 16th century and is still going today, if less furiously than before. The town was burnt down in 1747 and again in 1765, when fire brigades lacked the effectiveness of today's. On much the same subject, you should not miss out on the Honiton pottery, with its exhibition of the famous products of more controlled firing.

Broadhembury is a snug and settled, picture postcard village which nestles in the middle of lush dairy farmlands. It is a place which has retained its cosy rural atmosphere by a policy of preservation – the village remains much as it must have been when it was built.

The white-walled, thatched cottages give immediately on to the main street and to compensate for the lack of gardens, their walls come alive in summer with rambling rose, clematis and fuschia. There's Virginia creeper, too, and house martins nest under

the thatched eaves in the centre of the village, below the yew and chestnut trees which rise tall above the village square.

This is a conservation area and there are government grants to ensure that little is changed in the appearance of this pretty spot. It is an unspoilt village which is guaranteed not to disappoint the visitor. It's so quiet that almost any time a voice is raised in the main street, you can hear the echo.

How to Get There

By road take the A373 north-west from Honiton and turn right on to an unclassified road for Broadhembury (approx 6½ miles). *By rail* to Honiton. *By bus* the 361 goes from Honiton to Broadhembury on Wednesdays and Saturdays or alternatively catch the 363 on Fridays from Exeter.

The walk takes you from Broadhembury up to the heights of Hembury Fort and then back by a fairly difficult and overgrown path. Wellingtons are essential, as is a bit of fortitude on the homeward stretch.

The Broadhembury Walk

The walk begins in **The Drewe Arms** where, in the harsh winter of 78-79, various regulars were snowed in in the pub for five days after a wedding. Well, imprisonment had its compensations and it is believed that cheques for large amounts were cashed. Is it true, though, that all rescue attempts were resisted from within?

Turn right out of the ancient doorway of the inn, and head through the lych gate of the church, 20 yards away. You are heading left across the churchyard but break your journey to inspect the lovely church with its 15th century barrel roof, medieval bosses and the 14th century font with a pedestal. It also has a memorial to the Rev Augustus Toplady, the hell-fire preacher who wrote the hymn *Rock of Ages* and was vicar here from 1768-1778. The church now caters for the congregation of three different local parishes.

Go right, up the lane on the far side of the churchyard, passing over a stream on your way. The lane is signposted to Honiton. As you walk on, you pass an old chapel on the left painted a truly bilious green, the lane subtly taking you uphill and to a road junction. In the meantime, notice you are suddenly panting a little, or is it gasping, at the prospect of climbing Hembury Hill to your left. The view to your right (over the lowlands) is less daunting, a 'riot' of greens and more greens.

At the road junction turn left . . . be careful it's busy. Go past a mini crossroads and about 80 yards up, on the left hand-side of the road, there's an opening opposite a parking spot and a couple of road signs. Turn off the road here and follow the path up, Hembury Hill – it begins slightly to the right as you turn in. Four yards along this path (only 4!), branch left and drag your huffing and puffing body to the top. Gorse and bramble bushes may try and hold you back, don't let them, the view from the top is wonderful. On a clear day you can see to Halton Belvedere and Dartmoor.

At the top continue along the path to the left of the ramparts. Neolithic man lived here around 1800 BC and the ramparts are 1,000 feet long and 300 feet wide. The atmosphere of past deeds persists where much of the old fortification may have disappeared under vegetation. Many prehistoric items have been uncovered in excavations here, flints, pots, beads etc. Note also that it couldn't have been much fun carrying the shopping up here, as it's 900 feet high.

Follow the path along the left-hand side of the hill, taking frequent views over the ramparts. You will come to a gully – go down, then up again . . . repeat this down and up motion . . . then once more with a smile. This spot was probably the site of a prehistoric roller-coaster. Now, still keeping to the left of the hill top, you come out into a delightful beech coppice complete with magical light and shade.

Suddenly a road appears quietly on the left (depending on the traffic), cross to it and continue along it in much the same direction as before. There's an avenue of beech trees by the road, again the light is filtered through the foliage. When you hit open road, there's a majestic pig stye on your left with an amusing parade of straggling trees and snuffling inmates.

Next you come to a new stretch of trees and soon, to the left of the road, is a field in the midst of the trees. At the end of the field, there's a muddy track which turns left off the road. Follow this to the edge of the wood.

As you reach the trees, go slightly left – near the fence which marks the end of the field – and continue straight down a steep slope till you reach the path below which, at first sight, appears to be a stream running between two banks (i.e. you have now performed a slight deviation to the left before continuing on your original course). It is very steep here so be careful in picking your way down amongst the trees.

When you get to the path, turn left and follow it as it winds its marshy way along. It is often overgrown but never impassable – if, by chance, you have a light macheté about your person, now is the time to bring it out in readiness, as you move through a landscape of badger holes and fallen trees, with a brief glimpse of Broadhembury snatched through the scanty trees to your right. The path winds out of the woods and becomes muddier, it is still overgrown and tree-lined. At this point your correspondent saw two red deer – oh dear – which scampered up the path and scarpered.

Continue up the path, looking out for pheasants in the nearby woods to distract you from the brambles which are launching loathsome attacks on your flailing limbs. Console yourselves with the thought that these scratches and cuts can give you a very real sense of the immediacy of nature. After being forced to perform a quick spurt of limbo dancing, you will find that the path widens into a track; so brush the spiders from your earholes and pluck the twigs from your jumper. At the road, turn sharp right and follow the road past pre-Elizabethan, Broadhembury House, owned and occupied by Lady Drewe (not, in fact, the original Drewe family of Broadhembury but the one whose family acquired seigneurial rights over the village in the 1930s).

Now back in the village square, notice how the walk has taken a little of the edge off your appreciation of the village's beauty . . . The Rambling Rose you'd most like to see now is of the talkative barmaid variety . . . there is a remedy for this complaint and it lies not a million miles from the bar in The Drewe Arms.

The Drewe Arms, Broadhembury

The Drewe Arms presents a comforting face to the world, perfectly in keeping with the quiet atmosphere of Broadhembury. Not much escapes the notice of this old building which looks out over the village square. As you go through its low door you are entering a building which has been used for 700 years.

Inside it is plain and simple with authentic old wooden panelling. There are two bars, one distinctly and engagingly, small. Warm coal fires bring comfort in winter and should you, in leaving, glance up and see the red lion above the door, worry not, since this is not a case of the 'pink elephants'; the pub was once called The Red Lion. More mysterious is the origin of the large letter 'D' on the building – does it stand for 'Drewe' or 'Devon', or what?

There's gravity fed Whitbread real ale and draught Bass, keg Tankard, Pale and Mild, to reach the parts other beers cannot. There's also an à la carte menu which offers a tasty choice to eat and children can be accommodated (and kept quiet), in the room upstairs.

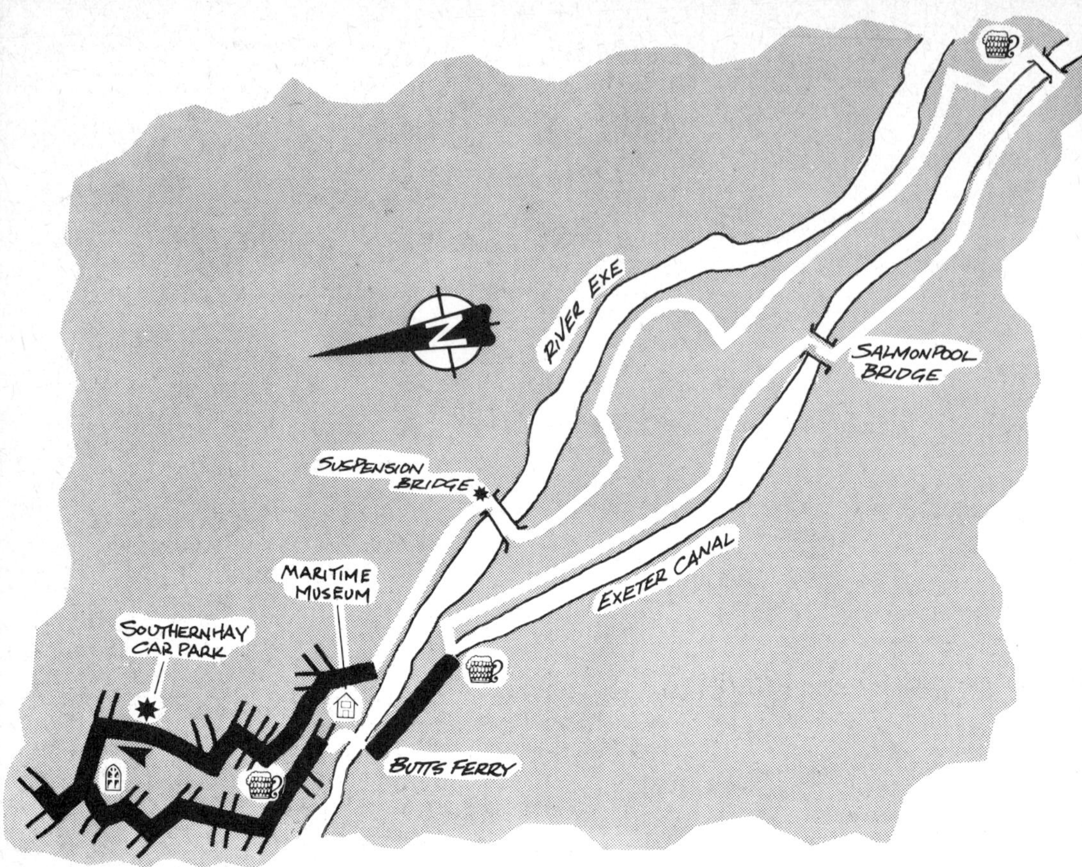

11 Exeter

APPROXIMATELY 5 Miles

The District

A shallow section of the River Exe marks the spot where the graceful Devon cathedral town of Exeter had its first humble origins in the 1st century BC as the home of the Dumnonii, a name which is Latin for the Celtic meaning 'the people of the land'. By a process of evolution, the people here became the men of Defenascir, then of Defnum and Defenum . . . you can see that all this was leading up to today's Devon. The city itself started as a small Celtic capital called Caerisc ('waterfort'), which was partly abbreviated (and then lengthened) to Isca Dumnoniorum by the invading Romans in the 1st century AD – or 'water of the people of the land'. Such longwindedness could not last forever! Further historical misadventure and a reversal of consonants brought about 'Exanceaster' in Saxon times and finally, in an age less close to the land, 'Exeter'.

Exeter through the ages has not always been the ideal spot to own a bit of property. Captured twice by the Danes and forcibly re-occupied by King Alfred, then taken in turn by William the Conqueror after a nightmare 18 day siege, a seizure which also marked the limits of the Normans' ambition in the West of England, the city has changed hands frequently enough. In 1549, after the Prayer Book Rebellion, an erstwhile Exeter vicar was executed and hung up for 4 years from the top of his church tower. The Blitz in 1942 also took a severe toll of the city buildings.

There's lots to see in Exeter and the walk takes you to the Cathedral and the Maritime Museum which stands by England's oldest canal, first dug in 1566 as an answer to the Countess of Devon's wayward line of argument which, in her spite at the city council, consisted of building a weir across the Exe to stop shipping at a place now called Countess Weir. This canal neatly bypassed the problem and on it, you may see extraordinary and exotic craft skimming, paddling or propelling themselves past you – a dhow from Bahrain, a South Seas outrigger or a Welsh coracle – don't worry, the Maritime Museum likes to keep its craft in working order.

You should also try to get to see the Roman ruins, the Royal Albert Memorial Museum and The Guildhall, Britain's oldest court. Oh and try the water here, ancient underground passages beneath the city bring a constant supply of pure, fresh water to Exeter taps . . . on second thoughts, it's also in the local beer.

How to Get There

By road Exeter is on the M5 (junction 30). *By rail* there is a frequent 125 service to Exeter. *By bus* there are numerous bus services in and around Exeter.

The walk goes from near the Cathedral down to the Maritime Museum, along Exeter Canal as far as The Double Locks, and then back, along the river Exe, into Exeter and your starting point.

The Exeter Walk

When you stand with your back to Southernhay car park toilets, you are looking at part of Exeter's old city walls. A plaque further on will tell you that the original walls were built by the Romans in 200 AD, but that they have been repaired by many other hands down the ages. You walk the small road past the light-blue garage doors and along the paved walkway with the city walls on your left, and soon you can read the plaque for yourselves: it's below the city's coat of arms. After the steps, turn left along cobbled Cathedral Close and pass under the quaint blue iron footbridge, which connects sections of the city walls, and soon you arrive at the west end of St Peter's Cathedral. On your right, there's an unspoilt row of irregular and misshapen houses, one being the Bishop of Crediton's residence. The See was moved from Crediton to Exe-

The Prospect Inn, Exeter

On the old Quay of Exeter and next to the famous Maritime Museum, the Prospect has one of the most interesting prospects of any urban pub. With a few modernities removed or covered, it was justifiably featured in the making of TV's *The Onedin Line.* It is between 200 and 300 years old, though bits have been added here and there, now and then and, interestingly, was once the prize in a Daily Sketch 'Win a Pub' competition.

It has just had a £12,000 tart-up, as landlord Mike Perkins puts it, but he adds that its old charm is undiminished. It's a pub with many nooks and crannies, stained oak panelling, a collection of old prints and pictures, Exeter Rowing Club trophies and, more practically, a children's room, back garden and front patio.

There are three real ales, all drawn on beer-engines – Whitbread Bitter, Bass and Royal Oak. On keg, there's Trophy, Tankard, Guinness and Grunhalle lager.

There's a cold table including salads,

ter in 1050 and he's been living here almost ever since. The courtyard of No 10 is worth a quick peep. Moving on past the late Elizabethan Mols Coffeehouse, you reach small St Martin's church. It was consecrated in 1095 though was largely rebuilt in the 15th century. You can go round the church, along small Catherine Street for a look at the ruins of St Catherine's Almshouses, which were founded about 1540. Then, return to the cathedral and enter it.

You can read much more about the Cathedral than I can write here, but of special note are the pale-yellow Beer stone pillars, the roof, which is the longest unbroken stretch of Gothic stone vaulting in the world, the minstrels' gallery, the 15th century clock and, for examples of early graffiti, find your way to the Chapel of Our Lady and there, on the smallish effigy of Edmund Stafford, you can see the handiwork of many amateur engravers, especially one, John Mogridge.

Leaving the Cathedral, turn left across the West Front into Deanery Place and then right down Bear Street to South Street. Turn left down down South Street and just after Concord House, turn right down Coombe Street. Walk on down, under the subway following the sign to the Maritime Museum. Leave the car park by the exit (!) and then go left down Lower Coombe Street and then left again down Quay Hill to the River Exe. **The Prospect** is on your left, so if you've been looking forward to the prospect of a drink, here's your chance.

This is one of the oldest parts of the city and was heavily bombed in the war. You may notice the plaque which explains how Exeter has traded since Roman times by means of the River Exe and since 1566 by canal – this makes it the oldest canal in England. Walk on past the warehouses (which house part of Exeter's Maritime Museum and well worth a look) and cross the river on Butts Ferry (3p adults, 1p kids and the last crossing is at 17.00 in winter and 18.00 in summer). On the far side, go on to the Maritime Museum proper. From here you can hire, between May and October, brightly-painted dinghies, so if you're feeling particularly lazy, you can row to **The Double Locks.** If it's winter and you're feeling energetic (you *should* be feeling energetic – this is a walk), walk round the canal basin past an old railway turntable and follow the railway line to the road by the Woof Boats sign. Turn left along the road and after Maclaine's Warehouse you can walk along the canal side, with its many boats, and on up to the swing bridges. Looking across canal and river, you can see The Judge's Lodgings which is where he stays when the Crown Court is sitting. To get to **The Welcome Inn,** a recommended move, walk up the right-hand side of the canal.

Being careful not to outstay the Welcome, retrace your steps and cross the swing bridge to the other bank. You now follow the canal towpath away from Exeter. You pass allotments and rather more gruesomely a factory with a tall chimney. It's an animal by-product factory, where they melt down hooves and bones for glue – the smell can be really vile, so hold your nose. Prettier and more wholesome are the ducks and canoeists, both hopefully afloat. At Salmonpool Bridge, cross the canal and if you want to visit The Double Locks – the best pub on the walk – follow the canal on the other towpath, crossing to the pub over the lock-gates.

Duly refreshed and invigorated for the stride home, walk back, on the pub side of the canal to the higher lock-gate and, 30 yards or so beyond, at a wide grassy area, turn right off the lane, down the path and over the broken fence. With your back to the fence, head slightly to the left of straight ahead(!) towards a tall chimney on the skyline and then soon swing further to the left towards the gasometers. The river curves to meet the path and often, through the sad ivy-clad dead elms, you can see disdainful swans gracefully gliding on this stretch. Rather more uncommon are the cormorants who follow the Exe up its estuary when they get sick of mackerel and fancy a trout for a change. You proceed up to a fence, climb over the stile and continue towards the gasometers. With playing-fields on your left, you cross the causeway to your right, over the River Exe flood channel, which is normally a wide grassy depression. You rejoin the river and continue upstream, along the stretch known as Countess Weir, watching for the Canada geese that ply up and down here.

Unfortunately, you have to leave the river bank and walk round the fence surrounding the very well-kept allotments. Walk under the concrete footbridge and up through the gate on the other side and then across the small suspension bridge over the river. At the path along the wall you turn left and walk past Pitts Hall and the Old Match Factory – now a house. Over the fence you can see round, carved stones, used in the old days for making wheels – well, that's my theory. Further along you pass Trews Weir and the old, but still functioning paper-mill. From the little bridge, take a look in the windows at the massive machinery which is presumably still partly worked by water-power. You pass the Rowing Club and Port Royal and behind the high stone wall beyond is The Judge's Lodgings.

When you're opposite the large funnel looming above the wall on your left, go up Colleton Hill to your right and at the cross-roads, go left along Colleton Crescent – a terrace of highly expensive houses reminiscent of Bath. Go right, up Friar's Gate, past the Salvation Army Temple and straight on up between modern flats to the traffic lights on your left at the top. Cross over the roads, towards the church on the far side and just before it, go right, up Trinity Street. It's now straight on up to the car park and depending on the efficiency of the traffic wardens and the amount you have paid and displayed, your ticketless car.

quiches, turkey pie, cold meats etc. and hot specials include rabbit pie, beef stew, basket meals and the like. Sausage and bacon butties complete the list.

The Welcome Inn, Exeter

A plainish, local pub between the canal and the looming gasworks, it is near where the coasters – rock-hoppers – discharged and loaded up. Apparently, the continental sailors wouldn't use 'the heads' provided in the pub but would simply discharge in the canal. No manners, sailors. Though it must be said that the crews would always surreptitiously leave tips when buying drinks. I'm sure Mr Fred Jones, the landlord, would be pleased to see the custom revived.

The Devenish beers include hand-drawn Wessex and there's a good selection of spirits and wine by the glass. Rudimentary bar snacks and pints can be taken out to the canalside or into the pretty garden, where children are welcome.

The Double Locks Hotel, Exeter

Built in 1702 on the oldest canal in England, it is therefore the oldest lockhouse pub in England. Due to Exeter's trade with Holland, the pub was built of metric Dutch bricks, which were originally used for barge-ballast. Its panelled bar has a very stong nautical flavour, decorated as it is with nets, models and pictures of ships, ropes, anchors, a ship's wheel and an old diver's helmet.

In summer, and with a week's notice, Alan Jones, the landlord, will arrange free boat trips to The Turf Hotel, five miles downriver, and back. If you simply want to sit, have something to eat and drink and relax, then take your pint and snack out to the canalside or large garden and listen for the parrot, in the orchard, who squawks 'Colonel Bogey' and watch out for the goat who eats crisps.

At any one time there are 4 or 5 real ales on offer – Famous Old Timer, Royal Oak, Wadworth's 6X and others which chop and change according to Alan Jones' whim. There's also cider and usual bottled beers and spirits. Bar snacks are of the sausages, pasties and sandwiches variety.

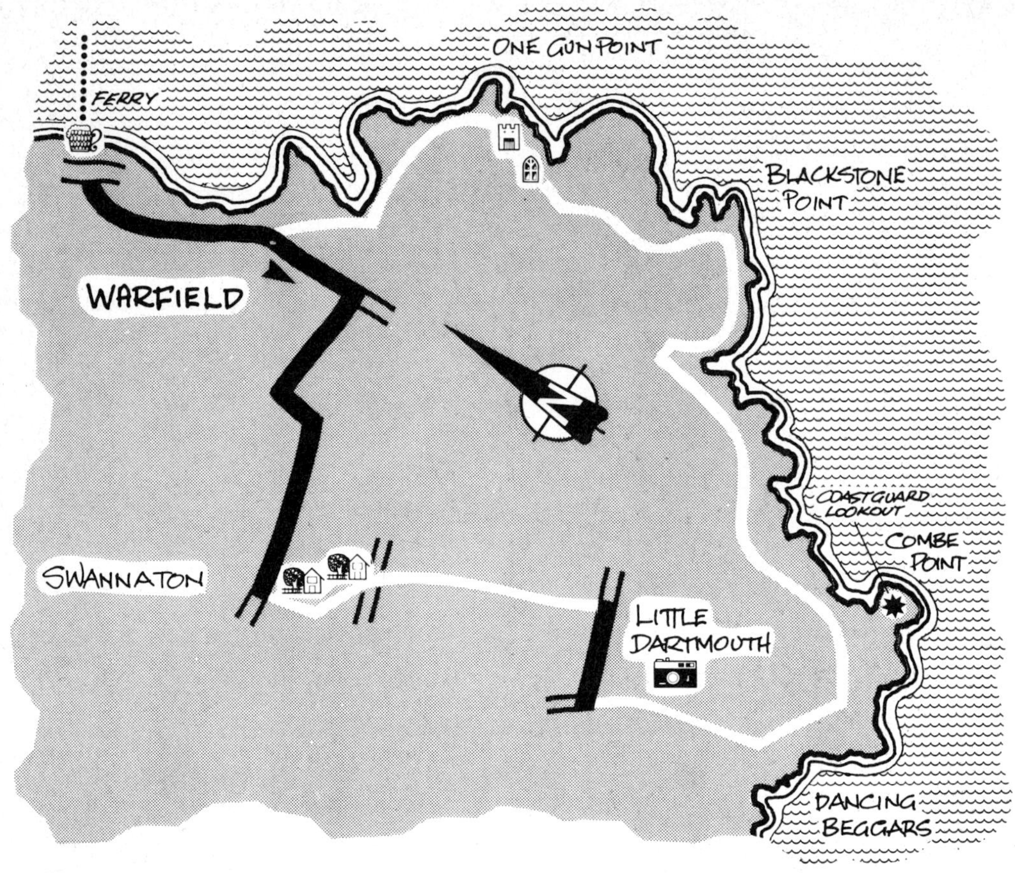

12 Dartmouth

APPROXIMATELY 4½ Miles

The District

Dartmouth had its heyday in the Middle Ages when it was one of the greatest seafaring places in the world and today, despite its decline in the nautical charts, maintains unbroken links with the sea by warmly welcoming seafaring types of all nations for business or pleasure. . . or both.

Dartmouth is a handsome town which stretches elegantly across the hillside overlooking the mouth of the River Dart. Its patient old houses all face down towards the river, as if waiting to see what the next tide will bring. A hunt for fine Elizabethan houses up the narrow streets of the town is a must for any visitor, who may, indeed see much else besides – perhaps local yachtsmen on the heights above town tinkering with sextants or muttering darkly over barometers and, lower down, retired admirals pottering about by sheltered coves sniffing the salty air nostalgically or gazing distantly out to sea. To ensure a correct continuation of the naval tradition here, Dartmouth College's authoritarian facade presides sternly over the whole town – this college has always had strong connections with royalty.

The best way to arrive in Dartmouth is by Ferry from Kingswear across the Dart Estuary (frequent service – £1.70 return). The view of the town will inspire you with a sense of history particularly if you read the following lines; this fine deep-water harbour has witnessed in its time:– the sailing of Rufus for Normandy in 1099 for a spot of

pre-EEC 'negotiation'; the gathering of the great European fleets for the second and third crusades; the sight of the 'Mayflower' forced back for repairs by Atlantic storms; a brief resurgence of glory in World War II when 485 American and British vessels collected here for D-day and the Normandy landings and, finally, the filming of *The Onedin Line.*

Much more graceful and dignified than neighbouring holiday resorts, Dartmouth sinks or swims on the attractions and resources of its river. The main local industries are small scale shipbuilding, crabbing and tourism. There's plenty to see and do in Dartmouth, but you must find your own way to the town sites and sights. However, the walk does take you past Dartmouth Castle and St Petrox church.

How to Get There

By road from the M5 (junction 31) go south onto the A380, then onto the A3022 and then right onto the A379 (approx 25 miles). *By rail* to Plymouth. *By bus* the 91 and 93 buses to Dartmouth from Plymouth.

The walk is more of a leisurely stroll up a gentle mountain slope out of town to Swannaton (shome mishtake here shurely), followed by a safe gambol by the salty brine back to Dartmouth.

The Dartmouth Walk

The Dartmouth Arms is set beside the cobbled quay and the Old Customs House which lends character to Bayard's Cove. It lies up the first road to the left as you drive off the Lower Ferry . . . but you'll be more than lucky if you find a parking space here. After a pint of what you fancy (a little of it does you good) in this friendly establishment which rejoices in the nickname 'Home Of The Stars', head right out of the door and follow

The Dartmouth Arms, Dartmouth

The Dartmouth Arms started in business 400 years ago as a cider house. Fortunately, the choice of drinks has improved considerably since those days and the pub offers warmth and hospitality to the modern guest.

The smaller end bar was once an archway into the next door courtyard, before the building was extended and it can still feel like a doorway in the nightly, closing time stampede.

The walls are cluttered with nautical memorabilia, including a ship's wheel, port and starboard lights and pennants. The corridor houses a collection of the photographs of the many stars who have dropped by for a drink, amongst them Twiggy, Kris Kristofferson, Sarah Miles and Meryl Streep.

The jovial staff here will furnish the paying guest with a selection of keg Courage beers and draught Guinness and cider. Snacks, sandwiches (including fresh crab) and basket meals can also be bought. This pub is not recommended for children who will nonetheless find it pleasant to remain outside in exciting Bayard's Cove.

The Olde Country House Inn, Dartmouth

The Olde Country House Inn is in the centre of Dartmouth by the Market Place, which is just round the corner from the Butterwalk.

the wall of the building till you get to some steps, hidden to the right of the garages ahead. Ascend and turn left up the street opposite The Trafalgar. Keep going uphill till a sign saying 'Above Town' appears on your right; here two lanes go off inland, take the second one, Swannaton Road, and follow up past houses which include 'Temeraire' 'Plimsoll House', 'Tap Scott' and 'Touch Down'.

Pass 'Lower Swannaton Farm' on a corkscrew bend and you're in the country. Climb the road up the hill, calling on muscular reserves you never knew you had, following the route as it zig zags. There's a straight stretch at the top with a row of farmbuildings, old and new, culminating in an extravagant modern garage marked 'Swannaton' and electronically operated. Immediately after the garage, turn left through a gate and follow the track which takes you past allotments and 'Higher Weeke' farmyard on its way to another road.

At this road, turn left and, in a few yards, first right with the public footpath which takes you over a stile to the right of Weeke Cottage.

Head for a gap in the hedge straight ahead up the field and then up to the top left-hand corner where there are three gates. Take the middle one and follow the track past a selection of barriers till you reach a row of white cottages. This is Little Dartmouth, so called because . . . well, I leave the explanation up to you.

By these cottages, turn right at the junction of the tracks and make your way between the long low outhouses old and new, and past the partly hidden tennis court to your right.

Soon, along this road, you get to two fine coniferous trees to your left by the road and 50 yards later there's a stile and a path labelled 'Coastal Footpath'.

Leap the stile with aplomb and head down for the sea. To your right is the town of Stoke Fleming and one 'golden' mile beyond Blackpool Sands (no misshtake here).

White bryony and hedge bedstraw are in evidence along the hedgerow here, together with many other wildflowers. Red admirals, (not the dipsomaniac naval pensioners of the town), rare fritillaries and peacocks (not the birds) flutter by with gay abandon. Swing left to follow the path along the sea and Dartmouthwards and now watch out for cormorants, kestrels and stonechats with their clerical collars. In winter you should see turnstones living up to their name and much else besides.

Along this path, there are plenty of seats where you can take a 'pew' and a view of the jagged rocks which jut like teeth from the sea and the yachts which bobble across the bay in preparation for the Annual Regatta. The path takes you to the Coastguard's look-out post at Combe Point, where you should dally on the veranda and scan the horizon. Then regain the path and walk the old Coastguard route into Dartmouth.

Keep along the path by the sea over several stiles and in a fairly up and down manner till by a plank bridge, you'll find a cave. Next you'll find yourself banking steeply up at Compass Cove and then you'll descend to Blackstone Point – the rocks to your right go by the collective name of 'The Mew Stone'.

Round this point, the path curves upwards. Below you, in the sea, are buoys marking lobster pots and parking spaces for boats. Up this wooded slope you can see mountain ash, hawthorn bushes, sloe bushes, deadly nightshade, (whose berries are not to be confused with sloe berries when making gin), old man's beard and philadelphiums, many of which are suffering from black spot, that fungus caused by damp.

The path becomes a track and hits the road at Compass Cottage. Turn right here and follow the road towards Dartmouth. Take detours for Sugary Cove (where the sand looks like sugar granules) and Castle Cove, where people fish for mackerel and pollock. Then visit Dartmouth Castle and St Petrox Church, the path to them is marked 'to the monument'.

After the castle take the road towards town, which goes right after the bridge near the Pottery (seen through trees on the left), past a quiet cove on the right (not a person).

As you walk down into town you will come to The Trafalgar on your left. Take the steps opposite and then take steps to sort out your thirst at The Dartmouth Arms, 'Home of the Stars'.

A free house abutting on the old market square, it is an old building with ceramic tiles on the outside walls and a porch pillar by the entrance.

Inside, the pillars are timbers from old shipwrecks and the walls are decorated with such diverse objects as shire horse traces and tractor snow chains. The atmosphere is genial and the clientele contains many members of the local crabbing fraternity. Many days of the week there is disco dancing till late and the pub is not without a certain modern outlook.

Among four draught bitters are Toby and Freo's and there's hand-drawn Bass from an old pump. The speciality here is American cocktails – try Bubblegum Shooter, a lethal concotion of tequila, crême de banane etc. The catering is good and the menu changes every day – e.g. hot chilli, minestrone and curry. Vocal entertainment comes in the form of 'Just Kate'. Who? The answer is 'Just Kate'. Who she is and what she sings you have to find out for yourselves.

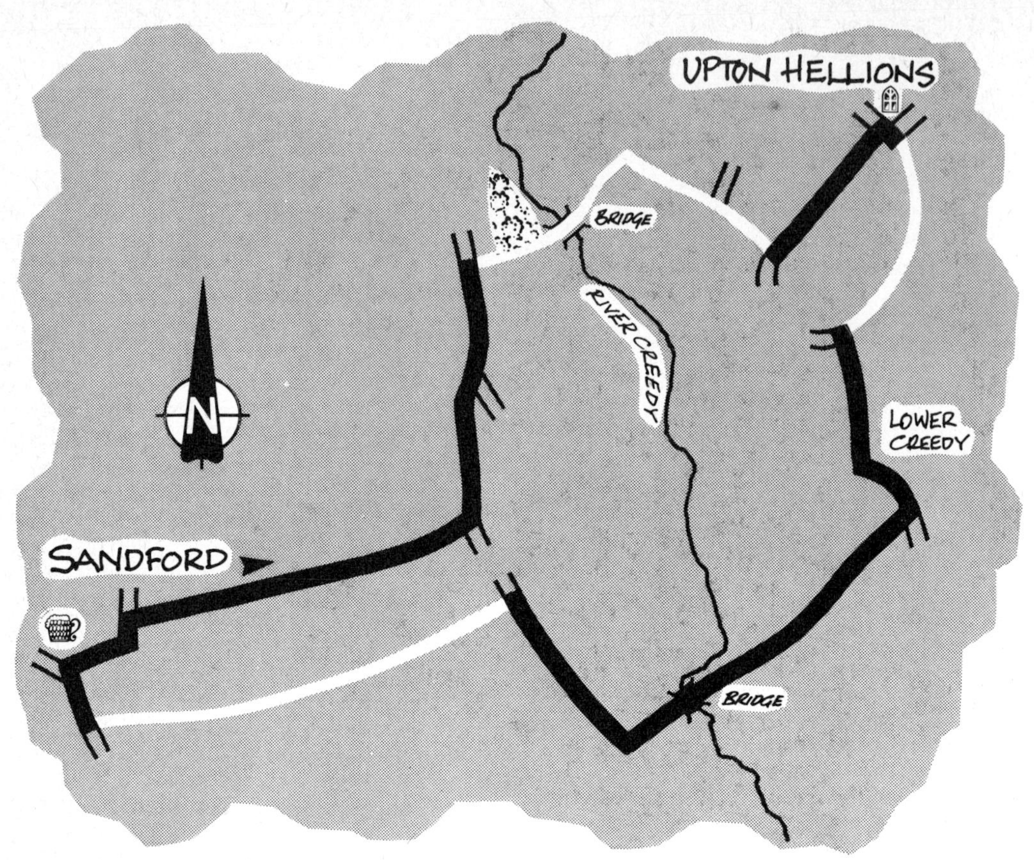

13 Sandford

APPROXIMATELY 2¾ Miles

The District

St Boniface is this area's very own home-grown saint. He was born in Crediton in 680 and as a young man travelled widely on the continent. He met and made an alliance with Pope Gregory II, who sent him to Germany to convert the pagans to Christianity. Having made much progress, he was martyred in Friesia with 50 of his disciples in 755 by hard-line heathens. He was a credit to Crediton and partly due to him the town became a medieval centre of religion and learning.

The town lies between the Rivers Creedy and Yeo and is a fine redbrick and sandstone market-town, though not much of it is more than 200 years old. In 1783, there was a disastrous fire in Old Crediton that had prospered through its wool trade and 460 houses were burnt down. This was in fact not uncommon in overcrowded and cheek-by-jowl Devon towns. There is an almost cathedral-like church and in fact the See was moved from here to Exeter as the latter gained importance as a port. There's a museum in the Chapter House and the 13th century Chapel of St Lawrence is now a school.

Sandford is mostly 18th century and, with its 15th century church and 16th century pub, is a charming village. Oddly enough, from the hilltop at Sturridge just north of Sandford, you can see eleven parishes without seeing a single church, all of which are hidden from sight by hills or trees.

How to Get There

By road the A377 runs north-west from Exeter to Crediton and an unclassified road leads north to Sandford (approx 9 miles). *By rail* to Crediton. *By bus* there is a weekday service, the 377, from Crediton to Sandford.

Short and sweet, this is a gentle walk of oaks, quiet lanes and two country churches in the tranquil patchwork of the Creedy Valley. The walk leaves Sandford, crosses the river to Upton Hellions and recrosses the river bank to Sandford.

The Sandford Walk

You turn left out of the 16th century **Lamb Inn** up to St Swithin's church. Its 1818 painted sundial, its old oak pews, all with little doors and its gallery, on either side of the organ, are only three features of this roomy but fairly small parish church. Returning to the small street, you turn left up to the Old Police House. It seems odd that a village as small as Sandford should have had a police house, but I suspect it was set up by a Ferguson-Davie, Bart, of nearby Creedy Park, to try to deter the villagers from poaching his game and to encourage obedience and loyalty with a little high-profile policing. Who knows? At any rate, nowadays you can pass the house with impunity and no fear of a "Ello, 'ello 'ello what walk are you going on 'ere then. . . ?"

Take the small lane between the old nick and the bottom of a row of very photogenic old houses and walk on, first passing an old News Of The World sign, then old houses and cottages and then Sandford Parish Hall. You're now leaving the village.

At the T-junction, turn left towards East Village and Poughill. This lane winds up down and around, until you pass on your left, a small ivy-clad building of stone and cob where you can prepare yourself for the next instruction. The next instruction is . . . just before the stable of the beige thatched cottage, you turn right down a grassy hedged track towards Upton Hellions. The hedgerows down here are made up of rosehip, ash, small oak, beech, bramble and bracken and amongst this profusion of growth lurk many wild flowers. Further on down, woodpigeons sit and coo in the branches of the taller trees.

When you reach the River Creedy, you can either cross the ford, (being sure to test your brakes soon after) or, if you are only

The Lamb Inn, Sandford

The Lamb commands the square in Sandford and you feel it was and is one of those pubs that the life of the village revolves around and depends on. Once a cider house, the pub has been licensed since 1780 and it's a fine stone and timbered building with a cobbled forecourt. Inside are paintings of how it looked when thatched, and the supporting pillar in the lounge used to be the 'shippings' outside – what the farmer of old tied his horse to, before he wearily trudged into the bar for his evening pint. The original beams, the open fires and the collection of various traps all combine to give the pub an air of rural warmth, and the oak-screen which predates the pub and is probably from the church and the old photos of past landlords make this rural warmth well-established.

The Lamb is a Whitbread's house and D J Seward, the landlord, stocks gravity-fed Huntsman's Royal Oak along with the more usual Tankard, Trophy and Worthington E. There's also Stella Artois.

The food range is very comprehensive and this is no doubt due to the landlord's son who is a chef de cuisine. Though it's not a restaurant, the menu includes trout, steaks, salmon, veal and curry.

And the snacks include scampi, pizza, pies, basket meals as well as sandwiches and ploughman's.

wearing shoes, you turn left (opposite a metal gate) through the tall trees to a narrow wooden bridge over the river. From the bridge the path goes straight on through bracken and back to the hedged track. However this next section of the track has been so neglected, that now it is very overhung and though it starts off merely muddy, it soon becomes a fully-fledged waterway – local wags call it the Sandford Hellions canal. So, in order to avoid this, turn right over the stile, into a field littered with derelict caravans and campers (vans, that is, not people). Keeping the hedge to your left, (this field is the occasional paddock of several horses and a disgruntled donkey), walk past a small gate, across the front of an impressive red stone house and then over a stile on your left onto a small metalled drive by a tall stone and brick building. Passing this on your left, you join a small lane which you follow.

At the S-bend you have a good view uphill of Hellions Church and the adjacent cottage. The oaks lining the lane provide many yards of perch for yet more pigeons and other birds and you may be lucky to see a pheasant arrogantly strut among the cows in any field near here.

At Barton Cross, turn left uphill towards the church and Upton Hellions. This hamlet can boast a famous son, of whom few people have heard. A certain John Parry, a fairly popular composer a century ago, was born here. He probably left soon after, but he went on to play violin at Covent Garden and composed such notable obscurities as 'The Bay of Biscay' before dying unhappily of dissipation. Woe betide all sons of the country who move to the city in search of fame and fortune to find happiness only in a bottle. This book bravely brings you completely useless information, other books wouldn't dare print. Personally, I feel rather sorry for him – would he have been happier here or even in Exeter? Ah, ambition.

To move on to something of more interest to the walker, go up the cobbled churchyard path and waiting for the nesting bird to leave the porch, go into the small church. Sober and unpretentious, it has a cool, calm air and the carved bench ends at the back are worth a close look. Unfortunately, if you're not interested in hedonistic composers or rural churches, Upton Hellions may be a disappointment – it's certainly small.

Leaving the church, go left back the way you came, aiming for the white bungalow ahead. Take the track behind it – can you read its name? – and walk on down a sunken hedged track above the small orchard. The track wiggles down under large oaks and over a small stream to a black wooden kissing-gate. The path, now narrow, leads up to a small metal gate by a white thatched cottage where you turn left along the lane. You pass Rectory Cottage, on your left, with its beautifully kept garden and old barn and then patchy cob field-walls on your right. Follow the lane round, past a row of cottages with a derelict section in the middle – was it a milking parlour, was the whole row farm buildings before? All these questions and more will be answered in our next edition.

A few yards further on, turn right down another lane, signposted Sandford and Crediton. This descends to the valley floor under large oaks to where it crosses the River Creedy on a lovely narrow stone bridge. Pooh-sticks may be played. Walk on along this oak-lined lane and, at Thornedges Cross, turn right towards Sandford and Poughill. Having passed thatched Mooracre, you take the next left; it's marked as a public footpath. At Furlongs (the rest of the walk is only a few from here), you go through the gate and along the track on the right-hand side of the field.

Just after an extraordinarily gnarled row of trees, now chopped and dead, go to the right of a large tree stump and through the small wooden gate. The path runs below a row of white modern houses and goes over a stile half-way along. At the end of the wire-netting fence, continue straight on and then swing very slightly right below a ha-ha. No joke this though, it's an ingeniously designed wall that is invisible from the house it protects, and consequently doesn't obstruct the view. Follow the ha-ha and leave the field through the ornate iron gate and walk down the path back into Sandford. As you emerge, you can see The Lamb dead ahead – well not literally, but going to the left of Jaclini Cottage, at a run by now no doubt, you can arrive at the bar in less than a minute.

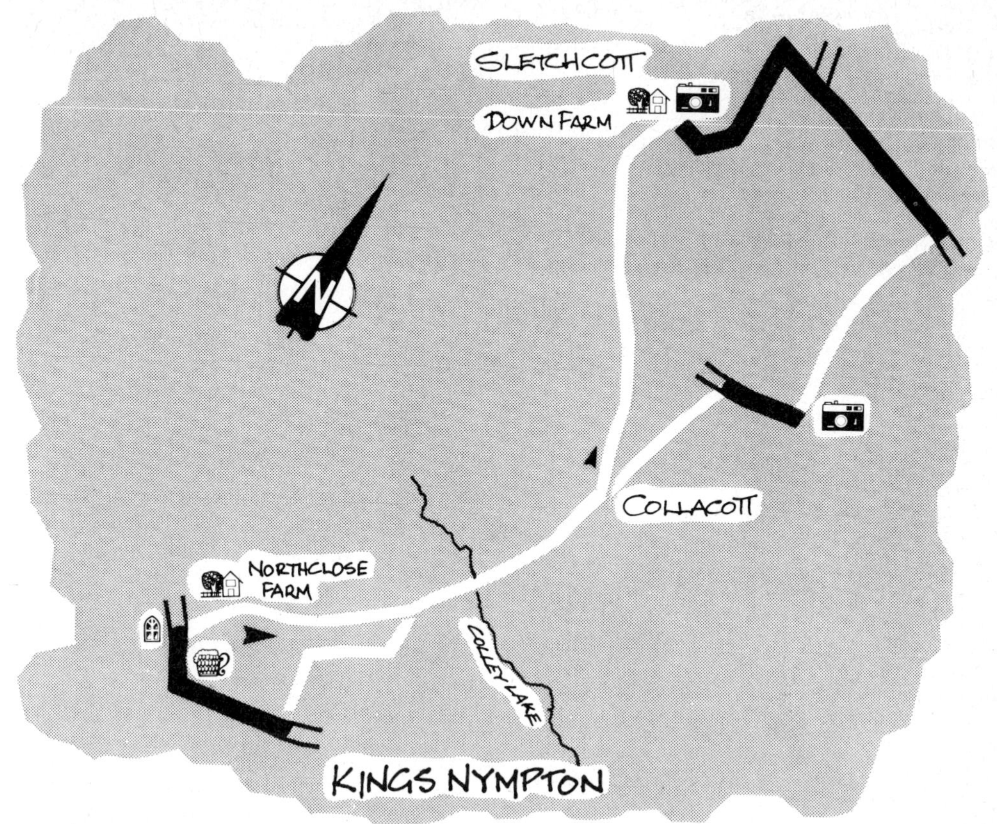

14 Kings Nympton

APPROXIMATELY 3½ Miles

The District

You arrive at Kings Nympton by a road which curves, climbs and plummets over the rolling Devon countryside – whichever direction you're coming from.

The fields are a criss-cross pattern of yellow (mustard), brown (moorland) and green (that which is always more so on the other side of the fence) all divided by dark lines of hedges and trees. The countryside is neat and tidy, a testament to years of agricultural toil and implies that Kings Nympton may be run along the same lines. It is!

Kings Nympton consists of old and beautiful thatched cottages which have aged gracefully in their cluster on the hill to the east of the Taw valley. The crowning glory of the village is its church with a copper tower. This building dates from the Saxon period and time off from walking should be taken to inspect it.

How to Get There

By road take the unclassified road southwards from South Molton and continue through George Nympton for Kings Nympton (approx 5 miles). *By rail* to Kings Nympton. *By bus* as the train runs direct, bus services should not be required.

There's no gamble about this ramble over peaceful and good-natured English countryside – it's a certainty you're going to enjoy it! Kings Nympton is a friendly place and this walk up to Down Farm and back is

calculated to put you in mellow mood and even encourage you to indulge in a mildly alcoholic, bucolic frolic on the hills!

The Kings Nympton Walk

After a quick 'starter' at the bar, turn right out of the inn and walk in the direction of the copper spire of the church. Follow the left-hand fork opposite a house called 'Nymet' on your right and then head to the right of Brewer's Cottage's fine aquiline profile and into the churchyard.

Here thin lines of old and greying gravestones await you and struggle to hold themselves erect for your inspection, despite the undignified squawking of chickens in the offing. It's a lovely churchyard and the church, which is dedicated to St James the Apostle, is just as nice. Go in, but only after looking at the sundial above the entrance, dated 1846 and which read 11 o'clock to my 12 (during British summer time).

Inside, the reredos is Georgian and interesting, the screen is medieval and there are multiple roof bosses, which is happily nothing to do with overmanning on repairs. Watch out, too, for the lineage of Sir John Furse, the roof painting dedicated to the Holy Trinity, a rickety old organ and the tomb of Sir Arthur Northcote of Haydon, who outlived his first wife, and then a second who passed away 'in full assurance of joyful resurrection to eternal life'. From the dates on the tombs, one can see how much life expectancy has changed since the 17th century. Behind the pews the avid church researcher can discover cans of woodworm fluid and realise the cost of upkeep of the building. Give generously and leave by the door with the toothsome coat of arms above it.

After leaving the church, turn left back at the road and march past Glebe House (to the left) and the church hall (to the right) till you come to a gate on the right marked 'Northclose'. Turn in here and follow the well used track towards Northclose Farm. Look beyond the farm to the hills for a view of undulating farmland and count the number of farmhouses in view. Just before the farmhouse itself, bear right of the building and go through the gate 20 yards from it.

By the farm there used to be a windpump bringing water to the farm but modern amenities have led to its removal. Proceed down the field following the track which moves slightly right towards a hedge. This field was once three smaller Glebe fields, part of the land owned and sub-let by the church. To your left is a Bramley orchard – nowadays cows eat these cooking apples since they're difficult to sell.

At the bottom of the field there's a metal gate, go through it and follow the track round to the right beside the stream. Keep well up from the bank since it can be very wet, its best to keep just below the hedge which will be to your right as you go. As you near the bridge (not far, but probably invisible), there will be a temptation to descend into a flat area by the stream – called Colley Lake since streams round here are called 'lakes' – don't; instead go straight on across a ditch and up over a 'treeish' fence. Here you'll find a track, go left and cross the stream ('lake')! by the bridge in 20 yards time. After the bridge turn left in the direction of the friendly yellow arrows which point you over the stile beside the house.

After the stile, go straight across the field to two metal gates at the end of a hedge. Take the one on the left and follow a path alongside the hedge on your right. As you go you'll probably see wrens flick and dart away before you. Look back now and see the church steeple behind, as well as the ragged fields of brown moorland and Northclose farm.

In doublequick time you arrive at an old wooden gate, not long for this world, so it may have been replaced by the time you get there. Go through it and continue straight along, following the hedge to your right up the field. To your left is forested valley and a sweep of serene English countryside – 'serene' may depend on the weather. Soon you come to a gate in the far right-hand corner. After this, follow the hedge to your left till you come to another elderly wooden gate. On your right is a lovely thatched house and, in the field you've just come through, a Dutch barn. Ignoring the gate on the left, follow a left-hand diagonal across the field to the gate in the bottom left-hand corner. Go through the gate and follow the track down, then up, to Down Farm – this is a walk of ups and downs. Again, as you climb, this is a time to enjoy the views of the local landscape with its trees and tracks and circling buzzards and crows. Sad, too, to see the number of wasted and boney elms ravaged by the evil weevil from Holland.

Go through the farmyard and take the metalled road up past a persistent and noisy sheepdog. The road winds past an overgrown tin storehouse and at a sharp corner a windswept old beech tree will nod you in the right direction, towards the parish road.

At the junction, bear right past cottages 1 and, presumably, 2. As you follow the telegraph poles look left for the view to South Molton. Kings Nympton used to be self-sufficient 30 years ago and now it depends on South Molton. Follow the road 600 yards or so then turn right down the farm track, again the forlorn sight/site of elm stumps.

Follow the track through and beyond the farm buildings as it curves left, then right. After a cattle grid, you see the Dutch barn once more – go into the field by the barn and follow the hedge on your left round to the far right corner where you came into the field the first time. You can see Northclose Farm again and the village spire. Go through the gate – you are now retracing your steps and follow the hedge to the next gate. After the gate follow a straight line to the next one – concealed till you get nearer. Go through it, aim just to the right of the house and go down over the stile to the bridge. If you are subjected to morose bovine scrutiny, it's not personal, it's just that you're standing in the way of the cows' trough.

Cross Colley Lake (a stream) by the bridge (again!) and take the path ahead which winds up the hill beside and under the trees. There is no shortage of magpies in the field but if you should see one on its own don't forget to say '7,6,5,4,3,2,1 Devil, I defy thee'. Head for the top right-hand corner of the field where there's a gate by a gnarled old beech tree. Turn right onto the track here and go to the parish road which will lead you past the modern rectory and into Kings Nympton.

At the junction there's a house with a sign saying 'Wychways' – the answer to that is right and it's 150 yards to **The Grove Inn.** Did you know that the thatching on one of these houses lasts for 23-25 years and that the ridge on the roof must be reworked every six? Ponder upon this fact as you pour that long awaited pint past that beckoning epiglottis.

The Grove Inn, Kings Nympton

Built 500-600 years ago as a coaching inn, The Grove stands roughly at the centre of the village. There used to be stables where the petrol pumps opposite now stand and perform, I suppose, a similar function in their stead.

From early in the evening, the locals gather to pass the time of day and, after a few pints, the chat flies thick and fast. If you want to borrow a combine harvester or a few bags of manure, then this is the place to come and ask.

The interior is spacious with walls from the local stone and a long bar. Behind the bar is a pile of cups won by the ladies' skittle team – the mens' is much less successful. The hunting horns above the bar reveal a connection with the local hunt which indeed meets here 4-5 times a season to sample the heat of the Norwegian wood burner before dashing off after foxes.

The beers are Whitbreads hand-drawn and keg Trophy and Tankard. A full range of hot meals and snacks is also available.

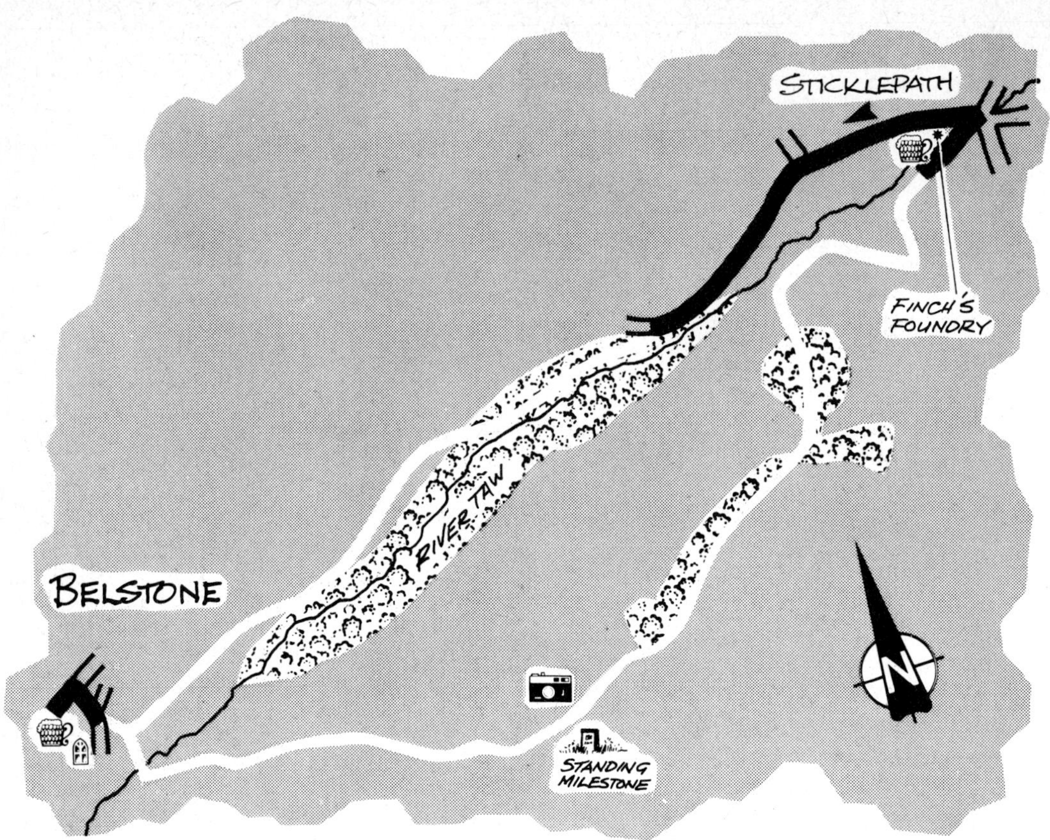

15 Sticklepath

APPROXIMATELY 3½ Miles

The District

The very bleakness of Dartmoor is thrilling – ask Prince Charles, he owns most of it – and, though the temperature is usually low and the average rainfall high, there's something about the moor which uplifts rather than dampens the spirits; it can hardly be the weather.

The 1000ft high granite mass of Dartmoor is what remains of mountains which overturned in the great upheavals of the earth of approximately 300 million years ago. Since then, the mountains have been weathered away and generations of vegetation have rotted to form the layers of peat bogs which make the area into a giant natural sponge and, conversely, the source of most of Devon's rivers.

It's a wild region of broad rolling hills and heather moorland. Mosses, lichens, purple moor grass, bog cottons and sedges cover the slopes beneath the curlews, sandpipers and lapwings who struggle across the sky against the raking wind. (Of course, with the wind behind them they zoom like bats out of hell!) It's here, too, you may see a rare merlin – like you, attracted by the solitude and open spaces. Below, the heather moor sustains the bogs – pimpernel, campanula and asphodel, the wort family – pale butter, St John's and the unsympathetically named louse, and to top off the list, lesser skullcap. These are all for flower people. Another comprehensive list from some well-informed sources contains skylarks, whinchats, stonechats, dippers and meadow pipits. Also occupying air-space, you may see dragonflies, the emperor moth, a marsh fritillery or even the very rare blue butterfly. Lists, lists, lists. Add adders underfoot – more afraid of you than you of them, the experts say – and the ponies who loiter by the road to avoid not only the flies, but also the tedium of their grassy hillside diets – please *don't* feed them – and you have a fair idea of the main population of the area.

An unusual feature of the moor is that the glacial tors attract diptera flies which gather at their summits like tourists. Scientists are investigating why there are flies on them (not on the scientists!).

Never far away on Dartmoor are prehistoric remains which have survived the ages in great numbers due to their granitic constitution and the fact that the moor (warmer in the past) was ideal for the primitive pastoral economy.

Unfortunately, Sticklepath is cut in two by the busy main road, but the beautiful Taw valley possesses that typical Dartmoor air of mystery and wildness. Skaigh Warren is the site of an old serge mill, once busy turning out uniforms for the troops of the Indian Raj and is surnamed 'warren' because of its former artificial rabbit burrows. These warrens were introduced by the Normans who brought rabbits, which they kept to hunt, to this country in the name of sport.

Belstone has a remarkable collection of 17 standing stones conservatively called the Nine Maidens. Legend has it that these are what is left of the nine local lasses petrified for dancing on the Sabbath. A smaller stone nearby. . . . who else, but the piper who played for them.

How to Get There

By road take the A30 east from Okehampton and you will find Sticklepath on this road (approx $3\frac{1}{2}$ miles). *By rail* regular 125 service to Exeter and then bus to

The Devonshire Inn, Sticklepath

Not only does this pub stand in an Area of Outstanding Natural Beauty, but, to a pub-lover, it is itself an area of outstanding natural beauty. From the thatch pheasant on the thatched roof, to the clome oven in the fireplace and the panelled cob walls, this pub is a fine example of a warm and friendly country pub. It stands just in front of a Quaker burial ground; in fact spirituality is high in the village – it has two chapels and John Wesley used to preach on White Rock. Spirituality of a different kind is supplied by Lady Gray who walks through walls!

The pub has a collection of hundreds of keys, so if you have any oldish keys you don't want, you could do worse than offer them to Mike Morley, the landlord, for his collection. His pride and joy is an old French wardrobe key worth £180.

The range of beers is excellent. There's Usher's Best and Courage Best Bitter on handpump, and either Ushers Ten-Sixty or Old Peculiar both from the wood by gravity. In summer there's also either Wadworth's 6X or Tawny or Eldridge Pope Royal Oak, all from the wood by gravity. Other drinks include local Tom Gray Farm Cider and fairly-local Inch's bottled cider, Tankard, Ben Truman, a mild and a lager on draught.

Food maintains this high standard with

Okehampton. *By bus* on weekdays the 173 and 383 operate from Okehampton.

The walk starts in Sticklepath and follows the Taw valley up to Belstone and returns to the start via the moor proper.

The Sticklepath Walk

You start the walk in the snug comfort of **The Devonshire Inn,** where the welcome is warm and the ales real and varied. The pub is just up the road from Finch's Foundry, a solid reminder of less technological days when fire and water were directly combined with brute force and grinding machinery to produce items for local trade, traffic and agriculture. The leat, carrying water to the wheels and therefore power to the furnaces, runs behind the pub and can be seen from the Ladies' window.

Leaving the pub, turn left up the main road, past two chapels and at Lady Well, where your dog can 'drink and be thankful', you turn left up the lane to Skaigh. You pass a row of cottages, cross a cattlegrid and continue past sloe trees between you and the River Taw. Soon you take a grassy path to your left that keeps you near the river, overhung here by straggling rhododendrons. Here the path winds through small silver birches, oaks and sycamores prone to black spot. Passing a weir and noting the peculiar redness of the water, you cross a small stream and continue up the river bank. In places this seems to be a walk for pigmies or limbo-dancers so low do the branches grow. So, hurdling and ducking all obstacles, you follow the fast-flowing Taw up its valley to where its divided waters meet again after passing either side of an island. Here you strike up to the right and, turning left onto a stony track, you then turn left again down a grassy path back to the river bank.

When you reach a wooden bridge, you turn sharp right uphill and then go left along a narrow stony path. Ignoring other paths to the left and right, you walk along the path as it roughly follows the contours of the valley-side until it swings up to a lone sycamore. Cast an eye back across the valley floor and opposite you will (in winter, anyway) see a small stream's waterfall tumbling down to be lost in the trees as it joins the river. From the sycamore, the path descends and then rises and, 50 yards or so before the wood ahead, it swings uphill again, opposite grey rock outcrops on the other side of the valley. Walk above marshy reeds and on up to a small open grassy field. This is a good vantage point from which to survey the valley below and, if you're lucky, the wheeling and circling buzzards eyeing up the free take-aways – rodentburgers – below. In this field there are often a few Dartmoor ponies; these are semi-wild, stocky and shaggy animals well-used to the rigours of Dartmoor's harsh conditions.

Walk along this field, keeping the wall on your right, until you must descend, down an obvious path at the corner, to skirt below rocky outcrops. You rise again to another grassy area and, still keeping the wall on your right, you walk along the top edge of the valley, with the Taw winding and twisting through the trees below. Soon you see Belstone up to your right and you turn right onto a track up into the village and **The Tors Hotel.**

If your children have been giving you trouble, you can threaten them with a spell in Belstone's stocks, while you have a drink at the pub and investigate the church of St Mary The Virgin with its fine stone pillars, its twin altars, its organ and the lovely arch which supports its tower. Belstone was given a degree of fame by the book, *The Belstone Fox,* and while the book's events happened here, the film of the book was largely shot elsewhere.

To continue the walk, go down the track that descends below the green, back into the Taw valley and at the bottom, just before the ford (unless you are wearing waders or are a duck) cross the small wooden bridge, turning left immediately after it, to join and follow a stony track. You may have to avoid a smallish 'lake' that often covers it here, but return to the track and follow it uphill, along a wall and under a spreading beech and a holly. The track follows the wall round and you stay on the main track as it swings right and uphill again. This now wends its, and your, weary way up the gorse-covered hillside. The climb is gentle but continuous, across numerous small streams and trickles, up to the peaty moorland. Often there are sheep here, sheltering behind the gorse-bushes and I saw quite a variety of breeds here – grey ones, like Old English Sheepdogs, black ones like untrimmed standard poodles and some rich-looking ones with brown coats, like expensive furcoats. The views get better as you rise and are best when you reach a tall milestone marked SZ1 (South Zeal – one mile) and DC1 (a mysterious and non-existent ghost village, also one mile away?). At any rate, you can see a lot further than one mile across Devon's hills towards Okehampton to your left and North Tawton further off to your right.

Here you turn right along a slightly sunken grassy path and then, at the crossing of tracks, go down the track keeping the wall and line of trees on your left. The track bends round two hawthorns and then continues in the same direction. Just before the corner of the open land you're on, go through the gate on your left, marked public bridlepath. Walk straight downhill with the wall and fence on your right. When the wall veers to the right, you go straight on, now with only the fence on your right. At the track, turn right and go through the gate and walk on through gnarled trees and summer nettles. The track, impatient to reach the bottom, turns sharply left, steeply downhill.

At the bottom, you turn right, through a metal gate and along a dank overhung track, which meets the river at one point, but continues on between hedges. You pass a field on your right, used, possibly, for the equestrian training of princesses and their spouses and the animals' stables on your left. You cross a Fiesta; sorry, that should be a small ford, and to your left is a house right out of TV's *The Good Life* – fully-functioning water-wheel, ducks and geese, kitchen garden and a braying donkey. You emerge onto the A30 and turn left, crossing what is in fact a rather fine bridge. Immediately seeking the safety of the pavement, walk back to The Devonshire Inn.

home-made steak pies and steak and kidney pud and also salads, ploughmans, pizzas, basket meals and sandwiches. In summer, there's an early breakfast on Saturdays, and cream teas in the afternoons (except Wednesdays).

All in all, just about enough to satisfy even the most demanding Grousebeaters.

The Tors Hotel, Belstone

Set in National Trust land on the edge of Dartmoor, it's only natural that The Tors should be made of the region's granite. It's a solid Victorian building with thick walls and a long bar. But the atmosphere is welcoming, there's an open fire in a stone fireplace and in summer you can take your drink and food onto Belstone's Green which overlooks the Taw valley.

The beers include hand-drawn Courage Best Bitter and Whitbread Best Bitter with Whitbread Britannia, JC, and Guinness on draught. There's also Tom Gray's Farm Cider.

Bar food is good with chicken, sausage burgers and a fisherman's platter, all with chips as well as ploughman's and hot and cold sandwiches.

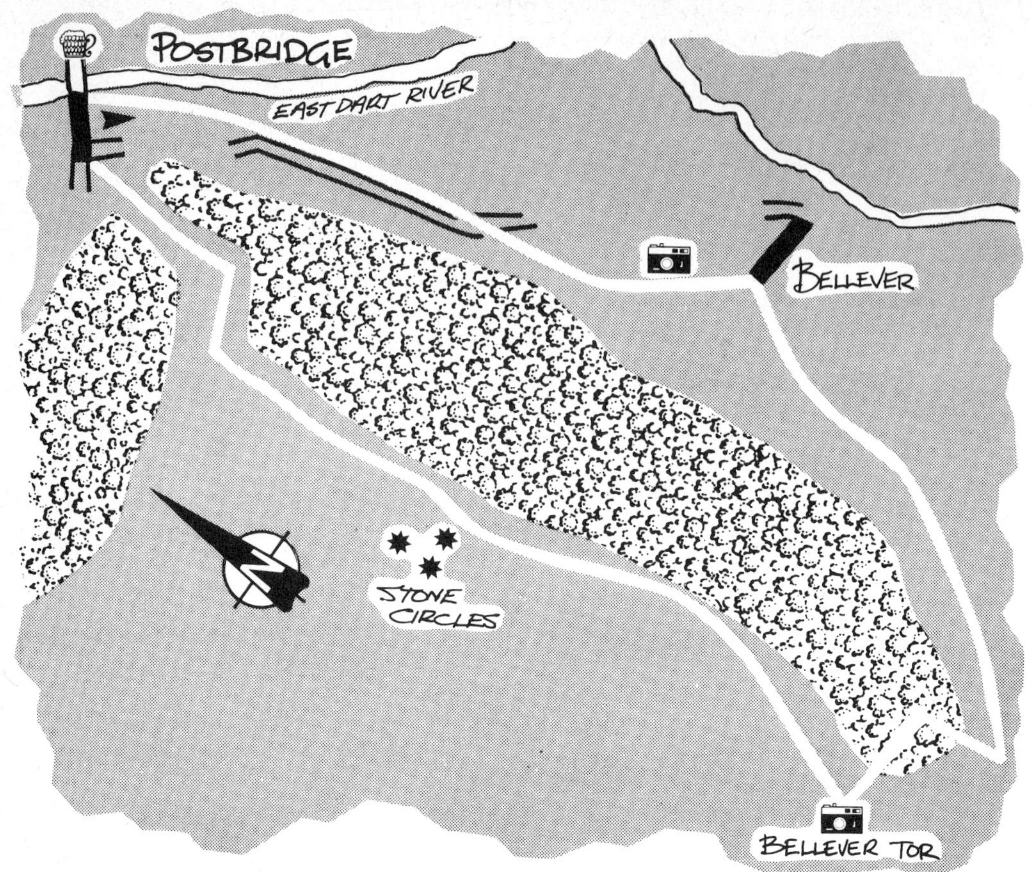

16 Postbridge

APPROXIMATELY 4 Miles

The District

Dartmoor has been inhabited by man since at least 8,000 BC when Mesolithic (middle stone age) hunters and gatherers first filtered into the old birch forests of the moor. At that time Britain was not yet an island and these people thus formed one of the first tides to reach the South of England.

In the meantime, lifestyles in this neck of the wood have altered somewhat and the majority of Mesoliths have migrated to the cities to become football hooligans and members of parliament leaving the vast open spaces of the moor to the elements and the present day population.

Dartmoor seems to exist quite separate,from its surrounding region. It is a wild, mysterious sea in an area which is generally calm, homely and prosperous. A bright day in nearby Bovey Tracey can turn into a dark and dank day on the moor with a mist that can chill you to the marrow. Conditions can, and do, change fast – the mist will descend like a dropped blanket and rain is seldom faraway – yet, almost always, somewhere on the landscape there is the sheen of sun on stream or a peaceful windless valley where cows contentedly graze. It is as if Dartmoor possesses its own meteorological zone where bright blue billows of clear sky are constantly chased across the heavens by gusting black clouds, and where persistent squalls of rain scrape low across the moors and hills in places it would be folly to walk.

Where better then to site a prison? Just

think for one moment of the poor prisoners who choose a night escape across these desolate wastes and bogs, with the roads sealed off and the bloodhounds baying in hot pursuit. Dartmoor Prison, near Princetown, stands stark and forbidding in the centre of this wild, mysterious moor. Since it first admitted French prisoners of war in 1809, it has become marginally more sophisticated as a centre of detention – the population of inmates is no longer decimated by regular outbreaks of typhus and, in fact outbreaks of prisoners themselves are rare, too. The prison is only 5 miles from Postbridge and is fascinating to see (on a fleeting basis). Except by special arrangement (possibly a bank robbery) you will be unable to visit the buildings themselves – be careful though not to run out of petrol since there's absolutely no stopping on any road outside or near the prison walls.

One last hint; should you ever get lost on Dartmoor, follow a stream, as it always leads to a road!

How to Get There

By road from the M5 (junction 31) take the A30 heading north and then turn left onto the B3212, passing through Moretonhampstead to Postbridge (approx 19 miles). *By rail* to Plymouth, the regular 125 service. *By bus* there is a service between Plymouth and Tavistock and from here catch the 619 (fairly infrequent) and in summer the 82.

The walk takes you to the village of Bellever over grassland and fields, then along a forest back to Bellever Tor from which you return over moorland to Postbridge. It is a straightforward, shortish and easy walk with a few choice slivers of archeological interest to entertain you on the way.

The Postbridge Walk

You'll find the **East Dart Hotel** near the clapper bridge which crosses the East Dart River. Under the protection of an avenue of beeches, the hotel has offered comfort to the weary traveller for centuries. Make for the Huntsman's Bar.

Safe enough by day, it's said that it is not always so by night. Once upon a Sunday night in the 18th century, the publican, J Webb convinced finally by the constant nagging of his teetotal wife and a hellfire sermon on the evils of drink from the local preacher, stormed out of the pub with his entire stock of alcohol and emptied it all in

Huntsman's Bar – East Dart Hotel, Postbridge

Whether you believe the legend of the black hound or not, there's no doubt that the East Dart Hotel has a fair bit of history behind it. The building dates from the 14th century and has been a coaching house and a temperance hotel in its time, a state of affairs which has now been rectified.

It's a typical old style country inn on the main street of Postbridge. It has a cosy atmosphere and unsurprisingly, there are frescoes of hunting scenes. Elsewhere you can see stuffed animals.

The catering is excellent with salads, flans, curry and seafood all on offer in the wine bar. There are plans to initiate real ale in summer as well as, at present, in winter. The beers include Whitbreads Mild and Bitter, Worthington E and Tankard. Children are welcomed and on Saturday nights you can join in a singalong by the piano – that's if your lungs are up to it after the walk.

The Warren House Inn, near Postbridge

The Warren House Inn is the third highest inn in England and is famous for its fire which has been burning continuously for 135 years in the old fireplace. It stands a few miles up the road from Postbridge on the way to Moretonhampstead.

the ditch opposite the building – down to the last drop. However this was not the end of the matter. Later that night a large black hound turned up to lap up the dregs and reputedly continues to put in regular appearances to this day. You see, the Devil takes many forms in the history of Dartmoor and you are advised also to keep clear of any headless goats you might see along with a tall hillwalker in a black kagoule. It's not for nothing that Dartmoor was the setting for *The Hound of the Baskervilles*!

Turn left out of the inn and cross over the road bridge and the East Dart River. To the left is a wooden gate, pass through it and follow the path. On your left is the clapper bridge, renovated in 1949 and so called because a 'clapper' is a plank in the local vernacular (granite planks?!). You come to a second wooden gate; after it, follow the path as it goes uphill through the middle of open land. Keep along the path ignoring all paths which cross it till you reach a point where a farm track joins the metalled road. (The road runs along by the edge of the trees to your right). This junction is marked, and obstructed by, a lonely looking barrier.

Move right and cross the road at the nearest point. Beside the gate opposite is an opening going left. Take it and follow the path by the wall for 40 yards or so till you turn right past a fence and through a gate, after which you turn left and find yourself in a field between two areas of tree plantation. (All this manoeuvering takes you from the road, round to the right of the trees on your left from your starting point by the road.). In the winter you find barrel-chested and befringed Dartmoor ponies here, they come down from the hills in search of food. They were once domestic ponies and are of no particular breed. Controversy rages over the annual cull of these ponies, a fair number of which end up in tins of dog meat.

Follow the left-hand side of the field to a gate and then continue along the track to the next gate directly opposite. All around are fine arborial specimens and beyond them views over valleys. After the second gate, head into the next field and downward to gate number 3. Through this and you're in an old once-terraced field, make for the moss-covered tree in the far left-hand corner. You're now on the outskirts of Bellever.

Detour: Go straight down the road through and past Bellever and you come to another clapper bridge, by the road bridge. It's not far. A story surrounds this pleasant spot and the two old spinsters who lived in a house nearby. Neighbours were curious to know how the two women lived; they never worked, they had no visible means of support, no-one ever saw them carrying food to the house. Then one day it was discovered they lived on snails and slugs that they found on the moor. Once this 'terrible revelation' became public knowledge, the two spinsters died of unhappiness – a real case of slugs and snails and locals' tales. Take a gander at the beautiful brown waters and a wander back up the road to the gate from the old once-terraced field. *End of detour.*

Not far from this gate and to the right as you walk down is a gate marked 'No admittance to Vehicles!' This warning need not deter you as you breeze through it and onto a forestry commission track which curves into the forest through the apparently closed ranks of the pine trees. The trees stand in rigid perpendicular rows and at their feet are ferns and moss, as distant birdsong echoes up the grey and musty corridors of the forest. You may see deer here.

Ignoring the marked nature trails, follow the track a fair distance till you come to a T-junction with a gravelled road. Cross the road here, make a hiccup in your route slightly to the left and roughly follow the line of the track from which you've just come. There's a pathway through the trees and up to the stone wall. Listen, for the river of sound flowing past you on the way, whistled up by the wind in the trees – you're getting near mysterious Bellever Tor.

You see patches of light appear through the wall, then the crags of the Tor to your right. Climb over the wall and head for the summit which is 443 metres above sea level. Here there are great slabs of granite, several shaped like grand pianos, and on top of the lot a triangulation point looking like an armless metronome futilely trying to control the wind which terrorises the Tor. This is a wind to bring the roses to your cheeks – hold on to your hat since even the birds around here have difficulty in the air turbulance.

This is an avenue tor whose centre was cleft by the pressures of the ice age, forming a clear walkway over the summit. It's an amazing place – with a 360° view around a vast natural basin in the landscape, where Dinkey cars criss-cross the moor on distant roads.

From the triangulation point go down to the 'walkway'. Turn right and there's a diagonal path leading to the edge of one of the two jutting sections of forest. Follow this path – starting with your back to the open moorland and facing the direction of invisible Postbridge – to just past the tumbledown stone wall. Turn slightly left to follow along the edge of the trees which will be just on your right and rippling in the wind as if terrified at the prospect of being mashed for pulp wood. Don't go into the forest and, incidentally, be wary of the adders which multiply around here in summer. 600 yards along the trees and across to your left are two stone circles. Sacred ritual sites or astronomical measuring sticks, no-one knows exactly. A bit further on, to your right and inside the forest, is a 'cist' or prehistoric burial chest, dating circa 1700 BC; it looks more like a modern picnic table than a grave. Follow the path down the clearing, with the trees to your right, till you come to the end. There are two firebreaks, take the first one to the right – not marked by a rowan tree like the other – and follow it to the forestry commission track, where you turn down left and walk 500 yards to the road. At the road turn right and head back to the Huntsman's Bar. Order a stiff drink . . . now's the chance to ask the locals to regale you with the tale of 'The Hairy Hands', a story too terrifying to tell before a walk over such numinous moorland.

The present building was constructed in 1845 and replaced the previous inn which lay on the other side of the road and used to serve the needs of the tin mining community and the travellers along the old pack horse trail. Apparently the old building was demolished because the landlord did not like it facing north.

This typical moorland building has two open fires, settle seating and one main bar comprising several rooms. There's a choice of 3 bitters and a choice of ten country wines. The menu is everything you could want and children are amply catered for.

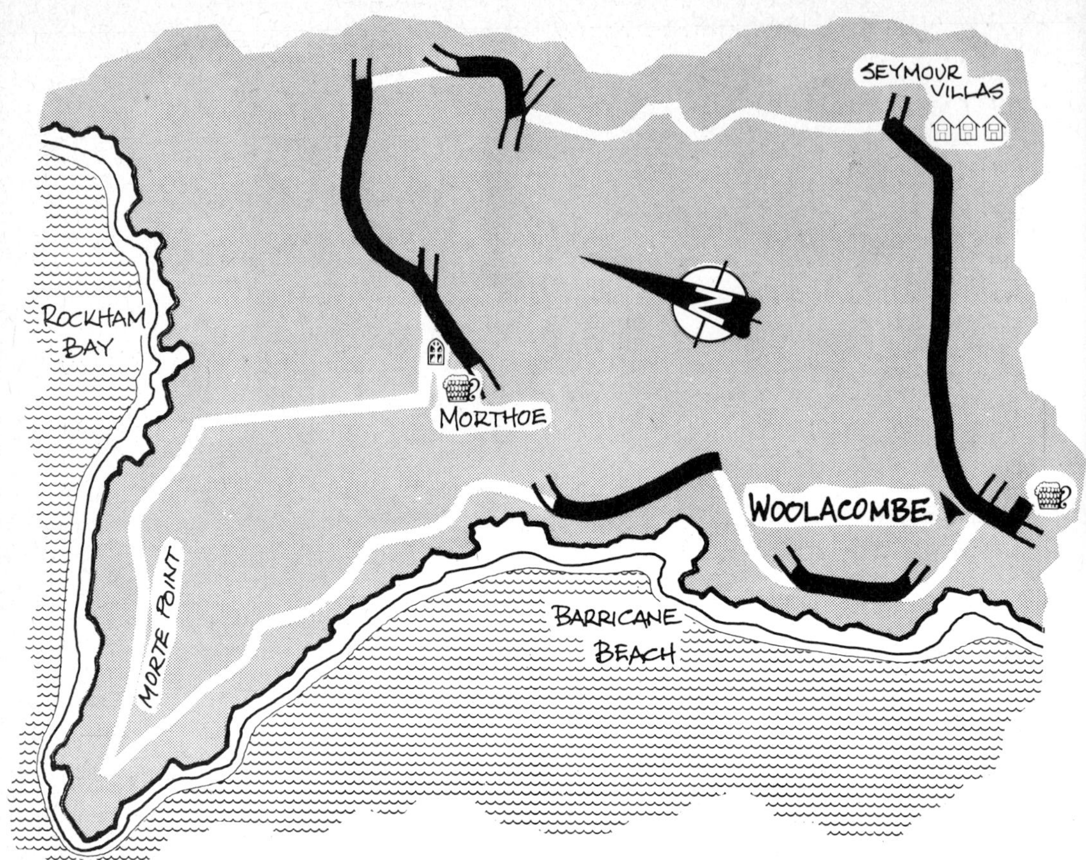

17 Woolacombe

APPROXIMATELY 4¾ Miles

The District

Were you to remove its hotels and all its other tourist amenities, Woolacombe would shrink to a scattering of homes, clustered in and around the bare combe that descends to the northern end of Woolacombe Sand. It is this seemingly never-ending stretch of pale yellow sand enclosed by steep moorland slopes which has attracted visitors (from coach-party grannies to avid, foolhardy surfers and, more recently, sand-sailors) for generations, and will doubtless continue to do so. By dramatic contrast to the beach and Woolacombe Down behind, with its carpet of wild flowers and flutter of flitting butterflies, Morte Point has been described by Dorothy Wordsworth as 'the place which Heaven made last and the Devil will take first'. Of course it depends very much on the weather, but in winter with fogs, gales and storms this promontory can be daunting in the extreme and, for sailors, highly dangerous. Indeed, in 1852 alone, five ships were wrecked on its forbidding rocks. The whole headland is owned by the National Trust and though the paths are distinct, care should be taken at cliff edges because the constant battering of the sea and wind makes them weak and crumbly in places.

How to Get There

By road take the B3231 south-west from Ilfracombe and then turn right on to the B3343 (approx 5 miles). *By rail* to Barnstaple and then bus to Ilfracombe. *By bus* the 300 and the 303 buses run between Ilfracombe and Woolacombe.

The best pub on the walk is about halfway round, in unspoilt Mortehoe, so you are advised to time your arrival there well before last orders. The walk climbs steeply out of Woolacombe and then unstrenuously undulates to North Morte, where it descends to Mortehoe. From here you walk out to the end of Morte Point and then back along the coast to Woolacombe. Except for the outgoing lane (which isn't too bad really), the walk is easy-going.

The Woolacombe Walk

From the Esplanade car park by the beach, you walk back, past the Red Barn Café, up a lane to the left of the Narracott Grand Hotel. This is the steep part, deliberately worked out to be at the beginning, when hopefully you have a full tank of energy. When you pass Sunnyside Road and Springfield Road, you are about a third of the way up – don't despair, trudge on, pausing to examine the wild hedgerow flowers and catch your breath.

At Seymour Villas with its herringbone-patterned wall, you can congratulate yourself and begin to think about planting a flag on the summit. Where the lane curves sharply to the right, just beyond the houses, take the marked public footpath over the stile and walk straight across the field (or, if there are crops, walk round the edge to your left) towards the unsightly caravan park that soon becomes visible. Just to the right of the far left-hand corner of this field, take the little path up through gorse, over the stile and into the caravan park. Turn left along the metalled drive ahead and follow it down and round past the toilets to a double public footpath sign, where you go left. Follow the direction indicated by the next sign, over the bridge and up the gravel steps through the caravans. Walk up between caravans E53 and E54 to meet another drive. Turn left up this and, immediately on the other side of caravan E23, turn right, over the stile painted with the words 'no kite-flying in any field – keep to proper footpath' – the angry thoughts of an irritated farmer. You immediately pass the National Trust sign with its more reasonably toned warning about dogs. Walk along the edge of the beautifully built slate and earth wall, ignoring two gates on your left and continuing in the same ➤

The Chichester Arms, Mortehoe

Parts of this warm and friendly village pub in the centre of Mortehoe, date back to the 16th century. Pretty from the outside, with white-painted slates and blue shutters on the old stone walls, the public bar is rather dominated by a pool table, but is nice enough for all that. The lounge is panelled and contains some interesting conversation-pieces – a globe, an hourglass, prisms from lighthouses and a propeller . . . from which hangs a tale. A wry barman told some customers that, in the war, an aeroplane had crashed into the wall, and though the propeller penetrated to the inside above the fireplace, the rest of the plane was still embedded in the wall outside. They even went to look!

Rather more sinister is the story that, about 100 years ago, a certain Cookie Watts was angered enough by her husband's continual presence in the pub (and therefore absence from home) to lay a curse on the building and its occupants. Suffice to say, the last 10-12 landlords and ladies have had disasters of one kind or another, such as death, divorce and a daughter's suicide. Your present landlord, Peter Bridgewater, is at the moment, an unsuperstitious man and sets little store by all this. By his own admission he's a jack-of-all-trades and seemingly a master of most, though you may be surprised to hear he's vice-president of the Vancouver White Caps (and running a pub in Mortehoe?!).

His wife runs the food bar in the lounge where the menu is extensive – especially recommended are the local crab and lobster salads, and these can all be washed down with hand-drawn Ushers Best, draught Mann's Brown, various Watney beers or Guinness, or, for the more adventurous, sloe gin.

Children are welcomed in the children's own bar, which serves soft drinks and kid's ➤

direction to and through a gate on to the road, where you turn right.

Just before the drive to Easewell Farm Camping Park you turn left up through a gateway – the public footpath sign is fairly concealed. The path meets Easewell Farm's drive and you turn left down it, admiring the view of hilly farmland with its backdrop of blue sea. Where the drive bends to the right take the marked public footpath 'stright across field' over the wooden ladder stile. Again keeping your dogs on leads, head towards the modern roofs to a stile by a white bungalow, turning right immediately after it along the path that winds down past the houses – watch your kagoule on the gutter. At the lane, turn left downhill, passing two slate barns in the farm to your right and the Rockham Bay Hotel to your left. Go on past the sweet old locals' cottages on your right and, where the lane meets the road at the Kingsley Arms ('a glorified café' a local told me), turn right and follow the road to **The Chichester Arms**, just after the church.

When the pub used to be cottages, one of the cellars was used to store dead bodies before burial. And there were many times when the cellar would be really quite full. This was due to the common and quite heinous practice of lighting beacons on Morte Point to lure ships on to its rocks. The villagers would then loot the cargo and, to avoid unwanted witnesses, kill the crew. This gave the local undertaker many weeks of solid, if somewhat gruesome labour. Nowadays, however, only beer is kept in the cellars, though several times the landlord has found that, despite a locked door, all his gas taps have mysteriously been turned off . . . could this be the beginning of a ghost-story?

Anyway, refreshed (or perhaps too scared to even enter), turn round to the right of the pub as you leave, through a little gate into the churchyard, or should I say, graveyard. If the church is unlocked, have a quick look (and a prayer) inside and then continue past the graves out of the lych-gate (a porched gate, where pall-bearers could put coffins while they caught their breath). From here, turn left up between the church and Rock Cottages, and, keeping Prior's Cottage and the toilets on your right, follow the lane to the, wait for it, cemetery. Of course, we know why a village the size of Morthoe needed such a large cemetery as well as the normal-sized churchyard. Enough of these morbid thoughts, hurry along the track to the right of the cemetery and go through the kissing-gate next to the large metal gate with stout pillars.

To reach the far side of Morte Point, follow the broad grassy path that heads off slightly to the left, alongside the patchy sections of crumbling wall on your right. As you get nearer the sea, stop and look behind at the view across Rockham Bay to cliffs and to Bull Point and its lighthouse beyond. Continue to a seat and then follow the stony path along the side of the headland to the Point. However, little detours to the cliff edge (where it's safe) are recommended for closer views of surf and rock and their eternal conflict.

After a few moments contemplation on the frailty of man (in rough weather only) head back along the stony path on the Woolacombe side of the promontory. This path becomes broad and grassy and soon you fork right along a well-defined path that keeps you nearer the sea. Bracken and gorse cover the slopes above. After crossing the stile in the wall, you continue along the grassy path ahead, watching all the time for oyster-catchers, cormorants and the many different types of gull. After about 150 yards, you fork right along the cliff, heading generally uphill, until you reach a stile and a National Trust sign. A narrow, but well-defined, path takes you along the cliff edge below an ugly white and red brick house and you wind along between the houses and the nasty drop below until you meet the road. Turn right downhill and, just after the Watersmeet Hotel, take the metalled public footpath to your right. Walk down through the garden and then again along the cliff.

Worth a quick look, if you can face the steps back up, is Coombesgate Beach – mind you, at high tide the beach is about the size of a handkerchief.

Again the footpath meets the road and after four yards (don't lose your way here!) your swing right onto grass, until you're forced onto the road again, and then right onto the grass again (like hopscotch, this). For another optional detour, you can go down to Barricane Beach, also known as Shell Beach, so rich is it in shells. And so, from the rocks of Morte Point, to the shells of Barricane Beach and on to the sands of Woolacombe Bay (smaller and smaller), you walk along the Esplanade back to the car park . . . and beyond to the Spanish Bar of **The Woolacombe Bay Hotel**, if your whistle needs re-wetting.

food and is actually run by children.

The Spanish Bar – The Woolacombe Bay Hotel, Woolacombe

This hotel bar is on South Street. The hotel was purpose-built by the Victorians, though the Spanish Bar has only looked Spanish since the 60's. Some very unSpanish games can be played here, namely – pool, darts, skittles and assorted fruit machines.

A range of food is available from the hotel kitchens from sandwiches, through pizza and ploughman's to chicken, burgers, plaice etc; all with chips. Liquid refreshments include Worthington Best, Mild and Hemeling (all keg).

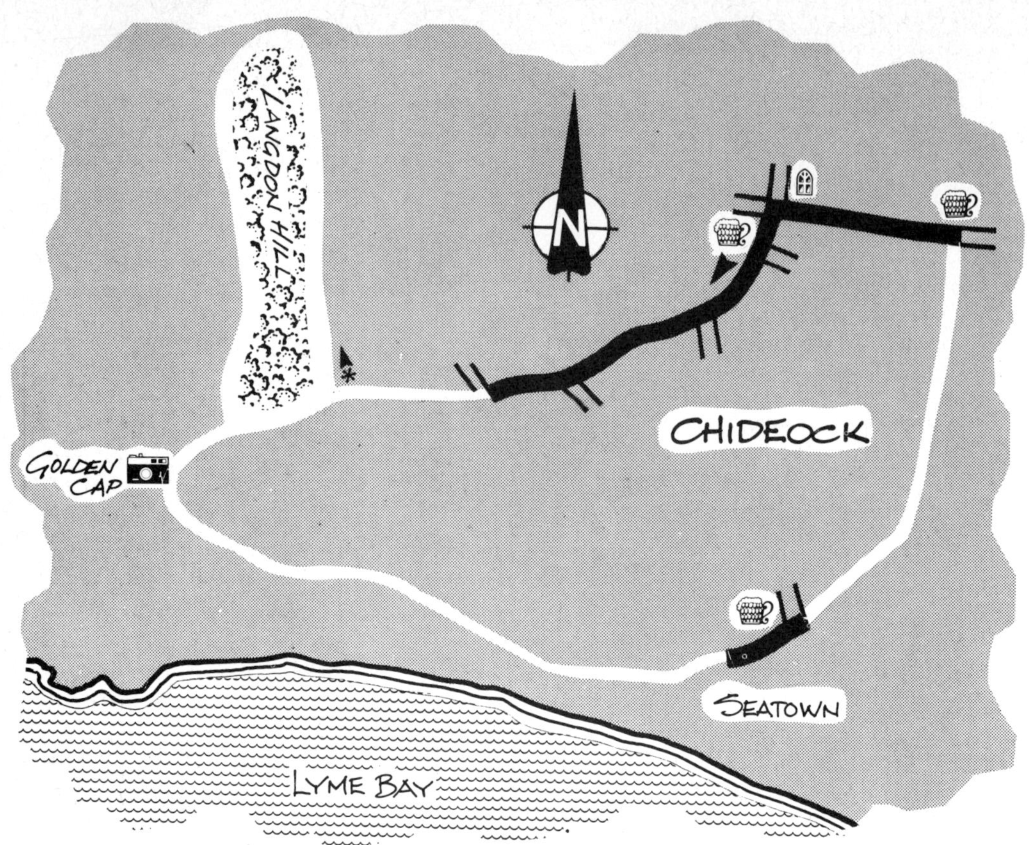

18 Chideock

APPROXIMATELY 4 or 2¾ Miles

The District

Chideock lies in a timeless part of Dorset and it is only the clamour of the steady stream of traffic on the main road between Bridport and Lyme Regis which reminds you that this is the modern age. Elsewhere along the walk, the landscape is so enthralling that it suspends the awareness of change.

The pronunciation of the place – say 'Chiddick' – can be a little confusing and this is hardly surprising since the spelling of the name has varied so much over the years; other versions include Coediog, Cidiok, Chydock, Chidiocke, Chiadick and even Cidihoc, as it was written in the Domesday Book of 1086.

An attractive, mostly thatched village built of the local sandstone, Chideock was a Catholic stronghold in Tudor times when two of the leading Catholic families, the Welds and the Arundells, held court here. This they did until the forces of General Fairfax captured the castle and the Puritan governor of Lyme Regis demolished it in 1645 . . . the killjoy, he was payed 39 shillings for his trouble.

Visit St Giles Church and you'll see the black marble effigy, possibly of Sir John Chideock a 14th century landowner, which lies in a typical Dorset church dating from the 13th century. During the Civil War, Roundheads placed a battery of canons in the churchyard, an act of grave desecration which is remembered to this day in what is still a strongly Catholic area.

How to Get There

By road take the A35 west from Bridport, Chideock is on this road (approx 3 miles). *By rail* to Axminster. *By bus* there is a regular service, the 495 and 496, betweeen Axminster and Chideock.

The walk is short and easy, it starts in Chideock and goes by wood to its highspot, Golden Cap, then along the coast to Seatown and back. There are magnificent views and 3 separate pubs to drink in – the problem is how to fit them all in, I assure you it can be done!

The Chideock Walk

The walk begins in **The Clock House Hotel** so clock in there at a suitable time (Dorset isn't that timeless). It's opposite St Giles at the upper end of the main street. After a preliminary drink, turn right out of the front door of the building, then right again in the direction marked Seatown.

Fork right along the lane just after 'The Swiss Cottage' – you'll be grateful to know the local hills are by no means the height of the Alps. Go past Cob and Anvil cottages on your right and Vin Cottage on your left. Ignore the road marked 'Ridwood' but go next right leaving 'Welderly' behind to your left. You are now in a leafy lane amongst oak, beech, holly and fir trees.

The road becomes a path, follow it to the left – if it's been raining a trickling stream will be moving in the opposite direction to you and it will almost certainly have been raining. When you join a farm track, carry onto the right following it towards Langdon Hill. When the track sweeps left into a field opposite a gate to your right, carry on up the path straight ahead. Soon you see the sea on your left, go straight on, ignoring the sign to the left for the coastal path, and continue till you reach the sign for Langdon Hill to the right before a gate.

Was this an old smuggling path? Well, probably, since just about everyone in Chideock used to be involved in smuggling. It's said that the local fishermen lived more by smuggling than by fishing and that groups of trees were planted on Dorset's hills to guide in French ships with their cargoes of contraband, choice brandy: Kegs were sunk off the coast and collected later when the coast was clear. Ingenious methods were used to avoid detection; bushes were set on fire to warn the smugglers of 'preventive officers' and local

The Clock House Hotel, Chideock

This inn has a thatched roof and parts of it are 400 years old. It is supposed to be haunted and two ghosts, a lady and a gent, wander along the sloping floors of the old corridors, no doubt in a search for kindred spirits.

There's an inglenook in the front room which is not short on flock wallpaper and there's also a blue rope noose which decorates the ceiling. The landlord, Mr Panter, is quite a character and rules the roost with a quick and ready tongue – so have a couple of witticisms ready for him..

There are plenty of real ales at hand – Watneys, Ushers, Ben Truman and Devenish's Wessex and there's a good restaurant, too. Snacks include the local crab and plaice and there's a cold buffet in summer. Children are welcomed and you can also play pool on the premises in winter.

The Anchor Inn, Seatown

The Anchor Inn is a stone's throw from the sea and has been a pub since 1860. It's a delightful inn whose toilets were once a smokery for local fish, just as the ice-cream kiosk outside was once a boat house. Seatown used to be a smuggling village and the Anchor has played its part in all that.

Nowadays it has two cosy bars with open fires and low ceilings. The atmosphere is very friendly and Arthur Banwell, the publican will tell you all you wish to know about the district.

villages were all in league. Now there are two separate wine importers in Chideock, yet you can no longer buy a cheap bottle in the village as in the days of yore when farmers, gentry and the clergy were such good customers for the smugglers, those early surreptitious import experts.

Back to the present ... at this sign for Langdon Hill ... the hyperactive members of the party will leap up the hill and go to work on an egg-shaped track which runs round it in a complete circuit. The distance is almost a mile and it will offer you marvellous views before leading you back to where you came in. On one side are views of fields of sheep and beyond Chideock to Epedown, on the other you can see straight across Lyme Bay and on a fine day to Start Point. In the opposite direction the view stretches as far as Portland Bill. In the spring the bluebells here are lovely. When you get round, go down the path to where the other members should be waiting. Turn right at the bottom and go towards the gate.

Pick up the (lazier, less able or more contemplative) other members of the party and head through the gate. Follow the path along the left-hand side of the field, ignoring the bridleway sign halfway across. In the corner of the field cross the stile and follow the path straight over to another stile. Pass the sign pointing to the coastal path, bearing in mind that it points in the direction of the recommencement of the walk, and struggle on up 'Golden Cap'. This used to be a look-out post for coastguards and you can see why ... at 619 feet it is the highest point on the South Coast. The view is magnificent – why have me describe it when you can see it for yourself? Dorset is a notorious area for witchcraft and apparently (and it probably is 'apparently') if you look carefully from here you will be able to see witches dancing in some valley or some shady nook in the countryside. (Or is this a smugglers' invention? Certainly there is a coven which still operates in the Chideock area.)

Descend from 'Golden Cap' and follow the coastal footpath down to the right, past a field with a crumbling edge to your right. The cliffs around here are extremely liable to subsidence and dangerous to walk on; so follow the path and be safe. Sweep round left and follow the coastal path to Seatown, past grassy slopes and windswept trees which seem frozen in the act of trying to uproot themselves.

Once at Seatown, you might wonder at the name of the place – 'Sea' is understandable but 'town' is a bit of an exaggeration. You see, it used to be bigger, there used to be houses on the seaward side of **The Anchor Inn** but the ocean is slowly encroaching on the limestone cliffs (at the rate of three feet a year at one point in the past.) The pebbly beach here used to be fine-grained, now the present day pebbles are used in the cosmetics industry.

This place is full of interest – many exceptional fossils have been found here and it was here, also, that Monmouth's advance guard arrived in 1685. Oh, it's also half way between Land's End and Beachy Head.

Turn left up to The Anchor Inn which is advertised quite literally as being a stone's throw from the sea. It's a lovely spot for a spot of 'Tally Ho'.

After re-fuelling at The Anchor Inn, head up the road and fork right leaving the caravan park behind on your left. On the concrete road you pass a second, then a third caravan site and then a house on the right with the homely handle of 'Frying Pan'. 50 yards past this house is a footpath signposted right. Follow this through a small park, over a bridge and to the main road. Turn right and, if you can take it, it's only 50 yards to **The George Inn** and the enjoyment of your next pint. If not, then turn left up the main street and walk back to where you started from.

Whether you sit outside on the terrace in summer or inside in the warmth in winter, the beers are very fine with Palmers Tally Ho, IPA and Sparkling BB. There's also Golden Cap whisky ($\frac{1}{2}$ malt, $\frac{1}{2}$ grain and, bottled in Bridport, named after the local peak). The catering is excellent (mentioned in Egon Ronay) and there's a special room for children. When you enter (or perhaps exit!) see if you can see the glasses above the door sway mysteriously – nobody knows why this is.

The George Inn, Chideock

The George Inn was built as a coaching house to serve the London to Plymouth route in 1693. It's named after George II and on the inn sign there's a picture of the battle of Dettingen, the last battle in which an English king took part ... George himself. Cromwell's troops stayed in the orchard out the back on their way to vandalise the local church.

The decor is traditional and plain with a small exhibition of butterflies and fossils. There's bench seating round the walls and the atmosphere is relaxed.

Enjoy top pressure Palmers IPA and BB and a good selection of spirits. There's also a good selection of things to eat and children are 'tolerated' if not welcomed. Behind the bar there's a jar with the ashes of a local cowboy's hat in it – ask the barman for the story.

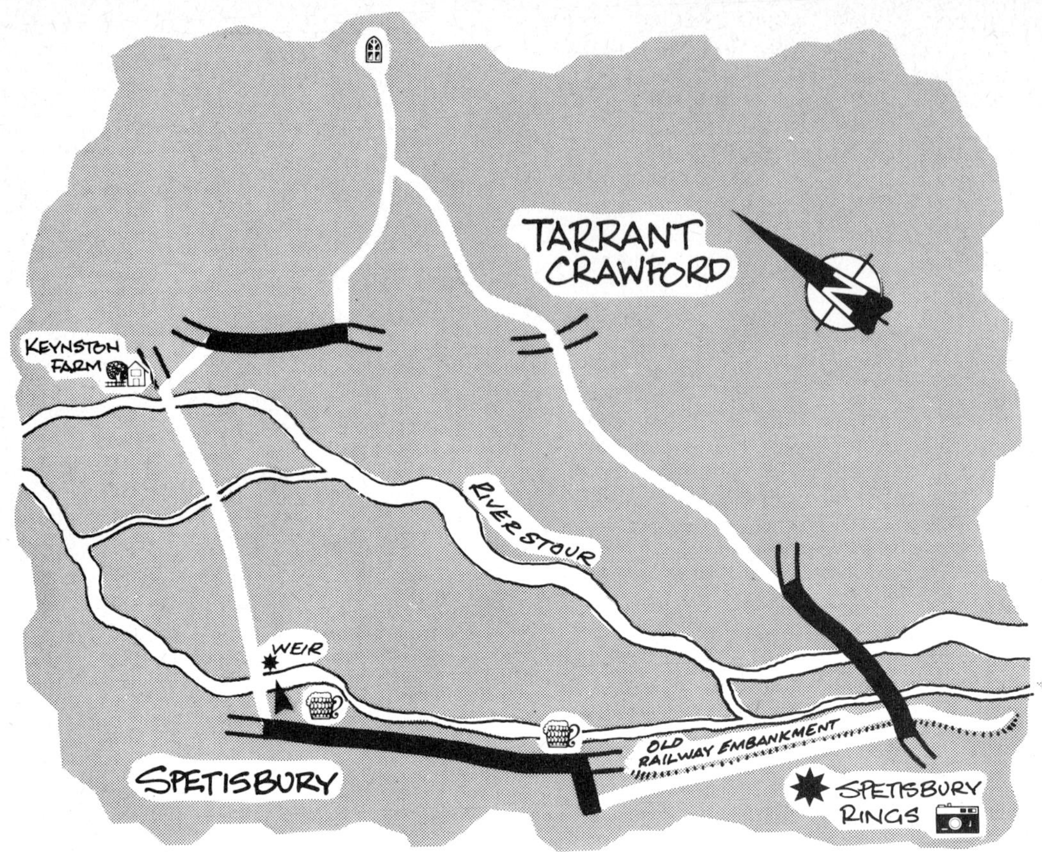

19 Spetisbury

APPROXIMATELY 3½ Miles

The District

The Bastards were responsible for the Georgian centre of the town of Blandford Forum. Let me explain a little . . . first about 'God's dreadful visitation by fire'. In 1731, the old town of Blandford Forum (the name is a Latinisation of Chipping Blandford) was almost completely destroyed by a fire which, fanned by a wind from the north, melted the church bells so they 'dissolved and ran down in streams', burnt all the local fire engines to ashes and reduced 400 houses to rubble. But it is an ill wind which blows nobody any good and the town was rebuilt by Act of Parliament, by public subscription and by the talented brothers John and William Bastard in a magnificent fashion. The result was the finest Georgian town centre in South-West England and a handsome crown for the rich, arable fields which surround it.

Follow the brown Stour downstream a little, or the A350 if you prefer, and you come to Spetisbury, a village, which is bisected at length by the main road and the start of our walk.

How to Get There

By road take the A350 south-east from Blandford Forum, Spetisbury is on this road (approx 3½ miles). *By rail* to Poole. *By bus* from Poole, the 139 and the X13.

The walk takes you from Spetisbury (pronounced Spetsbury) for a spin across watery meadows to the serene manor farm of

Tarrant Crawford, then back through fields to the heights of the Spetisbury Rings, once an Iron Age Fort. At all times the scenery is delightful and the walk is easy.

The Spetisbury Walk

Turn right out of **The Drax Arms** in the High Street, whose motto 'Mort en droit' (roughly 'die in the right') should not be taken as being any indication of the difficulties ahead. Head along the main (and busy) road past Cedar Court to the right and go to the church on the left.

Notable here are the pyramid gravestone (and the eulogy inscribed on it), the War Memorial in the porch and the cheerful evidence of the Sunday School in the church itself.

Back at the road, head left out of the churchyard – and then loop first right at the crossroads. This route is marked by a public footpath sign. Squeeze between the farm buildings left and the double-doored garage, onto a path which takes you over a spread of rivulets along the narrow spine of a concrete and hand-railed footbridge. From it you can spot moorhens panicking in the rushes and marsh and willow tits going rather more coolly about their business.

After the bridge, turn left by the white house which was once a mill and past a beautiful sluice gate which supplies the wear. This is canoing country.

Now follow the clearly defined path through a wooden gate and onto flat meadowland. All the time keep an eye open for swans and herons, willows and water rats, which variously glide over, paddle in, stand by and plunge into the bubbling water hereabouts.

Next you cross a stone footbridge and then head straight aiming for the house amongst the trees. In the field, which is marshy, go over a bridge of concrete and planks to reach another stone footbridge which will take you to the old building called 'Keynston Mill' and now a farm. Are the trees nearby part of the famous Keynston copse?

With this house on your left, turn right immediately and go through a gate into the paddock with the river to its right. At the far end of the paddock, part company with its frisky equine inhabitant, through the wooden gate. Head left under buzzing power lines for the metal gate beside the road.

The Drax Arms, Spetisbury

The Drax Arms, named after Admiral Drax, is a plain, simple pub just off the main road in Spetisbury. It was built in 1926 after its predecessor, a thatched building, had burned down. The decoration is modern and the highlight is the set of three flying Guinness toucans which adorns the wall behind the bar.

Despite the toucans, the Guinness here only comes in bottles. Nonetheless there's hand-drawn Badger bitter and Best and Strongbow cider on draught. There are sandwiches, snacks and basket meals, as well as fresh trout caught locally, and children can be accommodated in the garden where there's a swing.

The Railway Inn, Spetisbury

The Railway Inn arrived in Spetisbury with the railway workers of 1871. Originally it was a tally house, where Irish labourers who were paid in tallies, exchanged their tokens (or tallies) for food and drink.

Out of the windows of this old Victorian cottage building you can see the Spetisbury Rings above. Customers are warmly welcomed by Mr Burgess and his wife – the former is a member of the Handlebar Moustache Club – and on the walls and above the bar is a collection of prints which detail a

Turn right at the road and then first left a hundred yards or so up the road. On one side of the lane is an open field, on the other a copse. The lane curves right into Tarrant Crawford over a bridge and you see Tarrant Crawford House across the village green. Cistercian monks used to live here in the old abbey, parts of which are at the back of the manor house. The whole area has a tranquil atmosphere; this is a hamlet at peace with the world. Follow the road to the left past the old tithe barn on your left now used to store agricultural products and to the church ahead.

St Mary's is 12th century and has a plain and simple beauty to it. It is fairly well restored and retains an atmosphere of pious calm inside – its wall paintings are of great interest as is the tiny tinkly organ. The church is now regularly congregated by a flock of roosting pigeons who adorn its tower in place of gargoyles.

Out of the church, retrace your steps down the lane to the first farm building on your right. Opposite are two metal gates. Turn left off the lane through the second and rapidly you come to a third on a track which runs up the hill behind Tarrant Crawford House. This place is called Tarrant after the chalk stream which runs swiftly through it and you can plot the course of the stream by the number of places on the map called 'Tarrant'. 'Tarrant' means 'trespasser', look down once more on the serenity of the hamlet and the line of poplars to the left.

Go through another gate and follow the fence on your left straight through the field to the road, via a stile. Cross the road to another stile, heave yourself over and follow the fence on your right. To your left are the houses which constitute the remainder of Tarrant Crawford. Cross the two fences on either side of the concrete road and follow the grassy track which carries on. I saw a farmer here rounding up his cows in a tractor, Wild West style. Go between the legs of a pylon and fork left past the nearby gate to go through the next gate, 20 yards left and by a huge elm stump. Follow the fence on the right, then at the bottom of the field turn left towards the road – the field is a mustard field and there may be lots of pheasants hiding in it. A tasty mixture. Before you turn left to go to the road, look beyond the town to the Spetisbury Rings and their clearly discernible triangulation point.

Find the gate to the road – there is one – then turn right. Cross the River Stour by lovely Crawford bridge with its nine arches – stop halfway in one of its passing places to watch the river flow; for full pleasure dangle a piece of straw from the lips.

Walk up to the crossroads and go straight across to the railway bridge, direction Wareham and Dorchester. This, though now unused, is still inspected by British Rail. There's 12 foot of headroom here so even the tallest members of your party can proceed unbowed.

Just past the bridge is a footpath to the right and a choice. Either follow the public footpath over the stile to Spetisbury Rings . . . or go to the right up the steps over into the disused railway embankment. The track was closed in 1969 under the directions of Lord Beeching who did almost as much as Judge Jeffries in draining the region's life blood. It took the Old Somerset and Dorset Railway Company nearly three years to build the track to Blandford. Irish navvies used primitive tools in 1874 and you can see the difficulties as you walk along a steep-sided 'canyon'. When it gets less steep climb the escarpment to your left to discover the ramparts of Spetisbury Rings (or Crawford Castle) just above you.

This Iron Age fort was run by the Durotriges along with 26 other forts (including Maiden Castle) in the area. Around 42 AD it was overrun by Vespasian and his imperialistic cohorts, who became the ruling force of the region. Head for the triangulation point and you can see around for miles; $\pi r2$ – where $r = 25$ miles, to be precise. It's a wonderful look-out point, see if you can now retrace the walk.

Stunned, turn down the track to the left (as you face town) and go to the road where you turn right and go under the railway bridge into Spetisbury. At the main road, pirouette past the Gold Star Dancing Studio to find **The Railway Inn** on your right. After all that locomotion, this is a pleasant siding for all you old buffers with a little steam up to stoke up the boiler and stay on the right tracks with a spot of express oiling and a rest for those tender and overworked points.

To get back to starting point, turn right from the pub and follow the main road back to The Drax Arms.

fascinating history of old steam engines.

There's keg Badger Best and Bitter (the local brew) to assauge your thirst and a selection of snacks and meals to ward off your hunger. In summer there's a garden out the back. This is an unpretentious pub that I heartily recommend.

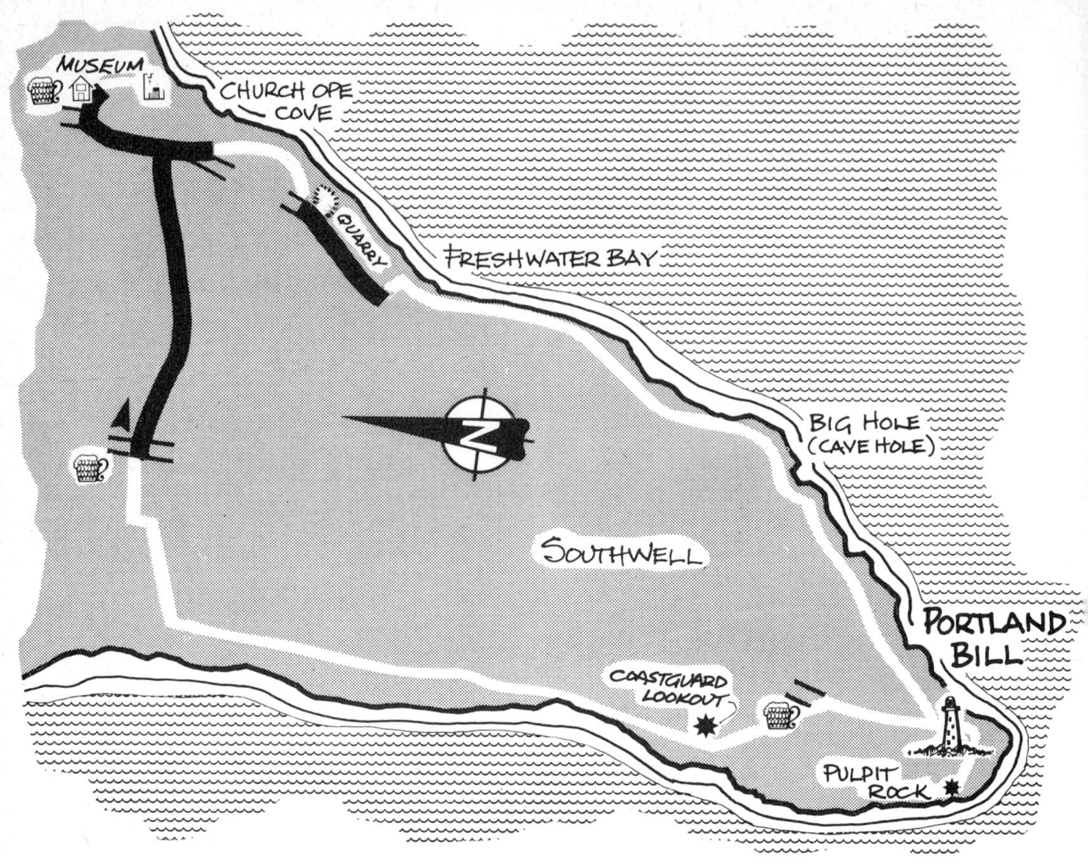

20 Portland

APPROXIMATELY 6 Miles

The District

Immortalised by Thomas Hardy in *The Well Beloved* as the Isle of Slingers and known locally as the Island, Portland is, in fact, a peninsula. It's connected to the mainland by Chesil Beach, an eighteen mile long bank of shingle, that stretches from here to near Abbotsbury. From Portland Heights Motel, the highest point of the Island, there's a marvellous, almost aerial view over Fortuneswell to this curving ridge of pebbles and its pounding surf. Chesil Beach is one protective wall of Portland Harbour, a huge calm expanse of water shared by bathers, yachtsmen and HM Navy.

Socially, the Island has a character entirely different from the rest of Dorset. It is perhaps rather over-institutionalised with the Navy, the Prison and Borstal and the age-old quarrying industry and its attendant traditions. Also it's a Royal Manor and consequently has enjoyed privilege for centuries. For example, when press-gangs roamed the land 'recruiting' for the Navy, the Islanders remained exempt from this inhuman conscription. Such privileges have made the Islanders fiercely proud, some might say to the point of chauvinism.

Geographically also, it is different; indeed its uniqueness separates it not only from Dorset, but from all England. With a deceptively treacherous tide-race off the Bill, it's a flat-topped, cliff-bound peninsula, that's treeless and boulder-strewn and can be bleak and windswept. It's pockmarked by the many quarries that dig and drill and blast for the pale, almost white, Portland stone under the turf. This high-grade stone has for generations been used locally, nationally and internationally – notable Portland stone buildings include St Paul's Cathedral and the Tower of London and the UN building in New York.

How to Get There

By road take the A354 south from Weymouth, turn onto the B3154 (approx 8 miles). *By rail* to Weymouth. *By bus* there are eight buses to Portland Bill, the 422 through to the 429.

The walk is about 5 miles long, but don't let that deter you – it's easy-going and involves no steep climbs or descents.

The Portland Walk

Setting out from **The Royal Exchange,** you turn right down the surprisingly wide main street of Weston, Weston Road, where you can often see children grazing and horses playing (whoops!). You may even see the 'Portland Punk' prowling around the horses. Reputedly, he was thrown and then dragged for a mile by a certain nag. He, as might be expected, suffered bad injuries to his body and mild derangement to his mind and has sworn revenge on the horse if he ever finds it. Go past the Post Office and at Weston Green, you turn left along Weston Street opposite the toilets. You are now walking to Easton and you'll have to forgive the locals their overpoweringly vivid imaginations given full rein when dreaming up place-names. The road takes you past a quarry on your right and terraced houses on right and left. Just before the large factory-like building, there's a deep quarry on your left.

At the T-junction beyond, you can turn left if you want, round past The Pennsylvania Castle Hotel to **The Mermaid Inn**, the Portland Museum and the way down to Church Ope Cove. Revived by the Mermaid's delights, take 10 minutes digestion time and have a quick look round the Museum (open 10.00 – 13.00, 14.00 – 17.00 except Sunday and Monday; 10p admission – OAPs, students and children free). In *The Well-Beloved,* the cottage that now houses the museum belonged to Avice who was the first of three women each in different generations of the same family, loved by Piers, the hero. Odd fellow.

The Royal Exchange, Weston

Naturally it's a Portland stone building, though it doesn't look it as it's painted white with green trim – Devenish brewery's colours. It's an oldish pub with thick walls and has two bars, a skittle alley and a beer garden. John Pope, the new landlord, is still settling in and, amongst other improvements and redecoration, plans to display his collection of pipes in the pub. One of these is a bamboo and metal pipe, crudely fashioned from the only materials available, by a prisoner of the Japanese in World War Two.

This Devenish house serves Devenish Bitter, Wessex, the new John Grove Bitter, Tankard and Guinness – all on keg. And food ranges from ploughman's and sandwiches to basket meals and, in summer, locally caught mackerel and other fish.

The Mermaid Inn, Easton

Near Church Ope Cove, the one beach on the Island, the old Mermaid Inn was a haunt of smugglers in times gone by. Nowadays, the newer (late Victorian) Mermaid is frequented by quarrymen, divers and naval types. Inside, the theme is naval with many photos of ships, the ships' crests and hatbands and the shell on the hearth.

You can drink your pint of Saxon, keg Mild, lager or Guinness here, swapping nautical anecdotes or repair to the garden with its large ammonite fossils. You may fancy a game in the skittle alley to work up an appetite for the excellent range of basket meals, pizza, ploughman's or, more simply, a sandwich.

The Devenish Arms, Portland Bill

By walking up the steps and into the pub, and by standing at the bar and ordering drinks, you are following in famous foot-

If you go down to Church Ope Cove you may, if you're lucky, notice on the beach some odd patterns made from small boulders and pebbles. This will be the handiwork of Winnie the Witch, who lives near the Museum and who may or may not be a witch. Certainly she owns no flying broomstick, but be it on your own head if you tamper with her pebble patterns!

To rejoin the walk, follow the roadside wall of the Pennsylvania Castle Hotel back to the T-junction. Incidentally, in the grounds of the Hotel wander a flock of Portland sheep, an ancient and hardy strain which you can see at closer quarters in the Portland Sheep Fair in Chiswell on Nov 5th and 6th – an annual binge of haggling, hard bargaining and much drinking. At the T-junction, follow the road straight on towards Southwell and Portland Bill. When it's possible, climb the wall and walk along the seaward verge. Once past the caravan park on your left, turn round for a look down to Church Ope Cove and the ruins of the Castle above. You can choose your own way now as you follow the road, but it's worth taking some paths to the edges (without descending) for glimpses of where the sea and the quarrymen have gouged at the low cliffs. Raising your eyes, you're almost bound to see little coasters, with 'salt-stained smokestacks', plying up and down the coast – small fry compared to Sealink's car ferries that churn their way to the Channel Islands.

You pass a rough car parking area and just after, you must skirt round the lip of a brambly quarry back to the road, which then runs between allotments on its left and a large quarry on its right. Southwell stands stark on the horizon on your right. Just after Cheyne House's drive, take the marked public footpath that heads down the well-used track towards the lunar-looking quarry. Has this ever been used as a location for Dr Who stories, I wonder? One thing is definite though – while walking here, do *not* mention the word 'rabbit' (I hardly dare write it), because these burrowing animals weaken the quarry-faces and have caused disastrous rockfalls. If 'that word' is heard by a quarryman, all the men will instantly down tools, so superstitious are they. All Portland you-know-whats are 'bunnies' – don't forget this.

You now follow the track, going left at junctions and forks to keep close to the cliff edges, which in the flowering months are dotted with little bursts of colour, by courtesy of the ragged robin, spur valerian, thrift, and of course Portland spurge, which somewhat mitigate the lunar landscape hereabouts. After a while, the track goes down, past large concrete blocks and then up again. You go past some fishermen's huts and ancient-looking cranes and winching gear. Though looking like derelict quarry cranes, they are in fact for lowering and lifting fishing boats in and out of the sea below. The fishermen ride up and down in the boats, which sounds like a frightening experience in anything but the calmest weather; but crab, lobster and mackerel are abundant in these waters, so presumably the risks have been weighed and found to be lighter than the profits.

You go on up, onto a grassy path and soon over a small stream. A large depression to your left is worth a quick look, through the bars down into Cave Hole. After the next crane, look back into Cave Hole or the Big Hole as its also known (yet more highly imaginative names!) though it in fact looks like three smaller holes. You continue along the cliff top and soon pass the first of the large beach huts, which proliferate here, despite the absence of any real beach. You are a very privileged Islander if you have a beach hut; they are handed down from parents to children and are regarded almost as second homes. The small rocket-shaped lighthouse to your right is now a bird observatory. Many migrating birds use Portland as a large signpost on their way in and out of Britain and their numbers, species and flight-paths are all logged in this 1869 ex-lighthouse.

Aiming for the red and white 1906 lighthouse, you can see a row of coastguards cottages to your right, and it's interesting to note that the chief coastguard merits a grander abode (on the far right) than his minions. You pass the Royal Manor and Lobster Pot cafés and a somewhat oddly sited telephone box and go round to the left before the lighthouse and out to the concrete Trinity House pillar. Swinging right, you pass a little stone hut with its huge slab roof, and then on to large, square Pulpit Rock, which if you've a mind to, you can climb.

Footholds have been provided by a thoughtful sculptor.

On a clear day, make that a very clear day, you can see Start Point from here and apparently it's really exciting to watch the Cowes Powerboat Race from the Bill. It's the most southerly point on the route from Cowes to Start Point and so much do mere fractions of seconds matter that the boats come dangerously close to the land and almost clip the rocks as they pass. Mind you, so fast do they move, that if you blink, you'll miss them. If you look to your right under the building in the MOD fenced property, you can see what is thought to be a 'raised beach' of sand and pebbles, left high and dry when, eons ago, the level of the sea dropped.

Walk back past the lighthouse and up through the car park to **The Devenish Arms**, a pub that can be packed in summer and deserted in winter. Stop here for a spot of glass to mouth resuscitation. Brought back to life enough to endure the homeward stretch, you walk up behind the pub towards the masts and when you're almost under them, you can see the Coastguard Lookout with its flagpole and large notice – aim for it. Naturally enough, there are commanding views all around, but especially along Chesil Beach.

You now aim for the big Naval block on the cliff ahead, leaving on your right the derelict old lighthouse, which someone has unsuccessfully tried to reopen as tea rooms. The coastpath is broad and grassy – eyes-skinned for those oddly-named cliff flowers mentioned earlier. You walk up to and beyond the Naval Underwater Weapons Research Establishment Centre. . . (torpedo factory, in plain English), with its huge window of white and transparent panes. At the further corner of its fence, you have a view across the Island of the old Prison which is now a Borstal. The Prison is now in the naval fort at Verne, but I don't know where the naval fort now is. All the fields to the south of Easton and Weston are farmed by Borstal boys. Follow the coastpath along, ignoring a track leading to a barn, and turn inland between stony fields where the path becomes a boulder-lined track. When the track turns left, you go diagonally left and then turning right rejoin the track, which emerges onto Weston Green. Find your car, tug off the wellies, and head home, tired but happy.

steps. Mr Dickinson, landlord of this 1954 Portland stone pub, has been host to Cyril Smith – for whom two chairs were necesary, the Goodies – forced to film as much as possible here by that maniac ornithologist Bill Oddie, the late Peter Finch – also on location here, Ted Tuckerman – of whom I have never heard, Francis Chichester – circumnavigator extraordinaire, Johnny Kwango – resting from wrestling, and, best of all, Charles Windsor – our handsome future king, who used to pop in for a swift pint with the lads and a quick game of Space Invaders while stationed at the Naval Dockyard. All were visitors with good reason, the pub is marvellously positioned and is warm and comfortable inside with oak panelling and a parquet floor. The public bar's fireplace pales before the carving of Devenish Brewery's crest–the lion rampant is rather demeaningly nicknamed Little Herbert.

Tied to Devenish (who'd have guessed it?) the pub serves Wessex, Saxon and Tankard bitters with Viking Lager and draught Guinness. There's a standard range of bottled beers and spirits, though you'll have to ask the landlord who has drunk the contents of all the miniatures. A wide variety of hot and cold snacks are available and if you're still not satisified, then have a game of bar billiards and calm down.

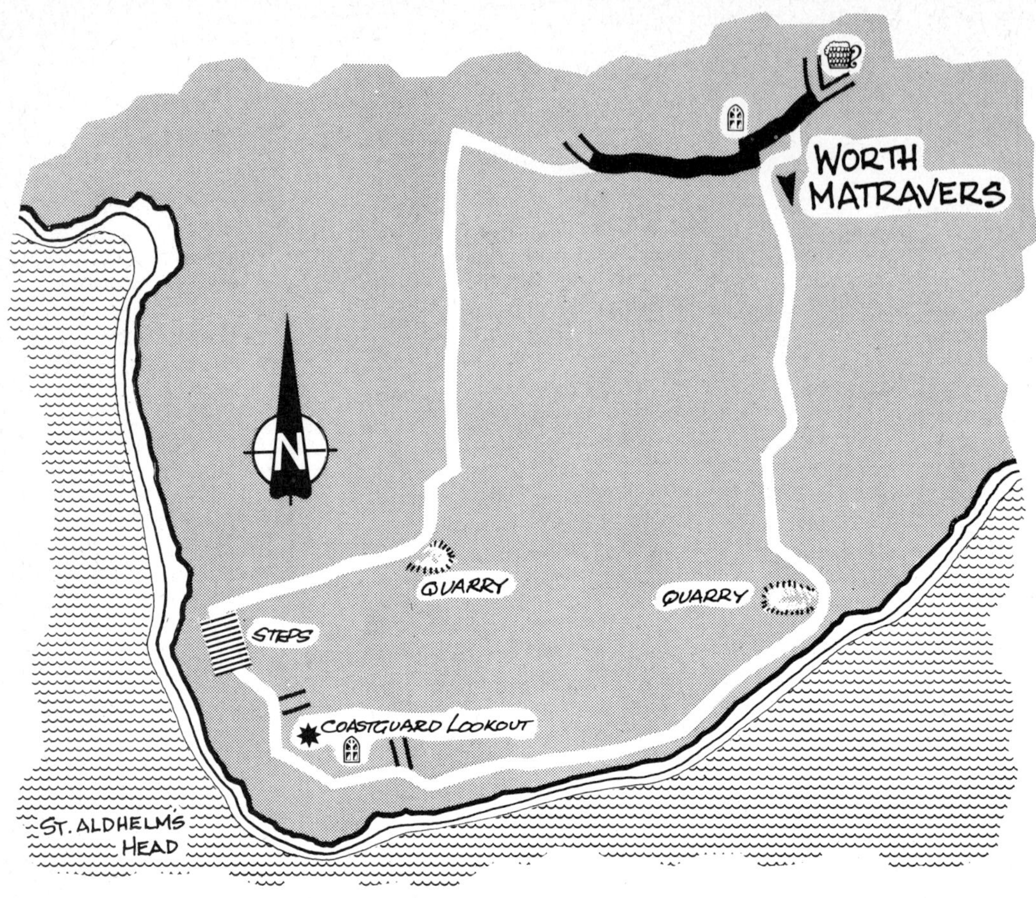

21 Worth Matravers

APPROXIMATELY 4½ Miles

The District

Worth means 'enclosure' or 'homestead' in Saxon but the Saxons were by no means the first settlers here. The area was inhabited several centuries before the Romans. From those first men of the Stone Ages, Worth has relied on the stone for ages and ages. Meaning it's a quarrymen's town and is completely built of local stone. Before it went out of demand, Purbeck marble was quarried as long as 700 years ago in Worth and was then sent to be worked at Corfe. The Black Prince's tomb in Canterbury Cathedral is Purbeck marble from Worth, as is the greater part of Salisbury Cathedral. Portland stone was quarried in nearby Winspit and Seacombe and now, above Worth, attention has been turned to Purbeck limestone.

How to Get There

By road take the A351 west from Swanage and turn left through Langton Matravers onto the B3069 and then left onto an unclassified road for Worth Matravers. *By rail* to Poole. *By bus* the 142 and 304 run regularly from Poole.

From the sun-trap village of Worth Matravers, almost folded into the hillside, the walk descends to Winspit, thence following the cliff to St Aldhelm's Head and a little beyond to Pier Bottom, where it ascends the almost 400ft plateau and returns via farm track and lane to the village

The Worth Matravers Walk

The walk starts in **The Square and Com-**

pass at the top of Worth. After a drink or two to prove your worth, and before you get the worth for wear in Worse (or something like that), leave the pub and walk down the road to the village green. The stone walls and roofs of the houses can in winter look sombre and grey, but in summer with their lichen, they look bright and fresh. The green has a serene tranquil air, with its houses looking contentedly over the pond and its ducking and dipping ducks. Walk past the pond and on down past the green telephone box, thoughtfully provided by the GPO so as not to disturb the eye. Below the telephone box are willow trees once used to make lobster pots for the renowned local lobster and crab trade. Talking of crustaceans, it's weird to find out that in 1920 or so a ship carrying pig-iron was wrecked off Winspit and that since then the lobsters caught there are not the usual true blue but are a red, almost cooked, colour, due to their diet of rust-tinted water.

Below the willows turn left as marked for Winspit and, after the lovely row of cottages, go left again down the marked path and over a stile. Leaving Worth, you cross a field to another stile. A well-defined path takes you off across this next field and gradually brings you to the valley bottom where you find another stile which, not unnaturally, you climb over. Flatter now, the path continues between hedge and fence until you reach a track just below a small Water Board building. This stony track was undoubtedly used to transport stone from the coastal quarries inland and stone from inland quarries to Winspit where ships, despite the absence of docking facilities or indeed even a beach, used to load stone.

The track provides easy walking down the valley and you can now more closely see the strip-lynchets on the hillsides. These are terraces to make ploughing poss-

The Square and Compass, Worth Matravers

This intriguing and unspoilt pub almost breathes stone. Completely made of it – roof, walls and floor – it had several name changes in its history, all closely connected with quarrying and the tools involved. The public bar has also been known as 'The Bank', due to its old function as the centre of the village stone trade where sales and barter were hammered out as the quarrymen washed down the dust after a day at the rockface. Occasionally they would even pay for drinks with stone carvings. Money is expected these days, though.

The pub's licence has been in the Newman family since 1907 and bohemian-looking Ray (or Charlie, after his grandfather) Newman has filled the rooms and bar with all manner of odd and interesting things – stuffed birds and animals, fossils, traps, old bottles, a collection of china and many pictures. Augustus John was a friend of old Charlie Newman and a sketch of him by the artist hangs in the larger panelled bar. In the smaller bar, dominated by the stone fire-breast, hangs a picture of Ray Newman's father and he seems to be in a little pain – you work it out. The pub has also played host to smugglers (quarrymen after work?) and in fact they often used the

ible on the steep slopes, though the necessity for them died along with the millions of victims of the Black Death – there then being many fewer mouths to feed. The track runs above a stream that waters the many hawthorns, brambles and ivy growing on its banks. At the gate, cross the stone stile and fork right to arrive at Winspit. You pass the signposted wall path to St Aldhelm's Head. It's worth having a quick, if not strictly legal, look at Winspit's little inlet and its quarry gouged out of the cliff with its deep and very dangerous chambers gouged out of the quarry. There's ample warning about the crumbling cliffs, but they are beautifully layered with huge blocks supporting gradually smaller and smaller blocks and slabs, topped by a loose covering of small broken stones and then turf. And it isn't only the land that's dangerous here – the sea has claimed the lives of many. On January 6th 1786, the East Indiaman 'Halsewell' was wrecked on the rocks and while the villagers managed to save 82 people, 168 lives were lost. Charles Dickens wrote of this disaster in *The Long Voyage.*

Go back to the marked coastpath and, taking no notice of the 'Coastpath closed at Chapman's Pool' sign as we don't go that far, climb shortly but steeply round the lip of the quarry where there are good views over the old stone workings to Winspit and along the coast to Anvil Point. The path now couldn't be easier – stray from it and you either cross the fence into the field (forbidden) or you veer right to a grisly death (rash and ill-advised). So you sensibly steer between cliff edge and fence, pausing occasionally to watch the diving shags which stay underwater for half-a-minute or more at a time and without snorkels too. Amongst other birds to look out for are the wheeling buzzards and hovering kestrels, the different varieties of gull and the little wrens nestling from the wind in the long grass and brambles. As you stride along picking the burrs from your jersey, you may be perplexed by the cabbages growing on the cliff edge, but presumably they simply escaped from the field above at a time when it was full of cabbages. While we're on wildlife... at the right time of year, you may see grayling and emperor moths flutter by and, if you're very lucky, the pine-hawk moth which is rare, but does frequent these cliff tops.

This nature trail (the path) rises with the cliff and at the corner of the field, you follow the fence as it climbs away from the sea. When the ground levels out, turn left along a track that passes a flight of broad steps and a derelict gateway, both on the right. These are the remains of an RAF radar establishment destroyed by enemy action in the war. Climb the long flight of concrete steps that lead up to the Coastguard Lookout. As you climb these steps, you'll see to your left the T-shaped rock, used, when this was a quarry, to gauge the amount of stone extracted. Continue up to the Coastguard Lookout and St Aldhelm's chapel.

Built on 354ft high St Aldhelm's Head about 800 years ago, the chapel is perfectly square with walls 32ft long and 3½ft thick. As well as being a place of worship, it doubled as a beacon to shipping before the Coastguard Lookout was built. A look at its atmospherically gloomy interior is well worth your while – especially if it's raining, as it's the only shelter for miles.

Walk back to the Lookout and continue along the cliffpath (again ignoring the warnings – we don't go as far as the dangerous part). You come to a flight of 211 steps, yes, I counted every one of them). From here the views ahead stretch past Hounstout Cliff and Egmont Point along the cliffs, past the not-visible Lulworth Cove and on to Weymouth and the jut of Portland. This is on a good day. In bad weather you'll be lucky to see further than Hounstout Cliff.

And so descend the steps and at the bottom (it's called Pier Bottom), turn right, climb over a stile and walk up the valley with its pure and naked slopes sweeping steeply down. You cross a stile and continue up to meet the quarry road where you turn left. You follow this and turn left onto the pale stony track which takes you between the bleak and, in winter, chilling fields until, shortly before Penscombe Farm ahead, you turn right over the marked stile along the public footpath back towards Worth. This path takes you along the edge of the field with the hedge on your left. You cross another stile and continue along the path to your final stile onto a concrete track by farm buildings. There you turn left and then, at the lane, right.

You follow the lane, passing on your left a pitch and a grand house, the possessor of the odd little potting shed/summerhouse with minute church-like windows. At (the) School House, fork left towards the church dedicated to St Nicholas of Myra, the patron saint of sailors. Reputed to have once calmed a storm, he was the Bishop of Myra, Asia Minor in the 5th century. The church is said to have been begun around 700 AD by Saxon King Ine. Of interest in the churchyard are the graves of a certain Benjamin Jesty and his poor wife. He was a pioneer of vaccination and he in fact beat Jenner to the needle, though his choice of guinea pigs seems somewhat shocking to us. He innoculated his wife and two sons with Cow Pox and yet the gravestone inscription credits him with 'great strength of mind'. Nowadays people would be jailed for much less. Turn left out of the churchyard, pass the village pond and head back up the hill to the pub for an injection of something a little more life-giving. I mean beer.

quarry tunnels to escape the long arm of the excisemen. Other customers have included Gerald Durrell and a ghostly lady dressed in grey, who has a spooky habit of moving coins. She doesn't steal them, just moves them.

The pub is a Whitbread tied house, but offers three different gravity fed bitters and a standard range of bottled beers and spirits. This is amply accompanied by a wide range of bar snacks. All this should keep you occupied enough to give you time to explore this interestingly unique and friendly pub. Whole-heartedly recommended.

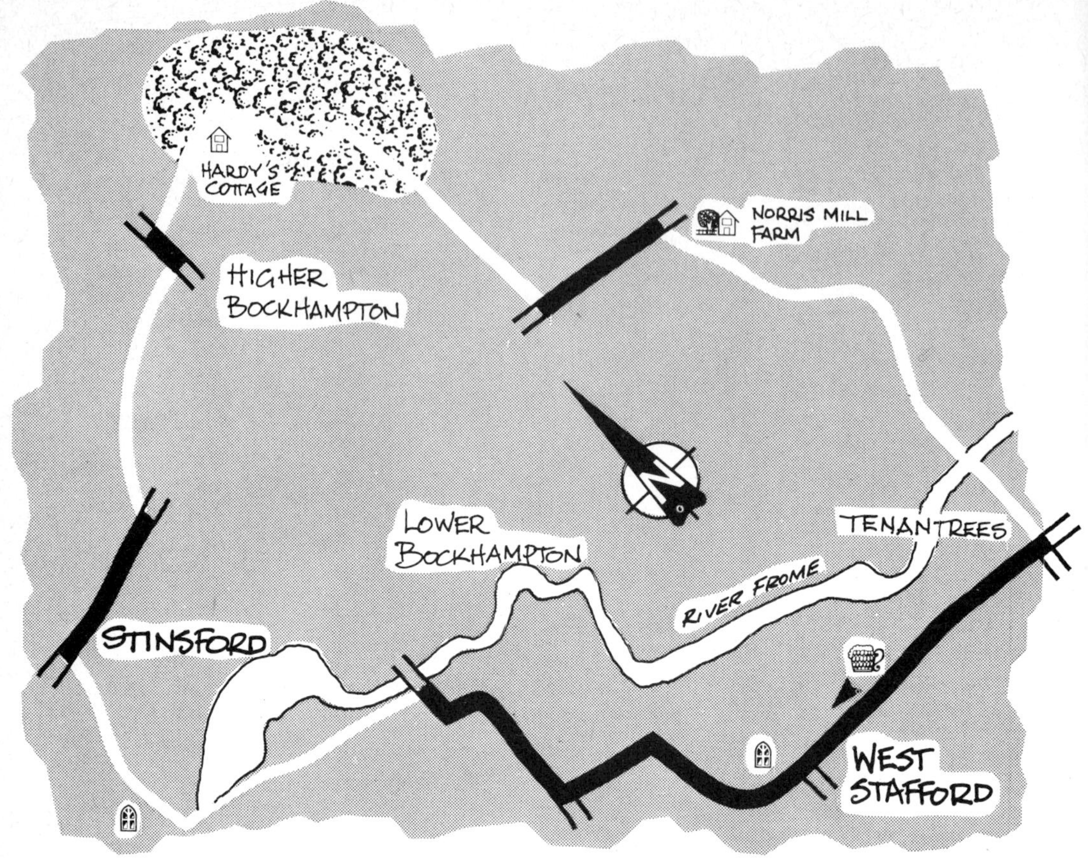

22 West Stafford

APPROXIMATELY 6 Miles

The District

Dorchester, on the River Frome, is the capital of peaceful and prosperous Dorset. But let's begin on a more morbid note. . . Since it was founded by the Roman invaders in 70 AD, Dorchester has had more than its fair share of suffering. The town's Middle Age spread was severely cut back by the plague and a series of fires in the 17th and 18th centuries, upset any architectural uniformity its buildings might have possessed.

In 1685, after the Battle of Sedgemoor, Judge Jeffries came to town and presided over a 'bloody assize'. He tried 300 of Monmouth's supporters, sentenced 290 to death and had 74 of them hung, drawn and quartered. This was all in a day's work for him. A little known fact about this misanthropic dispenser of justice is that he had a sack-like deformity in the lining of his throat which necessitated his spooning out at regular intervals any food which stuck in his gullet – no wonder he found it so difficult getting on with people.

Another famous trial was that of the Tolpuddle martyrs held in the Shire Hall (now a TUC museum open to the public). They were agricultural workers who earned 9 shillings a week, asked for 10 and received 8 as a result. When they formed a 'friendly society' (an early trade union) they were tried and deported to Australia. Later (i.e. too late) they were pardonned and all this helped establish the principle of free collective bargaining.

On the credit side, Dorchester is famous for its two Thomas Hardy's. The one, the admiral of 'Kiss me, Hardy' fame, the other the giant of 19th century English novel writing who dubbed Dorchester Casterbridge. . . but more of him later.

When in Dorchester, do as the Romans did, and visit Maiden Castle which Vespasian captured from the Durotriges in 43 AD. Two miles from Dorchester, the castle consists of 130 acres of earthworks first settled by Neoliths around 2,000BC maintained by men of the Iron Age, then occupied by a force of Romans until Durnovaria (Dorchester) was ready. These days visitors from afar no longer need huge sling shots to gain admission to see this fascinating fort. Two other sites worth seeing in Dorchester, nowadays a typically stolid English town, are the Dorset Military Museum and the Dorset County Museum.

How to Get There

By road take the A352 south-east from Dorchester and turn left and then right for West Stafford (approx 3 miles). *By rail* to Dorchester West station. *By bus* the 459 from Dorchester.

The walk starts in West Stafford, takes you to Stinsford, then Higher Bockhampton and back. It crosses delightful country, steeped in interest yet never too steep, past lovely meadows and lush grazing land, all divided up by the old irrigation system. For obvious reasons, this walk is a 'Hardy perennial'.

The West Stafford Walk

Turn right out of **The Wise Man Inn** after pondering over a drink whether the 'Hardy Poem' on the wall is, in fact, authentic. Was it *really* written by the great man? Head along the road past the church of St Andrew on your right. It dates from the 16th century and is Jacobean in character; the bells of the church were mentioned in Hardy's novel *Tess Of The D'Urbervilles.*

Continue along the road past the entrance to Stafford House on the right. As the road curves left, turn right over a bridge in the direction of Lower Bockhampton.

The old football pitch you have just passed, set in the field beside the road amongst giant oaks, was, so a sly local informed me, where Thomas Hardy used to play in derby matches for Higher Bockhampton Academicals. The countryside is

The Wise Man Inn, West Stafford

There is a poem by the entrance to the inn which is attributed to Thomas Hardy and which, in line with the pub's name, recommends a balanced attitude towards drinking.

The inn was built 400 years ago and may once have been the village school. It is a thatched building which contains a magnificent collection of mugs, toby jugs and antique pipes, gathered by a past landlord who sailed the seven seas.

There are two bars and an open fire. One of the bars is decorated just as it was when the pub was opened in 1920.

There's a full range of excellent snacks and hand-drawn Devenish and Wessex beer to quench your thirst in the pleasant and unchanged surroundings of this inn.

lush and green and alive with streams which flow like life-giving arteries through the grassy meadows. Water is a symbol of fertility here and is everywhere about; consequently the fields are rich and lush and full of birdlife, with pheasants and herons much in evidence.

Immediately before the bridge into Lower Bockhampton, turn left through the gap in the railings and walk along the straight path by the river bank with the Frome to your right. The river flows flat-surfaced and glinting and there's pasture land to your left. It's a compliant landscape, allowing the population around here a graceful life. As you go over a bridge, notice the bricks on the bed of the stream where the old ford was.

Before the gate (straight ahead) turn right and follow the railings to the churchyard of Stinsford. To the left is the sign for the Three Bears cottage – just the place for a spot of porridge, but don't hang around too long. Opposite is a gate into the churchyard.

The two wives of Thomas Hardy, his sisters and daughters are buried here, so too is C Day Lewis and also Hardy's heart which was buried in a biscuit tin – so it can indeed be said that his heart will always be in this part of the country. As a boy he worshipped at this beautiful old country church. Incidentally Hardy's ashes were 'heartlessly' buried in Poet's Corner, Westminster.

Leave the church by the other gate and go up the lane past Stinsford School. When you reach the road turn right and follow the road ½ mile past the lodge of Dorset Agricultural College, which is on the right-hand side. When you see a bridlepath sign to 'Waterston Ridge' (just before the road goes up with the Agricultural College on your right) turn left and go through the two gates ahead. Aim for the nearer clump of trees up to your right. Pass through the gate to the left of the clump of trees, then follow the track between the farm buildings. After the gate between the buildings turn right and walk past a row of huts on the left, used for making feedstuff for broiler chickens. When you come to a road, turn left, then right into Higher Bockhampton. Follow the signposts to Hardy's Cottage, where he wrote *Under The Greenwood Tree* and *Far From The Madding Crowd.* The thatched cottage can be seen by arrangement. (60p March – October) and is where Thomas Hardy was born in 1845. He almost didn't survive birth and was given up for dead till someone noticed he was just breathing. To English literature's relief and O-level candidates despair, he lived to the grand age of 88. It's interesting to note that Hardy was a keen cyclist and used to travel 50 miles in a day round the district.

Turn right out of the cottage and into the forest past the Hardy memorial. Take a sharp right turn after approximately 300 yards and go down a forest track which leads you to a gate by a pretty pond. It's a spot beloved of local birds and is a former passing place of the old Roman road. The track becomes a path and you follow this down to a field. Walk down the right-hand side of the field and then a track will take you to the road. At the road turn left and walk a good distance till you reach a house marked 'WBJ – 1925' on your right (just before Norris Mill Farm). Turn right along the signposted path just after this building and fork left by the first barn to turn right round the far side of the second barn.

Follow the track over a fence past a dung heap and over another fence into a field. Through a gate, you cross two small footbridges in the field, always following the track and ignoring the unsafe spindly foot-bridge to your right.

Follow the track to the far corner of the field and go through the gate and across a concrete 'tractor bridge'. Go straight ahead through the nearby gate to follow the farm track which has a ditch and a hedge on its right-hand side. Be careful, I fell on my face opening the gate here.

Soon you are faced with four gates, take the second from the right, a wooden gate, and follow the track between hedges. After the track has gone through two metal gates, head directly for the wooden bridge over the river. After this, turn left for a stile 50 yards away. Next head right for a flat sleeper bridge in the middle of the field. Turn right and go through the gate 20 yards away. Ignore the right turn here and go straight across the River Frome and onto the lane which goes post Lewell Hill on the right-hand side. Follow the land to Tenantrees crossroads and turn right for West Stafford, where you'll find The Wise Man Inn in the centre of the village after passing 'Talbothay's House' of *Tess of the D'Urbervilles* fame on your way. This may have been a Hardy walk but it was hardly hard and you hardly had to be hardy to do it, only to get through this sentence!

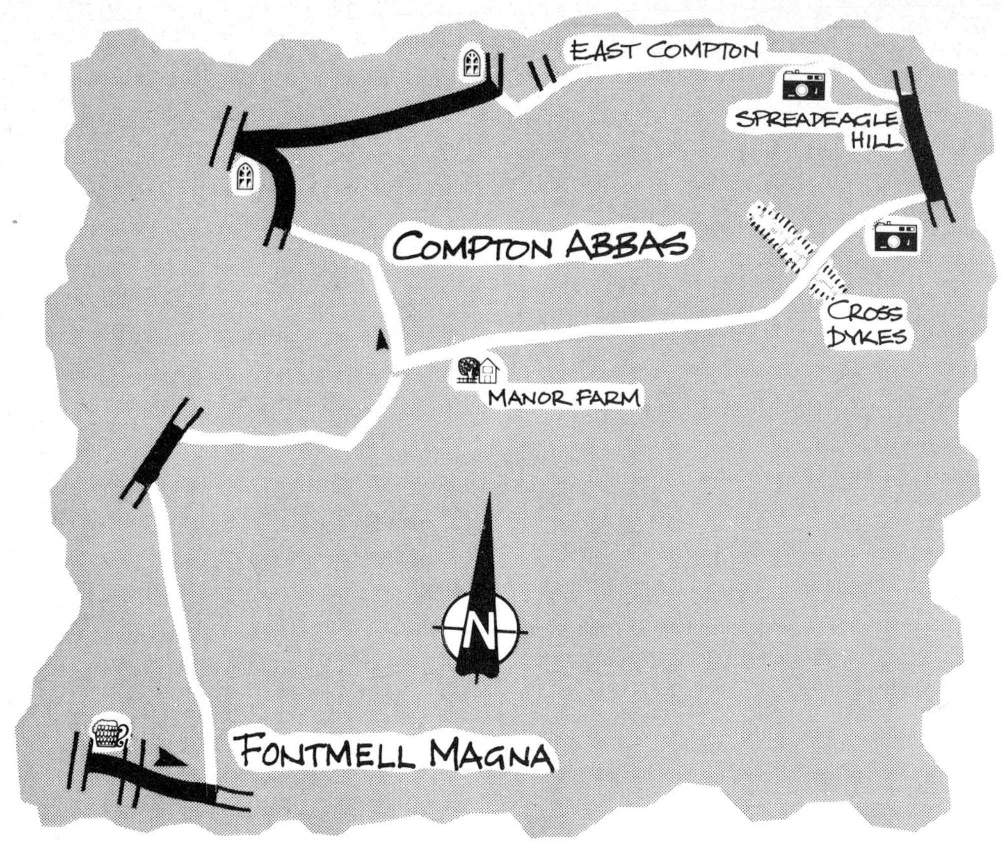

23 Fontmell Magna

APPROXIMATELY 5¼ Miles

The District

1592
Paid for 6 HIDGOGOS hds ....Is 0d.
1675
A Great Belly'd Woman with a Pass...........6d.
1719
Paid to a Woman Bigge with Child ....2s 6d.
1727
Paid for a Foxeshod, To Poleats and 3 Hoghogs Hods..2s 2d.

Brief scrutiny of the village of Fontmell Magna's churchwardens' accounts gives a good idea of the days when impoverished travellers and vagrants were hurried on from the parish with cash payments, and vermin were a prime source of revenue for those who stayed. Nowadays the spelling in what used to be part of Old Wessex has become more uniform and the word 'hedgehog' no longer appears in eccentric forms such as Hodgiogs, Headgiogs and Heggog Hod – yet all around the beautiful village of Fontmell Magna there are still many reminders of the past.

'Fontmell' means 'spring by the bare hill' in Celtic and the site of the village has been occupied since prehistoric times by men who left their mark on the landscape in the form of cross dykes and earthworks, saxon common fields, strip lynchets and the various millworkings which sprang up beside the chalk stream, which runs right through Fontmell Magna.

The church is interesting and was mentioned in the Domesday Book. In the yard there's a monument to a Rector's son who won the VC during the Indian Mutiny and there used to be, at one time, a maypole here before it blew down. The clock chimes the hymn tune 'Hanover' every 3 hours and as if this wasn't enough, can also be reset to play the National Anthem. The village shop is comfortingly antiquated and must be much as it was in the days of the famous Flower family, brewers and publishers, and the noted gardening Gardiners who brought forests to the surrounding slopes. For a place once dominated by Flowers and Gardiners, it's not surprising it's so peaceful round here especially as there is no longer any bounty on the head of the local 'Hidgogos'.

Neighbouring Compton Abbas, meaning 'valley by the abbey', at the head of the Vale of Blackmore, has its own sleepy beauty.

A few miles up the road, hilltop Shaftesbury gives wonderful views over Dorset and Wiltshire. Built in the time of Alfred The Great and called 'Shaston' in the novels of Thomas Hardy, the town has two museums, one of which is sited at the top of Gold St, whose cobbled slope has made it worth its weight in gold from the TV advertisers. Shaftesbury is a gracious English town and rich in history.

How to Get There

By road take the A350 south from Shaftesbury, Fontmell Magna is on this road (approx 4 miles). *By rail* to Poole. *By bus* the 139 and the X13 run regularly from Poole.

The walk is from Fontmell Magna to Compton Abbas, then up through East Compton to the heights of Spreadeagle Hill and back again to base. It's a fairly easy walk offering magnificent views of the rolling North Dorset downs and Blackmore Vale, which they enclose.

The Crown, Fontmell Magna.

The Crown adorns the pretty village of Fontmell Magna in a most suitable way. As one (pleasant) local put it, "it's a pleasant pub in a pleasant village for pleasant people who live in pleasant surroundings". Not to put too fine a point on it, The Crown is very pleasant.

It is fortunate, too, that Mrs Ball's tapestry of a crown, which she and her husband took with them when they moved their tenancy from The Crown, Shaftesbury, can still be displayed on their workplace wall.

An unusual feature of The Crown is that in order to pass water you must pass water. If this seems obvious to you, I should add that a stream runs between the main building and the ladies and gents. You'll be relieved (no pun intended) to know there is a bridge . . .

There are two low-ceilinged bars at The Crown and a log fire to keep everyone warm and happy. Across the road is a patch of grass to sit on in summer, drinking hand-drawn Badger's Best and the other keg Badger's beers on offer. An extensive menu includes home-baked steak and kidney pie. What could be pleasanter?

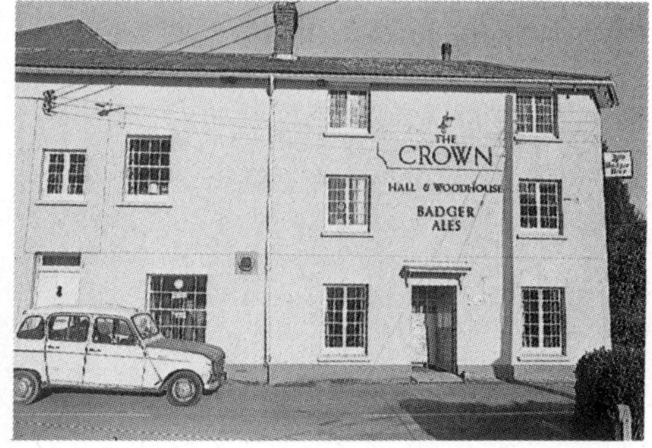

The Fontmell Magna Walk

Top up at **The Crown**, the pub, which stands at the crossroads of this handsome, thatched village and then turn left out of the door to go straight across the crossroads in the direction of Ashmore. On your right, babbling quietly to itself, is Collyer's Brook whose crystal clear waters are heading to join the River Stour as you go upstream past an old bridge on the right. Around you are busy buzzing beehives and quietly thriving apple trees, providing country goodness and an impression of industry for the otherwise sleepy country lane. You soon come to a lovely village pond on the right, peopled (if that's the right term) by the voracious village ducks and brown trout which can often be seen jumping clean out of the water after flies. This is Springhead (the brook rises from the green sandstone rock a few hundred yards up the lane) and along this stretch of water at least four herons live and hunt.

Opposite the pond and across the road, is a footpath signposted 'Compton Abbas' – go over the stile here. Proceed across the field to the far left-hand corner, where there's a double stile which takes you across a ditch – the second part of the stile is not in good shape, so be careful or you won't be either. As you cross the stile, there's a barn to the left and Compton Abbas church jutting up ahead in the distance.

Head slightly left across the field and follow the farm track into the next field. Now follow up the left-hand side, keeping well clear of crops. At the far end of the field, and it is quite far, is a stile beside willows. A little left over this stile and walk 20 yards to another stile, by the road in the right-hand corner – and a signpost which tells you which direction you've just come from.

Turn right at the busy road, past a house called 'Please Shut The Gate' and turn down right on the track to Manor Farm; this is a right of way despite the private sign. Swing left to avoid Manor Farm itself and to go through and past the outbuildings and then to the right of the pond.

Compton Abbas church is to your left as you fork left up a hedged lane with a loud

chattering collection of birds. Then, as the lane threatens to climb steeply and with a gate ahead through which you can see the sky, turn left over the fence into the thin patch of wood. The path is difficult to see at first. Go along through the trees stepping nimbly over the charming, yet ankle snapping, roots and branches.

At the end of the path, turn left into the field and go past a white metal gate on your left. Look to the hills for the spots of sunlight which rake the hard grained slopes like searchlights. As you continue by the fence and past the white metal gate, you come to a stile over some wooden fencing in the far left-hand corner. Beyond this, there's a path along a leafy lane, which becomes a track and takes you into Compton Abbas past a tiny unobtrusive duck pond (duck puddle) and a donkey field, full of braying asses.

Turn right at the parish road and then left just past 'Dairy Farm House'. Go uphill through the quaint old village and up to the main road, just beside which, to the left, you'll find some steps, which mark the entrance to the path to the church. Find your own way through the bushy maze by a deviousness of routes to St Mary's church, which is fairly modern and was built to replace the old church at East Compton.

From the church, turn right along the main road past the old school, taking care against the often heavy traffic. Unfortunately, Compton Abbas although beautiful, has no pub, so turn down right along the lane which leads to East Compton, soon passing 'Dove Cottage' on the right. (You narrowly avoid the lane you came up). The lane drops steeply, keep on straight, past the 'Old Farmhouse' on your right and through East Compton. On the left is the forlorn sight of the old and now neglected church, off the beaten track so business moved to Compton Abbas. Turn right along a track as the road dips and swings left just after the thatched roof of 'Homelands' and the rigid pheasants which stand rooted to its ridge. Don't go into the field by 'Homelands'.

At the junction of tracks, 100 yards from the turning, go left. At the next junction, head right past the sign which says 'unsuitable for motor vehicles'. On your left you'll soon find a house with a triangular birdbox and an unusual assortment of extras. Now follow the grey clay track steadily upwards; as you climb, the already exhilarating view gets better and better – of the serene valley and the beautiful hill across from you, whose ancient cultivated incline is now being tentatively invaded by gorse bushes. Keep right onto the road – this may or may not be the cue for a song. At the road turn right – before you turn, you will see the trees of Cranbourne Chase, the remnants of the old Royal Hunting Ground with its long history of deer poaching, highwaymen and smugglers, and, to the left, Shaftesbury on its hilltop site.

This is Spreadeagle Hill. As you walk, Compton Abbas Airfield is to the left but, just before the sign for it, turn right over the stile by the footpath marker. This is National Trust land and a very beautiful spot where you can feel on top of the world with dark forest left and the cultivated 'beyond' beyond and to the right. You're over 200 metres high here, even the bullocks have runny eyes, enjoy the bracing air as you make your way across the prehistoric cross dykes. Keep Rover under control.

Find the next stile by the fence to your right; after it, follow the fence (now on your left) downhill with 'where you've been' now beyond to your right. Keep going till you come to the gate by the clump of trees where the path is. Don't go through this gate, instead, in order to find the path again, go downhill to the right till you find the gate in to the field below at the end of the trees – it's hidden almost till you're upon it! Go through this gate and turn sharp left over a fence to find the path you came along in the first place. You're now retracing your steps back to Fontmell Magna.

Turn right at the end of the path and go past Manor Farm to the road. Turn left at the road and go over the two stiles at the far side of the cricket pitch. Now follow the right-hand side of this field, to go into the next field where you'll find the double stile to the left of the barn. Cross this obstacle, more a help than a hindrance, to get across the field to the stile by the pond. Now turn right down the road and straight across the crossroads to cap off your walk in a right royal way at The Crown.

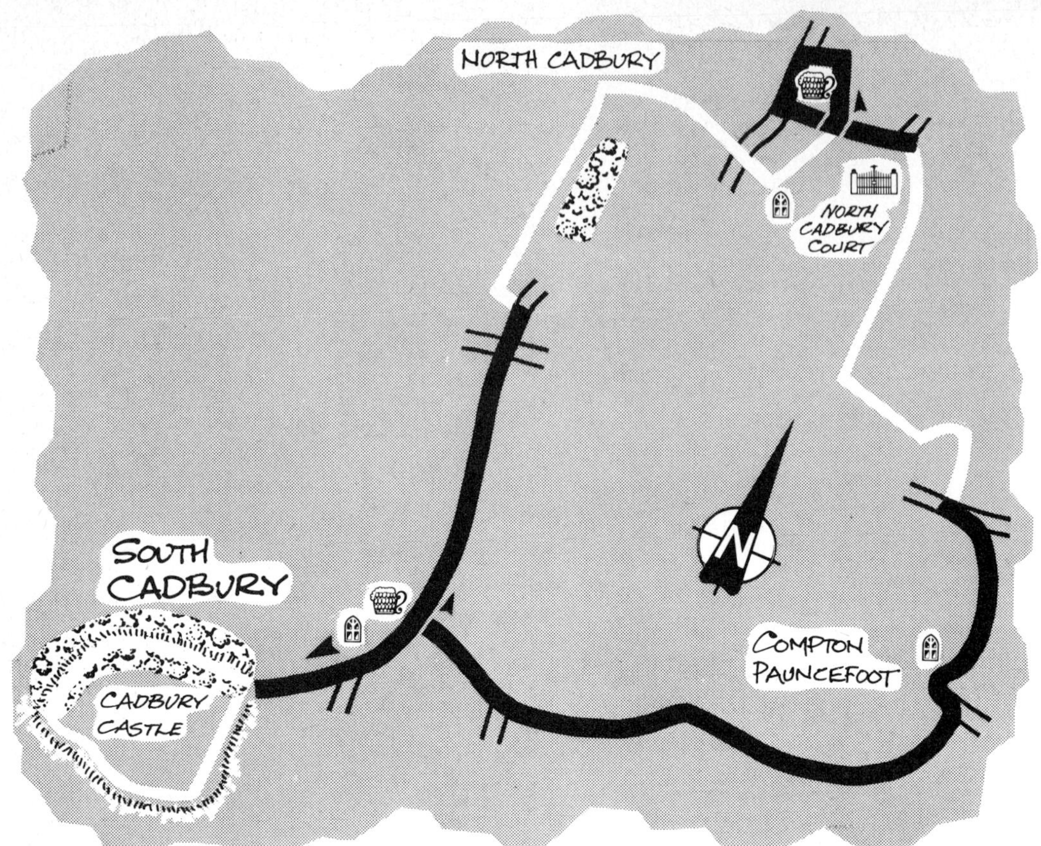

24 South Cadbury

APPROXIMATELY 5¼ Miles

The District

Not the twin centres of British chocolate manufacture as you might imagine, South and North Cadbury do however offer a delightful confection of a different nature. Tasty treats abound here. Most important is the probable site of King Arthur's semi-legendary Camelot – Cadbury Castle; it's a wood-circled hill, first used by the Neolithic settlers who saw its natural defensive advantages, namely that it was an island surrounded by undrained marshlands and was consequently well-nigh impregnable. But despite its impregnability, it was subsequently garrisoned by the Romans, the Britons, the Saxons and the Normans. Much excavation has been done to substantiate this; in a field to the west, bones of men and boys – probably victims of raiding Saxons – were unearthed in a trench and, in 1922, archaeologists found a cache of Roman coins (legionaries' pay, perhaps, being delivered by Securichariot?). Some say that silver horse-shoes have also been discovered, adding credence to the story that on St John's Eve in Midsummer, and on Christmas Eve, the pounding of horses' hooves can be heard as King Arthur and his Knights ride to water their horses at the spring at Sutton Montis. More fantastic still, is the tale, which many people believe (or have believed), that the hill is hollow and that fairies store their gold inside it. This was perhaps dreamed up to explain the noises one can hear at King Arthur's Well on the north side of the hill when someone closes the lid on St Anne's Well on the south side. Anyway, as always, the history of the Dark and Middle Ages is a heady mixture of fact and legend. If however, you visit in the summer during excavations, you may find someone who will guide you round the hill and perhaps help you separate the facts from the legends.

How to Get There

By road take the A303 west from Wincanton and then left onto an unclassified road (approx 6½ miles). *By rail* to Yeovil Pen Mill. *By bus* a private bus service operates from Yeovil to North Cadbury and from here there is a half mile walk.

The walk takes you from South Cadbury, up to the castle and then, back via South Cadbury, to North Cadbury; then through the grounds of North Cadbury Court to Compton Pauncefoot and finally back to your starting point.

The South Cadbury Walk

From the friendly **Red Lion,** turn right up to the village lane. On your right you see the little church dedicated to St Thomas à Becket. It sits peacefully in its pretty churchyard, which boasts yews, a tulip tree and a maidenhair tree – an extraordinary, primitive tree that has no living relatives – as odd, in fact, as the duckbill platypus. The church is modestly commanding and well worth a quick look.

Turning right out of the churchyard gate, look for two rival cockpheasants who never stray far from here and are never shot at. They stand haughtily, steadfastly refusing to look each other in the eye. Seen them? Well, they're on the thatches to your left and right. Almost opposite 300 year old Castle Farm, with its four mullion windows, on your left, you turn right up the stony track to Cadbury Castle. Ignoring a gate on your right, go through the kissing-gate further on ►

The Red Lion Inn, South Cadbury

It's a pretty pub with shutters and window boxes and a little red lion perched on the porch. Originally a farmhouse, the 200 year old building has been a pub since the beginning of this century and consequently has been the social centre of the village since then. A truly classless pub, it is fairly plain and unpretentious (its secret?) and on the wall are plates and pictures of horse-racing, a sport for all classes, and also it's run by Maurice Kavanagh, an ex-Metropolitan Detective Super, who obviously knows a lot about all kinds of people! The result of it all is warmth and friendliness.

It's a free house which stocks Gibb's Premium (from Salisbury) from the wood, gravity-fed Whitbread Best, Guinness and Best Mild on draught along with other more standard drinks. The bar food is also good with one daily 'special', scampi, home-cooked ham, cod, sausages, pizza, ploughman's and home-made soup and, of course, sandwiches. You can if you want take any of the aforementioned plus your children into the garden, which has a lawn and flowerbeds.

The Catash Inn, North Cadbury

There are two possible answers to the obvious question about the pub's name. Either it's named after Baron John Catte who around 900 AD mustered an army here to repel the Vikings. Or, it's a corruption of 'cad', as in Cadbury, which means a hill-top armed camp. Either way, North Cadbury is on the Pilgrim's Way that goes from Canterbury to Lundy Island. The old hostelry which preceded the present building, would have been obliged by law to give a pilgrim a glass of water if asked. The 1796 building has two bars, the public being big enough to merit, in winter, a stove at one end and a fire with three open sides at the other. The bar is ►

up and then, passing below towering trees that creak and sway in the wind, sounding like waves on a shore, you emerge above the tree-line on to the hilltop.

To get the best idea of how impressive and strategically important this 18 acre natural hillfort was, walk round the raised rampart – the amount of country it commands is staggering. A force invading the West Country had to pass here, in order to avoid the marshy Somerset plains to the north-west, the Dorset Downs to the south and the Forest of Pen Selwood to the north-east. As mentioned, excavation has revealed evidence of many settlements and strongholds. However, most interestingly, remains of a timber hall and a cruciform church, have suggested that Cadbury Castle was, in fact the site of Camelot, the court of Christian King Arthur's 5th century kingdom. The River Cam and nearby Queen Camel support the theory. If this was the site, and its claims seem more likely than Tintagel's, then it would have been no trouble for King Arthur, accompanied of course by his Knights of the Round Table, to nip down to Badbury Rings in 516 AD and trounce the invading, pagan Saxons. This battle was a fact. If Cadbury Castle was not Camelot, it was certainly almost invincible with its tiered ramparts, almost 40ft high in places. As such it was the crossing place for many ancient tracks. A mostly overgrown track, known as King Arthur's Hunting Causeway and still marked on maps, leads across the plain to Glastonbury, which is clearly visible to the north-west. In fact the views all round are magnificent with toy farms dotting the countryside and dinky cars driving across it. As you walk round, you'll see many holes in the ground – no doubt badgers or rabbits doing a little of their own excavation, looking for traces of their Iron Age forbears.

Retrace your steps back down the hill, past Castle Farm, a huge London plane tree and the church. Just before the pub you'll see on your right a peculiar little belfry on top of a garage – so watch for bats. Walk on down past the pub, between terraced houses and an orchard and you arrive at the A303, though you'll have heard it some minutes before. At the crossing there's a small thatched chapel with adjoining cottage – once a place for the weary Glastonbury-bound pilgrim to stop, rest and pray for a few minutes; nowadays, it's almost shaken to pieces by the thundering London to Exeter traffic.

On the other side, the lane crosses a bridge which crosses a stream and just after it you vault a gate on your left into a field of brussel sprouts. Follow the stream along the bottom of this field and when you are directly below a solitary beech tree to your right, turn up along the edge of the sprouts towards it. Of course the contents of the field will change with the farmer's planning but the chances are they will be of the cabbage variety. Go round the beech tree and on, now past cabbages, to a concrete track. Here you side-step right and then quickly left to walk along the left-hand side

of a long, narrow strip of woodland. Passing through a yellow-arrowed metal gate, strike out diagonally right on the faint track which curves round towards North Cadbury church. Go through the gate, over the lane and take the steps up to the field where you can see a stile under the church tower.

The church of St Michael, was built of almost glowing Ham stone in 1417 and is a good example of the Perpendicular style. A really lovely church like this deserves exploration and, if you venture inside, look at the rare 15th century glass in the west window and at the top, on the left, is St Apollonia – the patron saint of toothache-sufferers. Also rather amusing are the carved bench ends which often depict humorous scenes alongside religious and aristocratic emblems. One is dated 1538 on the back. Leave the church along the path that follows the back wall of a long building on which hang three interesting bronzes, between clematis and ceanothus. Turn left out of the lych-gate along the beech avenue to Woolston Road.

Here, go straight across and along the High Street which curves round to **The Catash Inn** at charming Woodforde Cottage.

Quenched, turn left out of the pub and then left again at its corner. This is to give you a little tour of the village and a chance to admire its Ham stone cottages. Turn left along Woolston Road and follow it past the Post Office and then go left at the tree set on its own walled triangle. Walk up the metalled road and follow it on to the concrete farm-track ahead. After you pass a line of trees, look right and behind for a good view of Cadbury Court, the house of a Mr and Mrs Montgomery. The track takes you through estate fields with their spreading trees and, at line of beeches, it crosses a bridge over the River Cam and swings left. Follow it along the river, passing a small derelict building and the sound of a waterfall above, just before the concrete bridge ahead, turn right along the right-hand bank of a calmer and quite deep stream.

At the road climb the wood fence and like a hedgehog at night, try to cross the dual carriageway. On the far side climb through the fence and turn left on to a lane and then right into Compton Pauncefoot. You pass between Weston Hill with its crown of trees on your left and a smaller, balding hill with its clumps on your right. Continue to the little spired church with its good yews and the newish half-doors on the porch. Perhaps the prettiest church on the walk, it is certainly the smallest. The font is 700 years old.

Going on along the lane under the high newish stone wall, turn right at the junction and wander on through the village proper. Again its built of lovely old stone – a pale yellow-grey colour topped off with a variety of different roofing materials, all of which are pretty. At the top of the village you pass an unpretentious but fine crescent of houses – perhaps built to house the staff of Compton Castle, an entertainingly over-castellated house set in front of a lake and amid beautiful grounds.

Just after the crescent, the lane swings right, so as to stay under the steep and wooded slopes of Pen Hill. Now you have an easy amble along this quiet country lane back to South Cadbury. Make sure you go to the right of East End Cottage and you'll pass old houses and farms, finally arriving at the pub and reward.

comfortable (with armchairs), interesting (with its original beams, its two large wheels from a hay-teasing machine and its sloping coat-rack) and, most importantly, friendly.

It's an Eldridge Pope tied house with Dorchester Bitter and Dorset IPA (strong!) on handpump. Old Highland Blend, Sextant Rum and Casterbridge sherries expand a standard range of other drinks to complete the list. If you want, you can take your drink and hot or cold snack either into the garden or into the amply equipped games-room.

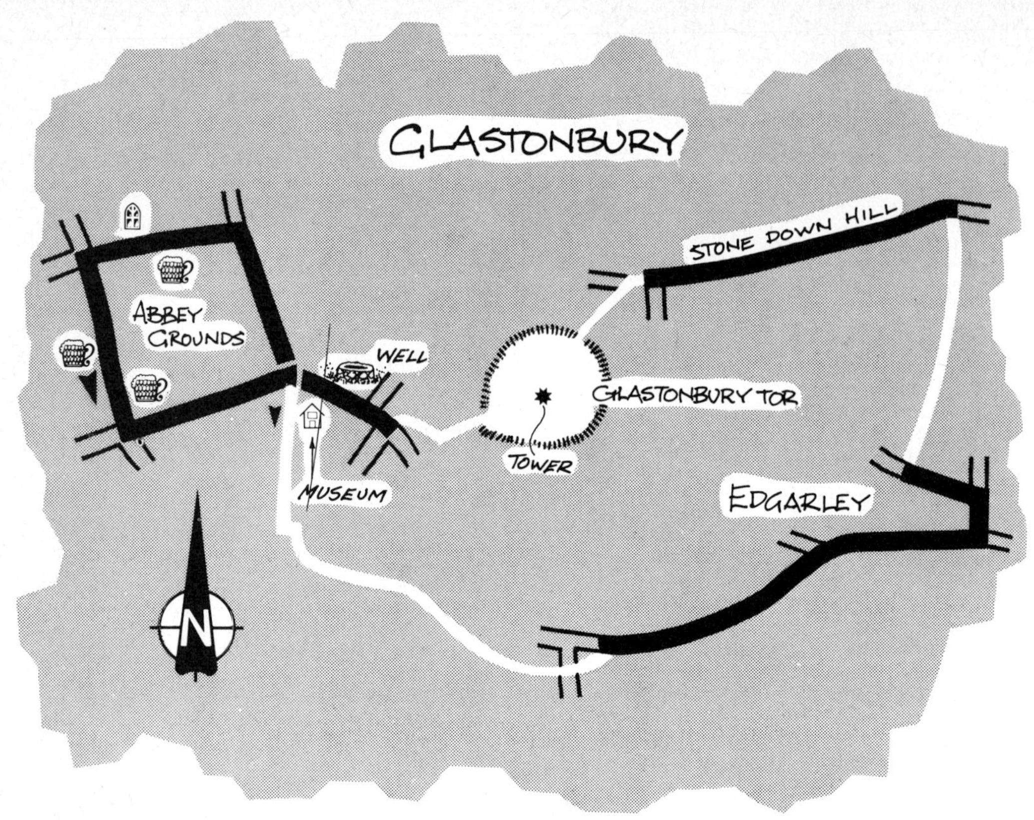

25 Glastonbury

APPROXIMATELY 4½ Miles

The District

The problem with Glastonbury's history lies in distinguishing fact from fantasy and extracting the matters of fact and the more substantial from the mythical and the mystical. Glastonbury seems to exist on two historical levels somehow mirroring the low-lying plains of the area and the strangely-shaped tors which form the line of the Polden Hills.

Ding dong – 'Avalon calling'. 'Avalon' was the ancient name for Glastonbury Tor and is much bandied about by those who depend on the tourist trade for a living and they are not afraid to use it liberally as a brand name for their products. It means 'place of apples' or, I read somewhere, 'Sleepy Island of the Blessed' – 'apples' seems more likely though there have never been orchards on the tor.

It is said that Jesus visited Glastonbury in the days before he became Jesus Christ Superstar. At the time of the crucifixion, the plains around Glastonbury formed a vast swamp with a system of lagoons and waterways which ran to the sea. There existed in these parts a network of lake villages whose internal and external communications were conducted by means of log tracks stretching across the boglands and boats hollowed from tree trunks.

Joseph of Arimathea, a dealer in tin and lead, came over to barter with the miners of the Mendips bringing with him the chalice from the Last Supper, the Holy Grail. Mixing business with pleasure, he buried the chalice on Glastonbury Tor and then also found time to conjure up a new strain of thornbush. In those days procreation could be achieved by the most eccentric methods, and, when he banged his staff on the ground of Wearyall Hill, it took root and sprouted into a Glastonbury Thorn, a species to be found nowhere else in Britain.

This was also a sign he was to settle here. (There's no guarantee this method will work for you if you bang your walking stick on the ground, after all, you never carried the cross of Christ).

From this point on, the Christian church began to flourish here, too, and by the Middle Ages the abbey had become the most powerful in the land. The abbey is said to house the bodies of St Patrick, St Joseph and St Dunstan, who was made abbot here in 943 and was soon to be tempted by the devil who appeared to him in the guise of a beautiful woman. He resisted the temptations of the flesh, however, and grabbed her (him!) by the nose with hot pincers, an incident which could have been highly embarrassing had he guessed the identity wrongly. Oh, and if you'll believe it, King Arthur and his wife are buried here, too; when they opened 'their' tomb in the 12th century, Guinevere's hair crumbled to dust. The abbey is fascinating, go there and find out for yourselves.

How to Get There

By road from the M5 (junction 23) go east onto the A39, Glastonbury is on this road (approx 13 miles). *By rail* to Taunton or Bridgwater. *By bus* there are regular bus services from both the rail stations, the 212 and the 266 respectively.

The walk begins from Glastonbury Abbey and takes you past the Somerset Rural Life Museum to Glastonbury Tor and then back. It is an easy walk presenting few problems to the reasonably fit.

The Market House Inn, Glastonbury

The Market House Inn was refurbished in the 1920's after years of providing accommodation and sustenance for 'cyclists, tourists, and commercial travellers' as you can see from the photo on the wall of the inn. The landlord here tells the story of little Jack Horner who apparently once worked as a bailiff for the abbot and delivered title deeds of properties, which (unusually) were baked in pies for secrecy – one day, he sat in a corner and started eating, well, the rest is nursery rhyme.

There's a piece of timber in one of the chimneys of the building which is 400 years old. There are two bars with, in one, an imitation log fire and covered beams. Beers include hand-drawn Directors and

The Glastonbury Walk

Turn right out of **The Market House Inn,** which you'll find opposite the abbey (all being well). Take the chance to visit the abbey with all its local and historical, secular and ecclesiastical history. Otherwise walk right along Magdalene Street and on the right you'll see the Old Pump House and St Margaret's Chapel, before you get to **The Globe** on the left.

Before your head starts spinning, turn left out of The Globe up Fisher's Hill. At the top of the hill, sweep left up Bere Lane. To the right the road goes to Wearyall Hill (see above) – the original Glastonbury Thorn was hacked down by a Roundhead who is said to have amputated his own leg in the process. Continue up the lane to the Somerset Rural Museum, a barn like structure on the right at the end of the road.

The museum concentrates on realistically portraying life in 19th century rural Somerset and you will be staggered by many of its revelations.

From the museum entrance (the house entrance) go half left a few yards and through the fence to follow the tarmac path downhill through the estate of new houses. Cross Actis Road and continue along the path. At the next intersection of paths, lead down the path to the right leaving house number 12 behind to the right. Very soon you see countryside ahead and release from this urban claustrophobia. Cross the road and just to your right there's a stile. Cross it, go left and accompany the power lines stride for stride across a huge meadow. Glastonbury Tor lies to your left and it's all flat and peaceful here.

As a hedge appears to obstruct your further peaceful progress, there's a stile to your left by a gate. Get over it – perhaps you could make use of the Fosbury Flop here, a bizarre backward high jump style – there are lots of stiles coming up so be zany in your approach to them. Be careful though this is a spot for courting couples and you could easily land on a car bonnet jumping over backwards like that.

Turn left up the lane and then right at the T-junction past Lower Edgarley Farm. After the visit to the museum, a life of 20th century farming seems much more appealing than the 19th century version.

At the road, the A361, turn right and cross by the pedestrian bridge. Follow the pavement downhill to the next village, past Edgarley Manor Farm. The first left after that goes to Wick – take it, then the first left again after 150 yards to go up a country lane. Once upon a time this area was completely underwater before they built the sea wall to the west on the present day coast – in fact pelicans – yes pelicans – guzzled their grub on this very spot.

Just after a sharp bend to the right there's a metal gate to the right. Go through and straight across the field to the stile opposite. Now begins a succession of six stiles in a row, roughly in a straight line. Do your David Hemery bit along this stretch, stopping only to look at the countryside. After the sixth stile you come into a field, head straight across it and out of the gate to go up a track to the left. By the gate there's an intriguing signpost to Gog and Magog – these are two oaks of great antiquity; sadly there's no time to visit the old timers.

The track to the left takes you up Stone Down Hill and this is a slope to get the kinks out of your legs – follow the high-banked track to the road.

At the road, turn right and 100 yards on the left go through the stile to get to St Michael's Chapel on Glastonbury Tor. It must have taken good Christians to walk up here every day. This Tor achieved a certain fashionability in hippy times as a focal point of 'cosmic forces' – See if you, too, can feel 'the vibrations'. At certain times hippies still plod up here in their never ending search for 1967. . . and you can see why, the view is stupendous – imagine the network of tracks across the marshes which used to be here.

To get to Glastonbury follow the spur of the hill, continuing roughly the direction you

came up the other side in. This will bring you to a gate, then another of the peculiar local kind, and then down a steep path to Well House lane – where 20 yards up to the right there's an outlet for the curious, curative water of Chalice Well, which has a rusty taste. Turn left, then right along Chilkwell Street and, if you like, visit Chalice Well, itself whose stream never runs dry even at times of drought. (This is open 13.00-15.00 in winter and 10.00-18.00 the rest of the year). Now continue along in a straight line, past the Rural Museum and the Abbey Retreat House till you come to a roundabout.

Turn left here and down Glastonbury High Street where you'll find The Queen's Head and St John the Baptist Church – both are worth a visit. At the bottom of the street, turn left and you're back where you started by the abbey. Thanking God that the water receded enough to allow the town of Glastonbury and its alehouses to flourish, go into The Market House Inn and order a pint of that other curative quaff.

Courage's Best and PA. There's also keg Bass and draught Guinness with 30 wines and 40 spirits to choose from. Snacks are good and children can be impounded in the other bar when it's not busy and out the back in summer.

The Globe Inn, Glastonbury

The Globe Inn is over 200 years old and is the centre from which the Goldfinch Carnival Club operates.

It is about to undergo redecoration and caters for a 'young trade'.

There's keg IPA, Tavern and John Courage and a reasonable choice of snacks. The outstanding feature of the pub is the juke box's selection. Children can play in the park next door while parents go round to The Globe!

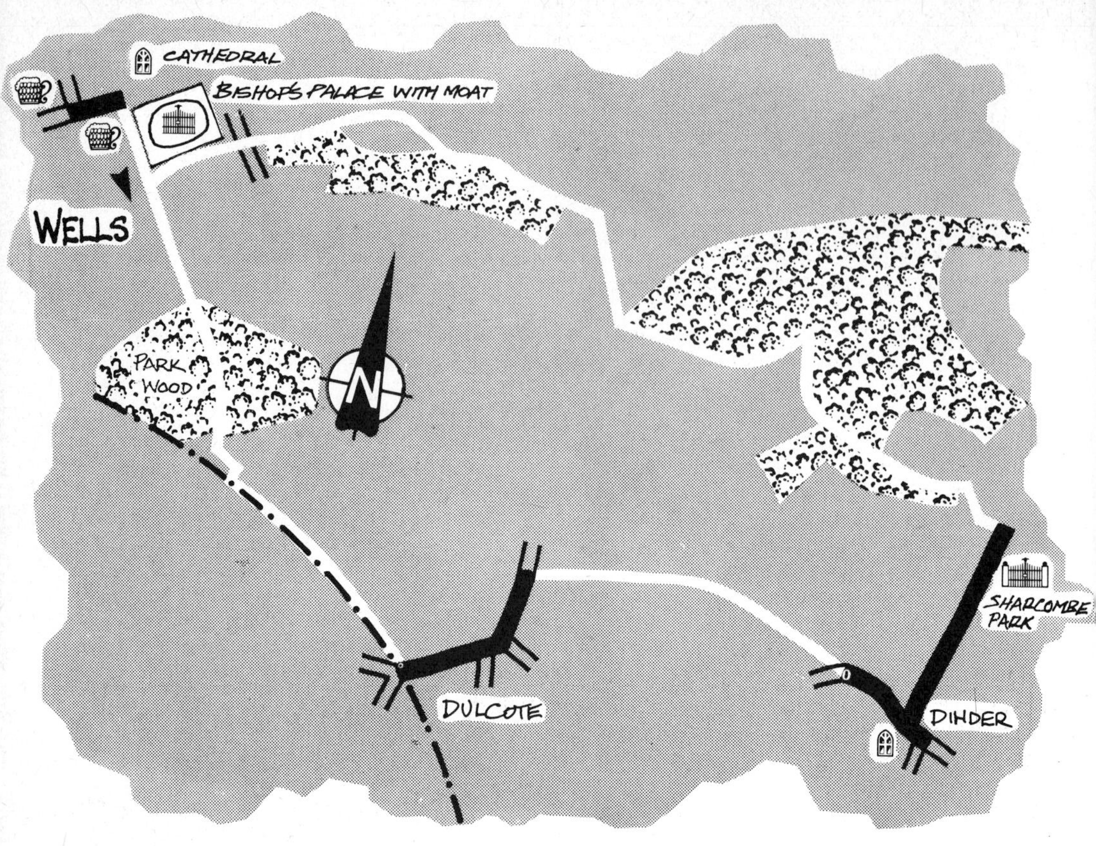

26 Wells

APPROXIMATELY 4¾ Miles

The District

If you ever thought 'there is nothing so beautiful now, as it used to be', then come to Wells to discover lasting beauty within the limits of the old city walls. Aesthetes, nostalgists, tourists and purists, will revel in the sites to be seen.

Riding across land, which had seen the comings and goings of King Arthur (probably a local warlord) some centuries previously, that grand old man of Wessex, King Ina, in a moment of inspiration, stopped off by the springs which seep out below the lead-bearing Mendips. Smitten by the view across the placid plains of Somerset and the prospect of continuing his journey to Glastonbury where he was in the process of building an abbey – after all it must have been a grating haul all the way from Cheddar (cheesey grin!) – he decided on the spot to build a church. Oh to be a whimsical royal .....

By 909, a Bishop's seat had been established at Wells and a city, which to this day sits above a honeycomb of water-hollowed rock, was built on the source, not the banks, of the river, St Andrew's stream. Wells grew to become the administrative counterpart to the mystical centre of the church at Glastonbury and it is interesting to note that Wells Cathedral has survived almost intact in the long run of history, whereas Glastonbury Abbey lies open to the skies; red tape can never be unwound.

Though built on watery ground, the Cathedral is magnificent and quite unique, with an unrivalled collection of medieval statues. These were fortunate indeed to survive the Duke of Monmouth's forces who stabled their horses in the nave in 1683 and proceeded to practice their shooting on the lower rows of statues – musket-ball marks can still be seen. If you have dental problems, try touching the tomb of Bishop Britton. When it was opened 600 years after his burial, his molars were still in fine condition and now it is supposed to have healing powers for toothaches. Make sure, also, that you see the medieval astronomical clock with the figure of John Blandiver – eternal percussion is his sad lot. Give yourself time to see lots in Wells including the Vicar's Close, the Bishop's Palace (perhaps the oldest inhabited house in England) and the local museum.

Nearby Wookey Hole offers spotlit caverns where troglodyte stone-agers once lived and loved in the damp and unsavoury conditions wrought by the action of the River Axe. Man actually chose to live here where hyenas had once laughed themselves to extinction and the spooky witch of Wookey stands petrified in stalagmite form. There's also an exhibition of Madame Tussaud's stores and rejects and a special fairground collection, too. Yes, it's a bizarre mixture at Wookey.

How to Get There

By road Wells is on the A39, between Bath and Glastonbury. *By rail* to Bath. *By bus* the 175 and 176 operate regularly between Bath and Wells.

The Wells Walk

Turn right out of **The Crown Hotel,** where you should have spent enough crowns to keep the proprietor happy and in business, into the Market Place and walk across, to the left of the Wellspring Bookshop to Penniless Porch, so called because beggars used

The Crown Hotel, Wells

Built about 1450 and added to, notably the front, by the Elizabethans about 1590, The Crown is an attractive urban inn with its timbered and leaded windows (look for the round ones with star-shaped lead) and its window-boxes. It was from one of the front windows that William Penn, the Quaker, preached in 1695, attracting a crowd of several thousand. He was arrested.

Inside there are two bars with open fires, original beams, photos of the city and a good collection of old prints.

There's also a good collection of beers, notably Wadworth's 6X and Royal Oak, both hand-drawn from the wood, gravity-fed Draught Bass and also Guinness, Theakston's Best, Courage Best, Worthington E and Grousch (lager from Belgium) all on draught. You might like to try Crippled Cox Cider or Sheep Dip Scotch (a malt) or even

to shelter here and beg from clergy and worshippers as they passed through to the Cathedral. You may pass through happy with the thought that begging is largely extinct now, until you reach the light blue pillar-box in front of the West Front of the Cathedral and pass the many collecting boxes within. It's clear however, that asking for money for the Cathedral is perfectly acceptable and indeed necessary for the never-ending restoration work that a building of this size and architectural importance merits and needs.

While the uncluttered heights of the nave and, by comparison the calm intimacy of the small chapels, hold universal appeal, every visitor will look for and enjoy different features in the Cathedral. Here's a list of some of the things that struck your researcher. First and foremost, the Chapter House steps, worn down through the ages by many a clerical slipper, leading to the light and airy Chapter House with its central column supporting the exuberant fan-vaulted ceiling. Then there is the 1380 clock, the second oldest working clock in England, with its knights who joust every 15 minutes and Jack Blandiver who rings bells with his hands and feet warning the knights to get ready and lower visors. The 14th century copes chest is a large fan-shaped wooden container and is still used today for processional vestments. And here's a test for you:– round the Cathedral are carvings of ten separate people all suffering from toothache. Can you find them? A clue – in the South Transept you'll find one, along with a cobbler at work and an old person extracting a thorn from their foot. If you can't find them, ask a verger.

After you've explored the Cathedral, leave the way you came and go back through Penniless Porch. Turn left here and left again through the old archway. In effect the walk goes in the Bishop's Eye and then later comes out of it (very uncomfortable for the old fellow). The Bishop's Eye is the name of the old archway. Turn right and walk to the corner of the moat which surrounds the Bishop's Palace. If you're lucky and the swans are hungry you'll see a swan, like the haughty aristocrat he/she is, paddle up to a bell near the drawbridge, ring it and be given food by some hidden lackey within. The swans were taught this by the daughter of a Victorian bishop and each new generation of swans has learnt it from their parents.

Walk along the moat keeping it on your left, watching the swans, geese, duck and gulls (in that pecking order) cruise and flap about. At the far corner continue in the same direction and go straight through the metal gate along the track, aiming for a wooden gate ahead. Here turn and look over the Bishop's Palace to the Cathedral – one of the many views of it on the walk. Once over the stile by the gate take the footpath straight on to Wellesley. Make for the stile by the gate leading into Park Wood. Nip over it and follow the track through this peaceful (except for the A371 traffic noise) wood with its pigeons high in its silver birch and oak. On the far side of the wood you see a gate ahead where the track swings to the right, go through it and following the fence opposite, to your left for 20 yards, climb through it (carefully – don't damage it) and scramble down the steep slope on to the disused railway track. Turn left along the stony track.

The track goes under a concrete bridge and when the cutting finishes and the embankment begins, you can see Glastonbury Tor on your right, Dulcote Hill ahead and the Mendips to your left. You cross the River Sheppey and when you reach the houses of Dulcote, turn round for another, different, view of Wells Cathedral. Immediately before the bridge at Dulcote, scramble down the left bank and out onto the lane that takes you through the village, past a lovely old long barn being renovated and out to the main A371 by a peculiar animal trough and fountain, both incredibly mossy.

Turn left along the main road (on the far pavement) towards Wells, walking past Dulcote's modest stone houses. Just after a house whose windowless end abuts the pavement, turn right through a white wooden kissing-gate and, following the line of the house and garden wall, head straight across the field. You go to and through a black metal kissing-gate and, turning left along the hedge, turn right to follow the tree lined stream. Go through another kissing-gate in the corner of the field and then again follow the stream, until, after 50 yards, you see a narrow concrete footbridge which you cross. Head now for a stile which is diagonally to your right, climb it and aim just to the left of the farm buildings ahead. Going through another kissing-gate (to the left of a large oak) you walk past the telegraph pole and on towards the church peeping above the farm. Once over the stile, you head in much the same direction along the lane into the village of Dinder; i.e. head for Dinder, dinderhead.

As you walk into the village, you pass a fine shell porch on your left and the little church that's almost as high as it's long, on your right. There's a good old print of it behind the pillar inside and its worth a look anyway by way of contrast with Wells Cathedral – from the sublime to the minute. The whole village is worth a few minutes wander – it's serene, warm, even sleepy with its stone houses looking out over the walled stream towards the A371. Go back to

Pig's Nose (a blend), but frankly I take no responsibility. For those with more usual tastes, there's an à la carte menu in the restaurant and in the bar, there's home-made pies, ploughman's and daily specials.

The Star Hotel, Wells

An astute innkeeper, way back when, decided to call his inn The Star of Bethlehem – thereby boosting his ordinary trade with that of many of the pilgrims who flocked to Wells and nearby Glastonbury. It was a coaching inn, built in the 16th century and, in fact you enter it along the old cobbled carriageway, now covered and hung with greenery. The stables were long since converted into a restaurant. The Hunt Bar has exposed stone walls with a collection of brasses, copperware and old prints and the older Tudor bar is wood-panelled with two fires, old pictures of ships, other prints and some clay pipes. It's warm and friendly downstairs, though upstairs there's a certain Mrs Stroud who occasionally appears clutching a cane stick in one hand and a red and white bottle in the other. She's looking for something, probably a drink, as bottles rumble in the cellar at night.

She's onto something but the drinks are dispensed in the bars and include Wadworth's 6X, Wadworth's IPA and Star Bitter on hand-pump with Guinness, Tartan Bitter and Carlsberg on draught. There's a good range of bar snacks in, yes, the bars, from sandwiches to steaks and the restaurant's à la carte menu in the evening is renowned.

the church and take the lane opposite uphill. Why is there a pavement here? Unless there was a former owner of Sharcombe Park who used to race his carriage dangerously down the lane – who knows? At any rate, you'll probably be safe as you walk up past the lodge and below the house.

Go left at the fork, through the gate, past a pillbox, between the tank obstacles and on up the track, past a small pine plantation to your right and into a field – almost an instruction a yard. Walk along the bottom edge of the field, with trees below you, towards the left-hand gate of two that lead into the larger wood.

Go through this small blue-arrowed gate along the well-defined, though sometimes muddy, path which winds through the larches, field maples and other trees. The path curves to the right at the far edge of the wood – watch out for roots here, just waiting to trip you up – and brings you to a gate, through which you go. Turn left along a broad grassy path below the treeline. Glastonbury Tor dominates the horizon as you go and it's possible that this path was an ancient pilgrim's way to Wells and thence to Glastonbury. If you'd come from Canterbury, this would be your first glimpse of Glastonbury and your journey's end. Certainly, it's ancient, evidenced by the stone slabs which show through in places.

At the end of the wood, just before the metal gate on your left, turn right up the two steps out on to the golf-course. Checking that no golfer is about to swing (and possibly end your life with a 70 mph golf-ball driving into your temple and prematurely finish your walk), go uphill to the top of the ridge and then aim for the bottom corner of the woodland diagonally to your left. Just near the corner is a narrow but defined path through bracken, that leads into the bottom of the wood. A few arboreal yards bring you to a stile which you cross and, turning left, strike out along the meadow. This is part of a nature trail (mainly in the trees of Tor Hill above), so watch out for nature, sometimes known as Flora and Fiona. Walk through the gateway, and passing through the lowing cows, continue in the same direction towards a modern bungalow by a stream which you leave to your right. Sidle through the kissing-gate and walk along the path between wall and stream.

Yet another aspect of the Cathedral heaves into view as you pass pitches on your right. Imagine old bishops taking constitutionals up and down here – "God bless thee", "And thee" etc. At the main road, go right and immediately left through the barrier. Walk along the wall and soon the moat, back to the corner where you left Wells. Follow the moat round and relieve the Bishop by leaving his Eye and entering the Market Place. Ignore your car – if you have a parking ticket, they won't give you another – and go straight ahead past The Crown Hotel and the fountain to **The Star Hotel** on the High Street for a pint of Bishop's Tipple which, if they sold it, would fit in very neatly; as they don't, it'll have to be the prosaic but tasty Wadworth's 6X.

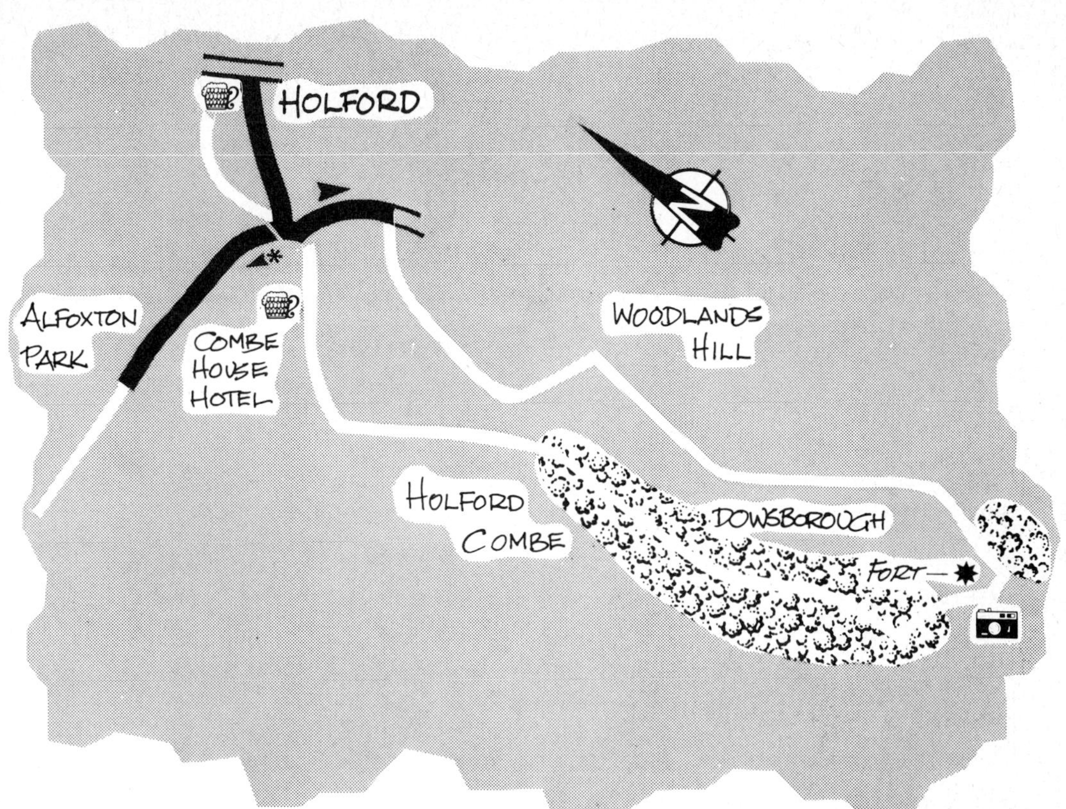

27 Holford

APPROXIMATELY 4¾ Miles

The District

"There is everything there, sea and woods wild as fancy ever painted". – Dorothy Wordsworth.

The Quantock Hills are only 12 miles long and 3 miles wide. They can be said to undulate gently rather than possess any more dramatic movement yet within their range there is enough wild and exciting scenery to please the most demanding country lover. The slopes down from the hills' twelve mile spine are covered with oak and beech trees in parts and elsewhere with gorse and bracken, generally in relation to the amount of shelter available. Everywhere along the length of the Quantocks are patches of whortleberry bushes and runt hawthorns and never far away are hardy sheep and wild ponies. In winter, red deer come down to drink at the silvery streams which twist through the sheltered, tree-lined combes, while higher upon the moors the adders increase unchecked in summer. At all times of the year, the visitor can see the 'wild simplicity' deemed so worthy of the Wordsworth's words.

Holford, at the base of the Quantocks, was once the home of William and Dorothy Wordsworth who lived at Alfoxden Manor (now the Alfoxton Park Hotel) for just under a year in 1797. They rented this house from the local St Albyn family for the sum of £23 a year – enough to pay a week's rent for one room in London in 1981! – in order to be near to Coleridge who lived in nearby Nether Stowey. The house was much

smaller in those days and certainly didn't possess a swimming pool.

It was Wordsworth's wont, and Coleridge's, to spend days and days out walking the Quantocks mulling over the problems of their poems, with the inspiration of the countryside and the perspiration of their steps to help. Poems that William Wordsworth wrote here include *To My Sister, Anecdote For Fathers, We Are Seven* and *Simon Lee the Old Huntsman.* Eventually he and his sister were sent packing from the district due to their unconcealed support for the French Revolution.

While Wordsworth wandered lonely as a cloud over at Holford, Coleridge lived for three happy years at Nether Stowey under the benevolent eye of Thomas Poole, his patron. *The Ancient Mariner* contains direct references to the neighbourhood and you can visit his cottage in Nether Stowey, open March-September. Doddington Hall, close by, is a fine Elizabethan House built beside the old copper mines – it is worth a visit, too.

How to Get There

By road take the A39 west from Bridgwater, Holford is on this road (approx 10 miles). *By rail* to Bridgwater. *By bus* the 215 operates between Bridgwater and Holford.

The walk begins in the charming winding lanes of Holford, goes past a church and a glen (an English glen) up to some beautiful bleak moorland and an Iron Age Fort. It returns alongside the stream which runs down wooded Holford Combe.

The Holford Walk

To put you in a poetic frame of mind, there's an imaginative selection of real ales at **The Plough Inn.** It's in the middle of the villlage and used to be frequented by that master of the spondee and dactyl, William Wordsworth himself. Having girded your loins in the suggested manner, make use of the Plough Inn's back door, from which you turn right up the lane which goes past Holford Post Office and general store.

Continue up this lane till you come to St Mary's church with its modern lych-gate. The church is 12th century with a gabled tower and is somewhat dark inside. Creaking doors and churchyard trees put you in mind of the fact that 'lych' in old English means 'corpse' and that the lych-gate was where the first part of the burial service was performed. After the church, proceed up the lane, watching over the wall to your right for the ivy-covered buildings of the old Huguenot silk factory. The spinney by the stream is lovely. When the industry went bankrupt many of the weavers turned to smuggling.

As the lane branches, fork left on the road to Holford Combe but only as far as the corner house called 'Ramblers' which you head around to turn hard left and follow the road uphill.

Just as you think you're doomed to join the A39 again, a sign for a public bridlepath appears to your right. Follow this track, marked 'To Crowcombe', which will take you straight up the Quantocks (much more pleasant than it sounds). Follow the track by a wood till you emerge on the moorish upland that is Woodlands Hill. The higher you get, the more the fresh breeze blows. As the track goes off in two directions to your right, keep to the left and make for the summit of the hill.

On your right and stubbled with gorse is Hodder's Combe; on your left is a flat prosperous stretch of rectangular fields which reach to the sea and Hinkley Point Power Station. Beyond this, you can see Barry in South Wales (a place not a person) and, if you swivel your neck, little Holford down behind you.

Over the top of this hill, Dowsborough, (or Danesborough) Hill comes into view, dead ahead. Just as you approach it, fork right to attain the summit. 'Wow' is the word up here – if not 'exhaustion' after the long haul up. You are now 1,000 feet up on the ramparts of the Old Iron Age camp, 10 acres in size. Little is known of its past since the site has never been properly excavated. Take time to take in some fresh air and the exhilarating views. The coppices of stunted oaks used to be cut in rotation every 40 years and then the bark was either used for tanning or burnt for charcoal to be made into gunpowder for the Royal Navy.

To continue, go right on the track which goes round the ramparts and exit first right along a track which leaves at an obtuse angle going downhill. The track descends, narrows gradually, then drops – there's a good chance that you are following the old pilgrim trail to Glastonbury.

When you hit a track at right angles, turn right and proceed a short distance to just past a grassy 'lay-by' on your right. After this you turn hard right down the path into a wooded valley. You have now performed an extravagant U-turn worthy of any politician, but you're not out of the woods yet. All around, now, the trees' deformed trunks suggest dancers rooted to the spot.

A stream appears to your left, listen to its restful murmur – you must follow it to the bottom of the valley in the womb of the forest. Avoid paths to the right and the left, always go downhill, at some points you have to ford the stream as you follow the broad path which meanders like a reflection of the vagaries of the stream.

Eventually you reach a pool, to the left of the path, where robins stand on twigs admiring themselves in the water and grey wagtails dive to drink. This is where the stream parts company with you, as you continue past a car park to a hedged path which proved to be a major flightpath for blue tits, great tits and robins. Soon you go past cottages on your left including the 'Quarry House' with its flower-filled windows and **The Combe House Hotel,** which used to be a mill for tannery. In the village itself fork left between 'Ramblers' and the thatched cottages.

Detour here to have a look at the Alfoxton Park Hotel, former home of the Wordsworths. Go sharp left after the thatched cottages and follow the signs to Alfoxton along Dog Pound Lane. By the gates to the hotel's drive, there is a public bridleway next to the sign 'Alfoxton Park Hotel' and 'YHA'. Follow the track uphill and eventually below to your right you will see the white house once occupied by William and Dorothy Wordsworth and the swimming pool where they never swam. Return to where the detour started in the village. *End of detour.*

Follow the road into Holford, branching left to go past Glen Cottage with its lovely views over the wall to your left. At the end of the lane is The Plough Inn and luckily its license is more than just poetic so you can march in rhythmically and order a cuplet or two.

The Plough Inn, Holford

On the main Bridgwater-Minehead road, the A39, The Plough Inn has recently become a freehouse and is now undergoing extensive refurnishing, but with a view to retaining its original atmosphere.

The building is 400 years old and used to be a hotel and coaching inn. It is said to be haunted by the ghost of an old Spanish merchant who was murdered for his gold 200 years ago when the inn was a stop-off point on the way to the then thriving part of Watchet.

The inn possesses two open fires and comfortable seating in its large main room. There is a central servery which dispenses hot toddies for walkers and there's home-made fresh food 'with a difference'. There's a selection of real ales including Sam Smiths, Royal Oak and Whitbread Bitter. Grolsch lager, the natural lager, is available in bottles and there's a skittle allley in the yard. Freshwater fishing on the nearby River Parrett is also recommended.

Combe House Hotel, Holford

The Combe House Hotel was originally a 17th century farmhouse, then became for 150 years the tannery whose old water wheel is still in place. It's a warm and comfortable country hotel and an ideal walking centre for exploring the contours of the Quantocks.

There's a small bar where you can buy draught and bottled beer and a comprehensive list of wines and spirits, as well as snacks. Children are welcomed and the traditional English cooking is of the highest quality.

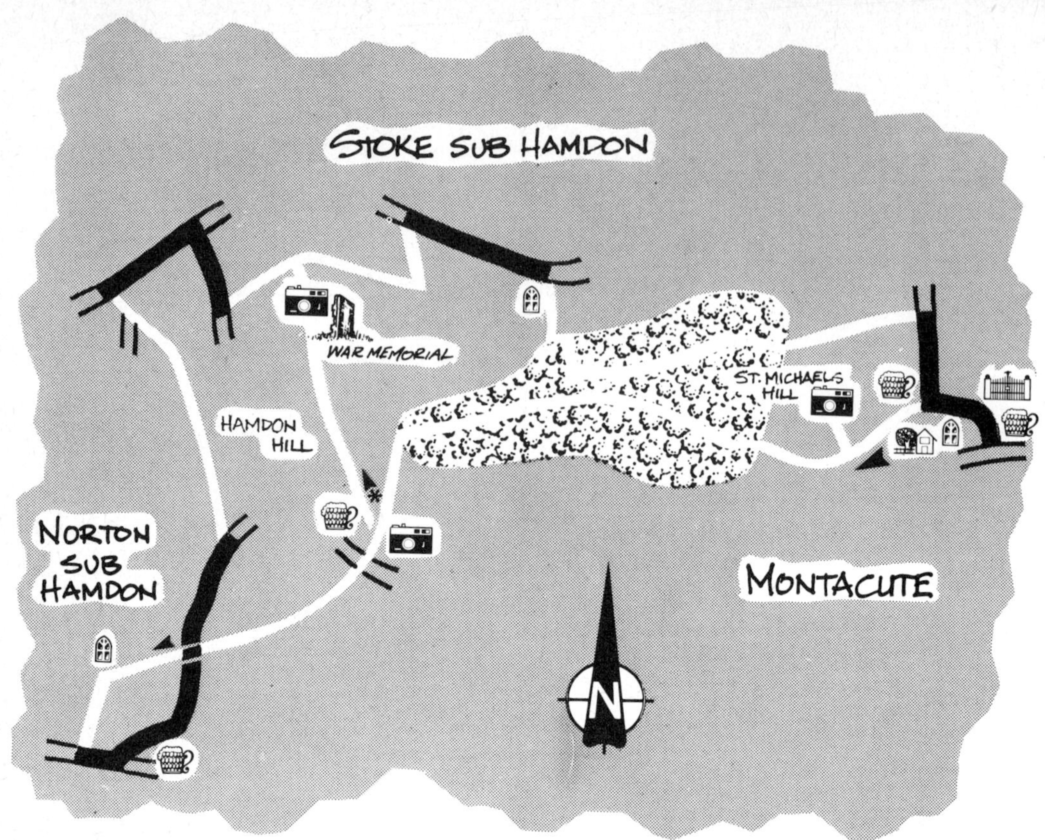

28 Montacute

APPROXIMATELY 5½ or 3½ Miles

The District

A proper introduction should begin with names and Montacute, near Yeovil, has had no shortage of those. Who knows what it was called before it was called Leodgaresbury and belonged to King Canute's standard bearer Tolfig (or Tofg). However in Tolfig's time, around 1035, the local sextant had a recurring dream in which Christ appeared and told him to dig at the bottom of St Michael's Hill.

Chanting a protective litany, the villagers went with the local priest to the hill and dug under a stone where they found a black flint cross, a book and a bell. These they put on a cart drawn by 12 red oxen and 12 white cows, as they debated where to send them. The cattle refused to budge an inch till the name Waltham in Essex was mentioned (where Tolfig had a country house). When it was, the cattle immediately leapt forward and went without stopping to Waltham where the cross now hangs in the abbey. After the discovery of the Holy Rood, Montacute became known as Bishopston by decree of the church.

This didn't last long, for soon the Earl of Montain, William the Conqueror's half-brother, was given the village and went and built a Norman fort on St Michael's Hill. This fort was dismantled when he was caught conspiring against Henry I but, in the meantime, he had changed the village's name from Bishopston (as it is mentioned in the Domesday Book) to Montacute. The derivation comes either from the Latin, mons acutus – pointed hill – or from an attempt to please his friend and battle companion Drogo of Montagus. In any case it's a pretty silly name . . . Drogo, I mean.

Be all that as it may, Montacute is a fascinating place with a long and checkered history behind it. The history features its Cluniac monastery (from Cluny in France), an abbey which was 'slighted' by Cromwell's cannons, Montacute House and the Montacute riots when the church bells were rung against the vicar's wishes in celebration of the local Friendly Society. This roused the solidarity of the locals against the Yeomanry and a war of attrition ensued; the next year the baker's wife was sent to jail for selling white bread to the working classes – at that time white bread was only for the upper classes.

The architecture of Montacute is exceptional and it would be a pity if you were to miss it.

How to Get There

By road take the A3088 west from Yeovil (approx 3½ miles). *By rail* Yeovil Pen Mill or Taunton. *By bus* a National Express coach (727) runs daily to Montacute from Yeovil and Taunton; it is a request stop.

The walks starts off in the village square, goes past a folly on the former site of the Norman fort and along wooded paths to Ham Hill, famous for its golden glowing sandstone. After that, you can choose to go to Norton Sub Hamdon or not . . . then back via Ham Hill to Montacute. Along the way there are four named pubs and a visit to Montacute House, an Elizabethan 'wonder'. It is, also, an easy-paced walk.

The Montacute Walk

Turn right out of **The Phelips Arms** and you come more or less immediately to Montacute House, a fine old Elizabethan House owned by the National Trust and open from April to October. You can visit it now or on your way back . . . or not at all, if you wish. It was built by Sir Edward Phelips, Speaker in the House of Commons and prosecutor at the trial of Guy Fawkes, in an attempt to impress the neighbours. This it manages by virtue of its height and symmetry, its massive windows, the golden glow of its stonework and despite its affectation of foreign styles and mock Renaissance details.

Turn right out of the main gate of Monta-

The Phelips Arms, Montacute

The Phelips Arms is named after the powerful village family who built Montacute House at the end of the 16th century and then sold it early this century. The house came into the possesion of the National Trust in 1931. It is, therefore, perhaps somewhat odd that the Phelips still think they hold proprietorial rights over the famous old house.

The Arms used to be a coaching inn in the 16th century and much of its history is the history of Montacute itself. During the Montacute riots, George Baker, the baker, the man who rang the church bells against the wishes of the vicar and his perverse point of principle, hid in the inn from the yeomanry who were trying to deport him to Tasmania. It's thanks to Baker's lucky escape that his great grandson drinks 6X in the inn today and not Fosters in some outback bar.

There's a ghost, too, a lady who wanders the corridors carrying a brandy shaped glass with a candle in it. Reports of recent sightings confirm that she leaves the smell of camphor wherever she goes.

There are two bars – one is friendly and comfortable, the other is friendly and comfortable and noisy. The inn is popular and there's usually a good cross-section of people here – when you see parties of peo-

cute House and go down Middle Street to **The King's Arms Inn.** An interesting fact about St Catherine's Church on your left is that the game of fives (like squash with a gloved hand) was once played against the outside wall, where the quadrofoils were planed off the south side of the tower specially for the purpose – by a former vicar – an act which seems irreligious today.

Turn left by The King's Arms and follow the road round to the right. Despite the 'private' sign, this *is* a right of way. Pass Abbey Farm, a quirky old building on your left, and go straight through the wooden gate on to a track which leads up the hill. As the track splits, fork right towards the trees for a detour up conical St Michael's Hill, over a stile to your right. From the stile keep climbing till you come to the St Michael's Hill folly, a tower which is some 200 years old, has a spiral staircase and is built of Ham Stone, otherwise known as inferior 'oolite'. It stands on the site of the Earl of Montain's vanished castle and this is where the last organised uprising of the men of Dorset and Somerset against Norman power took place. You should find the ascent a little less tricky than they did and at the top the view is very fine indeed. Incidentally, the hill is supposed to be where the Waltham Abbey cross was found and the tower is meant to be haunted by the daughter of one of the Phelips family who was imprisoned here for refusing to marry a husband of her father's choice.

Find your way back down to the stile and then turn right to follow the path with the trees on your right as you start. Head past a couple of telegraph poles till you see two stiles down to your left by the wall – one is by a gate. Take the right-hand stile and go into the wood. 15 yards later go left when you join a higher path. The wood is full of black spot, the tree fungus fuelled by wet conditions . . . disregard the black spot unless your name is Blind Pugh and climb a stile, then follow the fence to your right. After 100 yards or so, cross over the enticing stile to your right (just after a track joins you from the left). Follow the path for a good stretch as it winds its way along beside the top of Hedgecock Hill. Follow it, in fact, till it slowly uncoils itself downhill, gently to the right a bit. As you get down you're faced with a choice of directions – go left and a field will slowly appear through the trees on your right. And then you'll see on the brow of the hill to your right . . . **The Prince of Wales,** not in person but 'in building'. To get there you turn right at the end of the field, go straight across a track and follow the path. A few yards after the track, fork right aiming for the building on the hill. Then by the other side of the field, fork left up a minor gully which takes you to the Prince of Wales and a 'pint of crazy water' as the locals call it . . . well, some of them.

The Prince of Wales is owned by the person of that same name. It stands on the site of the old Roman fort on Ham Hill and the old quarries which have been worked for over 1,000 years.

If you want to shorten the walk here, instead of going to the pub, head right (oh well, in addition to going to the pub) along the top of Ham Hill to the War Memorial and resume the walk from the paragraph beginning 'From the War Memorial'.

By The Prince of Wales there's an old Roman Well 170 feet deep and it's an excellent spot to while away some time watching birds such as kestrels flying low over the quarries as well as the noisy helicopters from the naval base at Yeovilton.

Leave the pub and turn right past the 'tombstones' which stop the unwise and unwary from hurtling over the edge of the hill and swing right to get out of Ham Hill Country Park and to the road.

At the road, pause by the old iron seat for a view of midget cows and doll's houses in the valley below, then take the steep downhill path, almost opposite but slightly to the left of the road you came out. Below half left you can see Norton Sub Hamdon.

Take this winding path down to the trees in the bottom right-hand corner of the 'field'.

At the bottom of this 'field', cross a path and carry straight on to the path in the 'tunnel' of trees, which you follow till you get to a stone stile on the left, opposite a track to the right. Climb over the stile and head half right for the gate in the far corner of the field, roughly in the direction of Norton church tower. Go through the gate and then through a gap in the hedge opposite.

Now you follow through gaps in hedges and over troughs and past a football pitch and a ditch to the back door of the church. If you see Norton Sub Hamdon's tall and beautiful 15th century church stone glowing golden in the dying light of a summer sun, you will be fortunate indeed. Don't miss its circular pigeon house which contains 400 nests – well, you won't since you must exit by the front gate to go into the village.

At the main village road turn left, go over a bridge and arrive at **The Lord Nelson,** where you can sample the glowing local hospitality.

Turn right out of The Nelson and continue up the track through the farmyard and beside fields with Ham Hill now to the right. In 1661, four agricultural workers, out early one Monday morning to pick beans, reported hearing the sounds of battle here in the dark – noises of drumbeats and clattering armour and the groans of the dying. At dawn, the noises ceased, leaving the four terrified at this ghastly, ghostly occurrence, for there had been no battle there for years. Coast along the track till you come to a stone stile where the track (now a path) curves right. Go over the stile and head straight for the gate, beside which you'll find a lumpy old kissing-gate. Bill and coo your way past this obstacle and follow the track to the main road of Stoke Sub Hamdon – Stoke means 'dairy farm', Sub Hamdon means 'under Ham Hill' – and turn right.

Go past the Fleur de Lis pub and turn right past the old post office on a road which goes past the old Half Moon pub. Once you have crossed a cattle grid, turn first left by some houses and go up the track which curves left. 50 yards up, take the track which goes up under a canopy of trees – ignore the path to the right and go up to the War Memorial with its wonderful views all around.

From the War Memorial, bear off to the right as you look down on Stoke Sub Hamdon. Follow the ramparts in the footsteps of long dead Roman legionnaires. The folly

ple leaving mysteriously and being replaced by other similar social groupings, don't be disturbed, it's only changeover time for the skittle alley.

The landlords are justifiably proud of their beers, 'the Bishop's Tipple', Wadworths 6X and Old Timer are hand-drawn and there's John Smith's on keg. The menu is good and the snack list likewise.

The King's Arms Inn, Montacute

The King's Arms Inn used to be a cider making house for the old abbey and was re-modelled in the 18th century when the three storey building became a two storey building, by a change in the floor arrangement.

It's a handsome Hamstone building with mullioned windows, which the visitor enters to be greeted by the roaring fire in the hallway. The interior is tastefully elegant and the panelling in the main bar came from the remains of Coventry Cathedral. There's a back room for the more boisterous customers and their singalongs.

The beers are gravity fed draught Bass, keg Bass Special and Worthington E and draught Guinness. The buffet at lunchtime is very good with home-made guides, Dorset pâté and local fish to be eaten with home-made bread rolls. (Warning; it is fairly expensive). There's a garden out the back and children are welcome there, though not in the bar itself.

The Prince of Wales Inn, Ham Hill

The Prince of Wales is the only building on Ham Hill. The materials for its construction did not have far to come since it stands bang

appears dead ahead in the distance. As the rampart bends right, take the steep left-hand path towards East Stoke, down then up the outside rampart . . . . then down a nettled path and into a wood where you turn right to go under a tree shaped like an arch. Go on to a stile of metal bars and logs. Clamber over and follow the path which curves a little left at first then goes straight into a field below where you strike off half right till you come to a half-concealed gate by the hedge. Next to the gate is a stile – follow the track behind it with hedges on either side, into East Stoke. Watch out for strange breeds of sheep here.

Turn right at the road, go past a police station on your best behaviour, slowing down at the 40mph sign, and turn in to East Stoke Church which you'll find on the right. This, like Norton's church, is devoted to St Mary the Virgin and dates from the 11th century. Again it's made from the beautiful local stone.

Turn right from the road at the end of the churchyard and follow the path with the church on your right. The path becomes a track and sweeps left under an oak, keep following the track into the woods and turn left when you get into the trees, so that you follow the track just inside the wood. Back towards Montacute with the outskirts of Montacute visible to your left through the trees, you come to the broken remains of a wooden gate, just after which you turn right, then left in five yards, to cross a fence near an oak and into the field occupied by St Michael's Hill. Go down then up a dip and bear left of the clump of trees. As Montacute House comes into view, turn down left along the footpath to the metal kissing-gate in the direction of the cricket square. Gallivant through the gate and head for the wooden kissing-gate, after which you turn right past a playground for the road. At the road, turn right and proceed to The King's Arms, near which you turn left up Middle Street and to the village square, called the Borough, and The Phelips Arms where you started. After all this, you might like a drink.

in the middle of Ham Hill quarries. It was built 150 years ago as a cottage for the quarry manager and only the ends of the present building have been added since. Come to think of it that's quite a lot. The walls inside are of exposed hamstone and the warmth of this material is complemented by the log fire which heats the bar.

For your delectation, they serve hand-drawn Ushers Best Bitter and Hall's Harvest Bitter. There's also Bass Special and Ben Truman on keg. If you like malt whiskies the landlord offers a selection of 20.

Tasty snacks are on sale with a choice of 20 different cheeses. This is a good, well-run family pub, and so it should be since it is owned by the Duke of Cornwall; namely Prince Charles, heir to the throne.

The Lord Nelson, Norton Sub Hamdon

The Lord Nelson is the village pub of the beautiful Somerset village of Norton Sub Hamdon. It is a 17th century building which was renovated three years ago to leave it with a pinewood ceiling and wall to wall comfort under subdued lighting. During the war it was the centre of illegal traffickings in alcohol, with all the whisky being reserved for American servicemen who could pay higher prices. Nowadays, the publican is more patriotic.

The beers – Bass, Toby, Worthington and Guinness – are all on keg. There is an extensive à la carte menu and children are welcome.

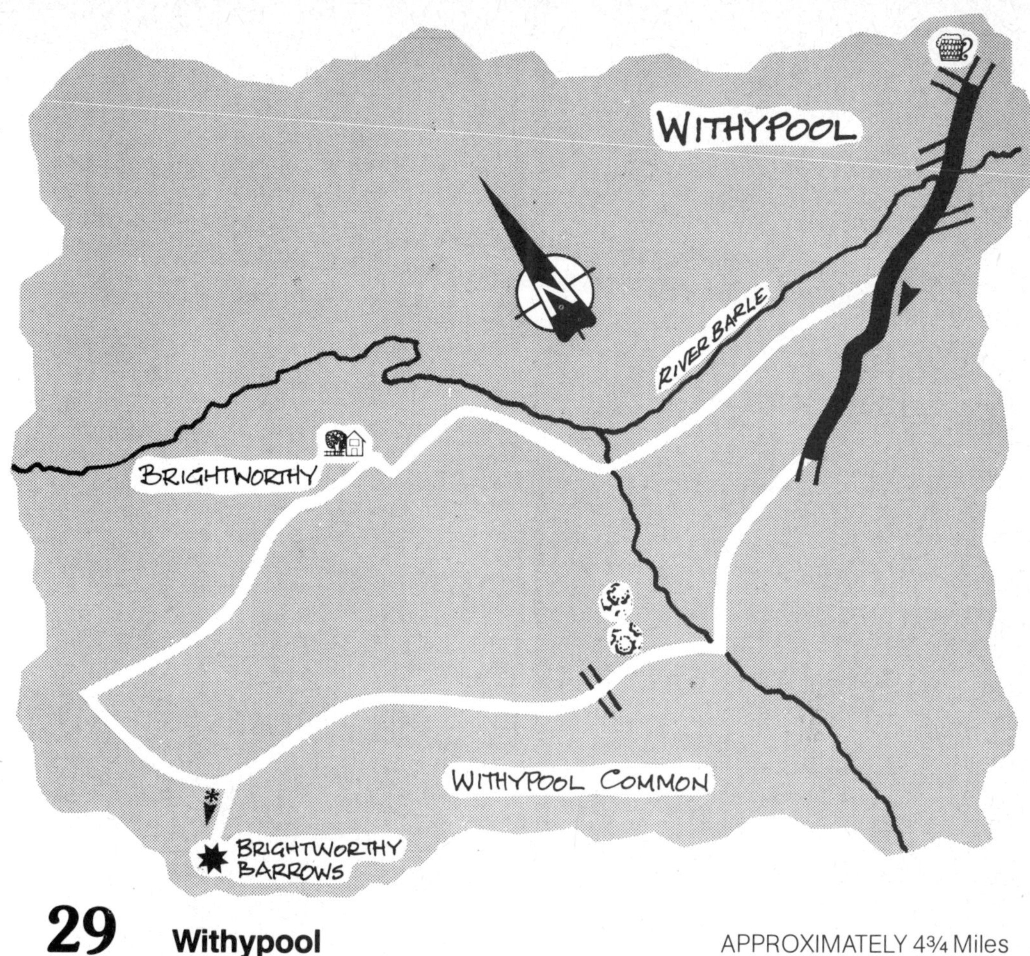

29 Withypool

APPROXIMATELY 4¾ Miles

The District

Meaning 'the pool of the willow tree', Withypool is an unpolished diamond set in the cluster of Exmoor's undecorated but graceful moorland hills. Right in the middle of the moor, Withypool was once the chief village of the Royal hunting grounds. And horses, stags and foxes are still very much in evidence as a quick look inside The Royal Oak will prove. Exmoor was immortalized by R D Blackmore in *Lorna Doone* – indeed he stayed in The Royal Oak while writing it. He created the popular image of Exmoor in his writing, though it must be said that nowadays much of the moor's steep slopes are either cultivated or provide enclosed grazing for cattle and sheep (mostly Devon and cross-breed cattle for beef and Exmoor Horns and Closewools for wool). But prehistoric features such as Withypool Hill's stone circles and the numerous other Bronze Age earthworks still remain and the tough and wild moorland ponies still graze where they will, watched only by red deer and buzzards.

Though the walk never takes you very far from civilization, it's as well to remember that the weather here can be whimsical and instantly changeable and that when it's bad, it boasts the worst weather in southern England. Be warned.

How to Get There

By road take the A39 east from Minehead and turn right onto the A396 and then right onto the B3224 at Wheddon Cross. Turn

right onto the B3223 after Exford and then right again onto an unclassified road for Withypool (approx 16½ miles). *By rail* to Taunton. *By bus* a National Travel coach leaves Taunton at 17.10 for Weddon Cross. Unfortunately this is the nearest you can get by public transport (it's 6 miles from Withypool).

From Withypool, the walk climbs up towards Withypool Common, and, before descending the hill towards the River Barle, there's a detour up to Brightworthy Barrows. The walk returns to Withypool along a Public Footpath that runs through Brightworthy Farm and then back along the Barle.

The Withypool Walk

The walk starts with that ancient transaction – an exchange of money for ale – over the counter in **The Royal Oak.** With a lighter wallet (and head), walk out of the pub, turn right and, to visit the church, turn right again through the gate to St Andrew's church. Largely restored in the 19th century, it has had baptismal rights since the 12th. Modest if plain, the church sits squatly in its churchyard (note the restored medieval cross), watching over the village with a woeful eye. Turning left out on to the road again, go on down past the Post Office to the fine old bridge over the River Barle. After a quick game of pooh-sticks, walk on over the cattle grid and up the road to Hawthorne Bungalows where you turn right. Passing the stables, on your right, you leave Withypool.

For some way now you 'take a walk on the wild side' as to your right there will be cultivation and habitation and to your left the uninterrupted sweep of the moor's bleak horizons. Moorland streams, cutting their own ditches, trickle down to the road here and just beyond the aptly named Waterhouse Stud Farm gate you take the red-marked path to Landacre, off to your right. The path heads off in the arrowed direction across the grass to a huge tree by a brick incinerator and, though muddy to start with, becomes stony. When you see the pine copse ahead, pause and scan the sky for buzzards who may be circling the sky scanning the ground for you. Or maybe for small rodents. The path curves round into Knighton Combe and runs alongside the babbling brook which is seemingly in a hurry to meet Mother Barle. At the red-marked tree you should see stepping-stones across, depending on how vandalistic the cows have been but, at any rate, the stream is narrower further up and leapable. Scramble up the steep path, forking right to meet the path which leads you round the top of the pine copse.

You will now be guided by red daubs on trees, boulders, stones, telegraph poles, gate-posts and stiles. If you get lost despite the red-marks and this detailed walkround, then you should have stayed at home in the first place.

As the moor gets more moorish, you continue along the beech-topped wall, over the lonely drive to Knighton and Brightworthy, and on to Landacre as marked. The path becomes a track (and sometimes, after rain, a stream) and then swings away from the beech-topped wall and skirts round the top of a line of beech-trees, shading a stream. It continues stonily up and out on to grassy moorland. Keep near enough to the hedged wall to easily hear the wind whistling through the leaves and just after the highest point of the hedged wall, you arrive at a gate.

So far you have merely pecked the cheek of Exmoor's romantic beauty – now's your chance to wholeheartedly embrace it. For this fling, turn left up the faint grassy track straight up the hill (where there are no red-markers). When your leg-muscles say stop, stop. Turn and look back across the woods and fields across to Dunkery Beacon, the highest point on the horizon and indeed all Exmoor. Continuing up to where the slope levels out, you can see the long bump of Green Barrow ahead, at the right-hand end of a line of windswept trees. When, you can see the 428m high triangulation pillar of Brightworthy Barrows peeping over the heather at you, head towards it. If you can stand on it, you get slightly better views than if you don't, but they are breathtaking anyway, as is the wind. Then retrace your steps back to the gate with its double red arrow.

The arrows and the wall and the path all lead you downhill now and soon, to your left, you can see plain, noble and remote Landacre Bridge over the wide Barle, looking for all the world as if it belonged in Scotland. At the red-marked footpath sign, go right through the wooden gate despite the Withypool arrow. You walk along the track to another gate (red-marked) and on along the sunken track to and through a gateway with sleepers and tyres. This is the first of many obstacles for horses that you will see. The track continues to the next red-marked gate, where you climb the stile and go downhill now, past a pink shed, over a stream and down to another stile and gate.

Walking round the back of the corrugated-iron roofed farmhouse, you follow the red arrow right, past the pretty and unchanged farmyard stables on your left and out of the drive gate. Turn left through a red-arrowed gate into a field, where you head for the nearest telegraph pole and guess what's painted on it? Correct. Continue across the field aiming for a red-marked tree and nip through the gap and down to the Barle.

You now head downstream back to Withypool and though the path is level and easy, it can be boggy and wet, due mainly to all the moorland streams that feed the river. You cross one of these numerous streams by a gate and soon you cross your first riverside stile. To your right you can see what, at first glance, seems to be a modern circular barrow but, on inspection, turns out to be a drainage area to make the riverbank

The Royal Oak, Withypool

A hunting pub through and through -- four packs of hounds meet here; ask 'dashing' young publican Mr Bradley which and when. It's decorated with antlers and there's a collection of hunt-buttons (apparently the best in Britain). It was probably a hunting centre when R D Blackmore stayed here during the writing of *Lorna Doone.* Another example of his writing hangs behind the bar in the lounge. Sir Alfred Munnings was also a famous customer; he had a studio over the stables in the thirties. A little later, Eisenhower took time off from planning the winning of war, to nip down here from his moorland billet for a relaxing pint or two (of bourbon?). Withypool has more horses than people and therefore more stables than houses. The Royal Oak however offers accommodation for creatures both equine and human.

And for the humans, drinks on offer include hand-drawn Ushers Best, gravity-fed Taunton cider, Guinness, a good range of wines, sherries and liqueurs and a selection of 12 malt whiskies. There is an à la carte menu in the restaurant, but the bar meal menu is, in a word, excellent and includes pâtés, soups (both home-made), home-cooked ham, lobster salad, fresh local trout in season, prawns and a daily 'special'.

less marshy. If you approach quietly, you may see a lonely heron fishing or just mournfully standing there.

Walk on along the riverbank to your second stile and then cross a wooden footbridge to the third stile. Once over the stone slab bridge over the trickle, head along the river above the trees to a footpath sign and fourth stile. Keep above the marshy area and two hawthorns and go to and through the metal gate. Just to your left is your fifth stile into a field. Pausing only to nod at the horses – it's their field, after all – walk along the top, somewhat boggy edge and then down to a red-marked gate.

As you walk along the side of the riding school building you may eavesdrop a lesson with a stentorian voice booming 'shoulders back ... knees tight, Jennifer, I can see air between flank and knee'. On your left, more obstacles for horses litter the field, but you proceed to the next red-marked gate and along the hedged wall for stile number six which leads you on to a sunken track. You pass a derelict building and, once you're through yet another red-marked gate, you rejoin the riverbank – which takes you to your seventh and, phew, final stile by a massive alder. Recross the bridge and, hoping you haven't dropped your wallet crossing one of the umpteen gates and stiles, walk back up to the pub where I can see no reason for you to discontinue the tradition you practiced at the outset. Can you?

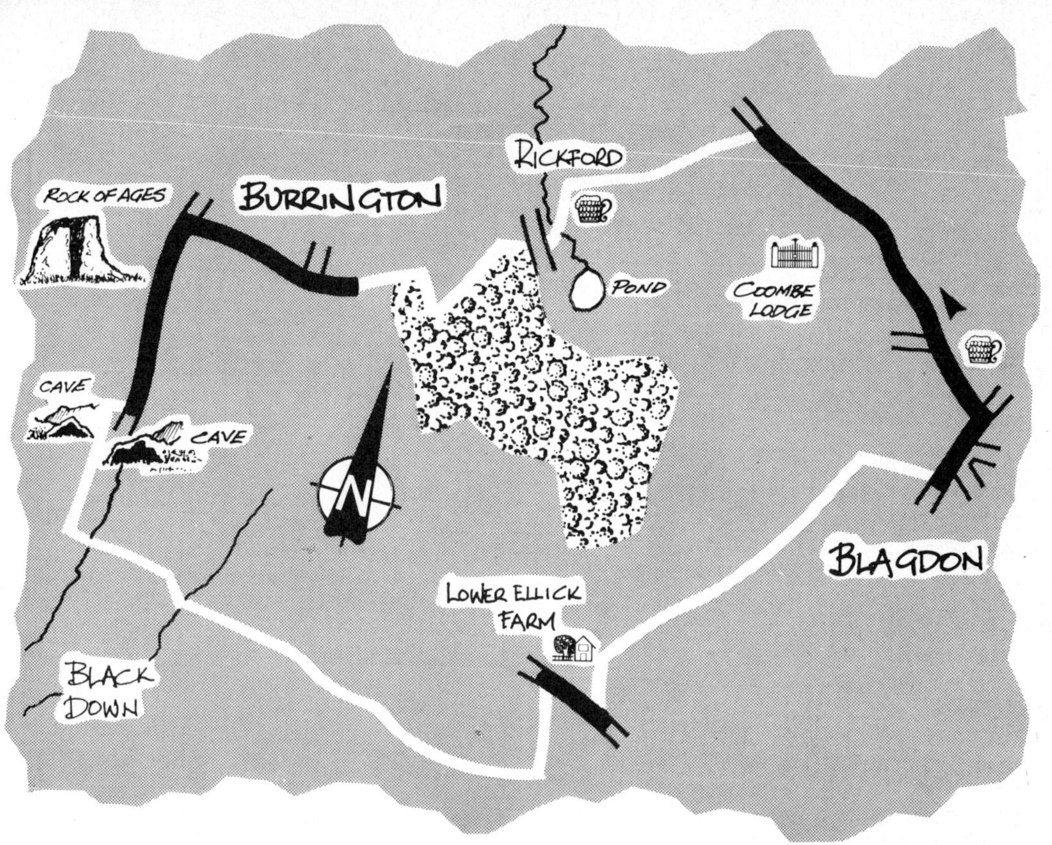

30 Blagdon

APPROXIMATELY 3½ Miles

The District

The word 'Blagdon' can mean either 'black hill' or 'black valley', depending on whether 'don' is a corruption of, respectively, 'dun' or 'dene'. So it's appropriate that the village of Blagdon stretches from the valley, up the steep slope of the north side of the Mendips, to the top of the Mendip plateau. The village church, restored this century and worth a visit, stands about half-way up the hill, looking down over the Yeo reservoir (as it's known to the Water Board) or Blagdon Lake (as it's known to everyone else). This 'lake' was very well landscaped with plantations of trees round its edges, giving it the look of any natural lake. It is however no more than 14ft deep and for this reason produces brown and rainbow trout of prodigious size. Indeed there is a trout hatchery at Ubley and, so successful is it, that trout ova are sent all over the world, populating rivers from South America to Kenya, Ceylon, New Zealand and the Far East. The lake also provides what seems to be very good conditions for duck, though obviously all English weather is OK by them. On one December day in recent years (it was probably pouring), 2,000 birds were counted. They were mostly wigeon, but large numbers of teal, mallard and tufted duck and smaller numbers of shelduck, pintail, shoveler, golden-eye, scaup and smew were also seen, though scaup and smew sound more like Dickens characters than ducks. Enough ornithology – on to the mineralogy paragraph.

➤

The Mendips were a very important lead-mining area right up until 1850 or so and it was on a Blagdon farm that a lead ingot was found: after its motherlode had been traced to nearby Charterhouse and it had been dated to 49 AD, it became evidence of the earliest known smelting in Britain. These hills may have been worked prior to the Roman invasion and in fact, it's claimed by some that Jesus, nephew of Joseph of Arimathea, had accompanied his uncle to the Mendips before he began his sensational career as an early Christian and martyr. Anyway it was the Romans who were the first major miners, exporting lead in bulk and making the Mendips 'gruffy'.

'Gruffs' were/are grooves, following veins, dug to extract the lead ore and claims were decided in a rather odd fashion. A prospective prospector, usually working on his own, dug a hole to waist-height and then, taking hold of a digging-tool, threw it as far as possible along the vein on both sides of his hole. The point where the tool landed showed how far along the vein he was allowed to mine. To standardise procedure, one special kind of digging tool was used: it came to be known as a law hack and was used only in this ritual.

How to Get There

By road take the A38 south-west from Bristol and turn left onto the A368, Blagdon is on this road (approx 16 miles). *By rail* to Bristol. *By bus* there is a regular bus service, the 124 and the 129, from Bristol to Blagdon.

The walk starts in Blagdon, goes down lanes and across fields to Rickford. From here it goes behind Burrington and half-way up Burrington Combe where it climbs and wends its way between Blackdown and the Combe and then descends back into Blagdon.

The Blagdon Walk

Having supported local industry (i.e. having sampled Butcombe Bitter, brewed just across the valley in, believe it or not, Butcombe), you may now leave the **Queen Adelaide** and start walking. Leaving the pub, turn right, down the Bath to Weston-super-Mare road and just after Clander's Batch on your left, go right, down Menlea. As you descend, Coombe Lodge looms into view ahead. A bit of a Victorian monster, designed to impress and succeeding, it was built as a home by the Wills cigarette family, though why they didn't buy The Embassy, No 6, Park Drive, Old Holborn, Chesterfield, I don't know. This laboured joke is almost endless – but I'll spare you more. At any rate, the home is now a College of Education and, as mentioned, it looms into view. Passing a covered well on your right, you go straight on along Bourne Lane at the letterbox. You walk under a high wall and to your right Blagdon Lake stretches back up the Yeo valley.

You pass Ridge Farm and just after a large metal gate on your right, you climb over a stile by the wooden gate on your left. Walking neither up nor down you follow a line of stumps, dead elms (soon to be stumps?) and field maples amongst others. This leads you to a gate and into a second field. Continue in the same direction to another gate and a third field. Aim for the house ahead and cross a stile to its left. You are now on a tarmac driveway which descends past bijou gardens to **The Plume of Feathers** – to your right at the stream. Rickford is rather a damp hamlet – so what more appropriate then a drink.

Refuelled, leave the pub and turn left up the lane along the stream, past the sluice house and on up to the main road by the pond. Turn right along it and after 20 yards or less, take the wooded footpath left uphill. At the gate ahead, where the main path curves right, go up to your left through the trees on a defined but winding path. Where you can see a brackeny area to your left, stay on the wooded path which soon emerges onto a stony track. Here you turn right and walking below pines, you curve round behind white Orchard Cottage. Just after a ramshackle garage, soon to be overwhelmed by ivy, on your left, turn sharp left.

As you walk up this track there are more good views over the Yeo valley and down towards Weston-super-Mare. Up to your left is the commonland of Burrington Ham. At Hollywood, the track becomes simply metalled, and not paved with gold as you might have expected, and then descends, passing two squirrels eating nuts on a branch at Hillgate. At the fork with its triangle of grass, go left, thereby passing above the village of Burrington. At the junction with the road that goes up the bottom of Burrington Combe, turn left uphill and pass the Nursery and arrive at The Burrington Arms – a rather busy (in summer) tourist café-restaurant with a license. So if you're feeling thirsty, peckish or just weary, enter.

If not, then go on up through its car park and up the Combe proper. Just beyond the toilets there's a long fault-line running from top to bottom – evidence of geological upheaval way back in the mists of time. The rocky slopes were worn away years ago by persistent streams that ran down off the Mendips. Indeed there is a theory that the Combe is simply a huge cave with no roof.

Soon you see on your right a huge bluff of rock with a large split down the middle. This is where Reverend Augustus Toplady sheltered from a storm and was inspired to write his one and only number 1 hit – 'Rock of Ages, cleft for me, Let me hide myself in thee.'

'Cleft for me' might sound rather self-important but on a wintry evening, with only a narrow track winding down the wooded combe, the combination of the rugged rock and thunder and lightning must have been potent to a preacher, indeed to a hell-fire and brimstone preacher, vision-inducing.

Opposite the Rock of Ages a very steep path climbs the slope up to Burrington Camp – earthworks dug and defended presumably by Iron Age boy-scouts. Just beyond this path a large cave descends darkly

Queen Adelaide, Blagdon

Queen Adelaide was the wife of William IV and it's thought that the building – it was a farmhouse before – was converted to a pub and given her Highness' name after a Royal visit to or even simply through Blagdon.

It's a simple and modernised, but warm and friendly, one-bar pub. It has no ghost and since the Royals has had no famous customers to speak of, except maybe Pincher.

But, and it's a very big but (you ask Pincher), Ronald Clarke stocks a very good range of drinks which includes Butcombe Bitter, Draught Bass, Courage Bitter and Best Bitter (all on handpumps), John Smith's, Guinness and Blackthorn cider on draught, various keg beers and lagers, Old Bush Hills Irish Whiskey, Southern Comfort, a bourbon, and a selection of French, Yugoslavian and German wines. The food is every bit the equal of the drink, with a range of bar snacks, both hot and cold, including soup, cottage and steak and kidney pies, ploughman's with local cheddar and stilton, pâté, salads etc. Just don't forget you have a walk to go on.

The Plume of Feathers, Rickford

Rickford was mentioned in the Domesday Book, but the farmhouse, later to become the Plume Of Feathers, wasn't mentioned

and deeply (I think). It's known as Aveline's Hole, though all I know about it is that 50 neolithic skeletons were discovered in it in 1797 by two young lads chasing rabbits and that its impressive stalactites and stalagmites have since been completely vandalised.

When you see a break in the gorge to your right and just before the gorge swings left, go up the stony track, which soon becomes a path, which soon becomes a stream. On your right is Sidcot Swallet – a tiny entrance leads to several chambers but some of the tunnels are, in cavers' language, very 'tight'. Continue up the path/stream to the spring which is surrounded by a low concrete wall. Strictly speaking it's not a spring – a swallet is where an underground stream meets rock it can't cut through; so it surfaces and thereafter behaves like any normal stream. So, just before the Swallet, go up a steep rocky path which climbs past a little cave entrance, to the entrance to Goatchurch Cavern. This entrance leads to an extensive maze of passages, chambers and underground streams, and you can walk for 300ft or so before it gets 'tight' and you have to crawl. Not recommended for the walker though – it's dirty and can be dangerous without guides and equipment, not to mention that inside it's as black as pitch. It's said that a dog was once put in the cave, only for it to emerge three weeks later in Cheddar – 4 miles away – with all the hair rubbed off its body and no doubt extremely 'cheesed off'. Well, you know that fict is stranger than faction.

Go back down to the Swallet, if you ever left it, and take the path up towards the bracken and in a few yards, fork left to follow the valley up. At the crossing of paths, take the left one which dips into the valley bottom and out, and then remains level with a sea of bracken on both sides. Above the bracken on your left you can see the scarred rock faces of Burrington Combe peering menacingly out of their gorge at the heights of Black Down to your right.

The path dips into another stream's wooded valley and this trickle, if you were to follow it down, soon goes underground only to pass through Goatchurch Cavern on its way who knows where. Got minds of their own these Mendip streams. The path continues, now climbing very slowly and with fields on the left. Look back every now and then to see if you can spot Wales across the Bristol Channel or indeed whales in the Bristol Channel. Just after the path begins to descend as gently as it climbed a broad grassy track joins it from the right. At the crossing of paths and tracks a little further on, go left downhill, more steeply now, along a very wide track flanked by trees and bushes. This track descends to Ellick House, where you turn right, along the road.

Pass on your left Lower Ellick Farm's drive and before the isolated building beyond, climb over the fence and head slightly left, across the field to the gate to the right of the farm buildings. Once through, follow the line of telegraph poles to a stile and clamber over it. In this, your third field, continue in roughly the same direction, i.e. diagonally to the right, between the two woods, towards a holly-tree by a gate and its yellow-arrowed stile, which you climb. Enough orientation across this field for you, dear walker? Fifty paces (exactly measured for you) in, again, the same direction, i.e. diagonally left, lead you to another yellow-marked stile. Vault this and walk downhill, to the left of the Mendip Hotel, to another stile. Climb this and then onwards down the path to the next yellow-marked stile by a gate. Once over, follow the path straight on to a gate. You go through it to another, 20 yards or so on – and then to a stone stile to the left of the house. The path runs along the wall of the house and down steps, with their somewhat religious barrier, to a road. Turn left and walk down, passing the Seymour Arms and, joining the Bath to Weston-super-Mare road, on downhill. The road curves to the left and leads you back to the Queen Adelaide where you can toast this oft-forgotten lady from the cobwebbed corridors of history. Can I have my Booker Prize now, please?

until about 400 years ago. Built of Mendip stone, it's somehow appropriate that it should be frequented by cavers who come to the Mendips to explore its labyrinthine cave-systems. In fact, these cavers often squeeze themselves under the benches in the bar as part of their limbering-up exercises.

This unpretentious pub has one sizeable bar with two open fires – one in a large stone inglenook fireplace. It's roomy and friendly and caters for a fairly youthful trade – this may be to do with its games room and is certainly to do with the proximity of Coombe Lodge College of Education.

There's Courage Bitter and Best Bitter on handpump and other Courage beers and lagers and Guinness on draught. Food is of the ploughman's, pies and pasties variety.

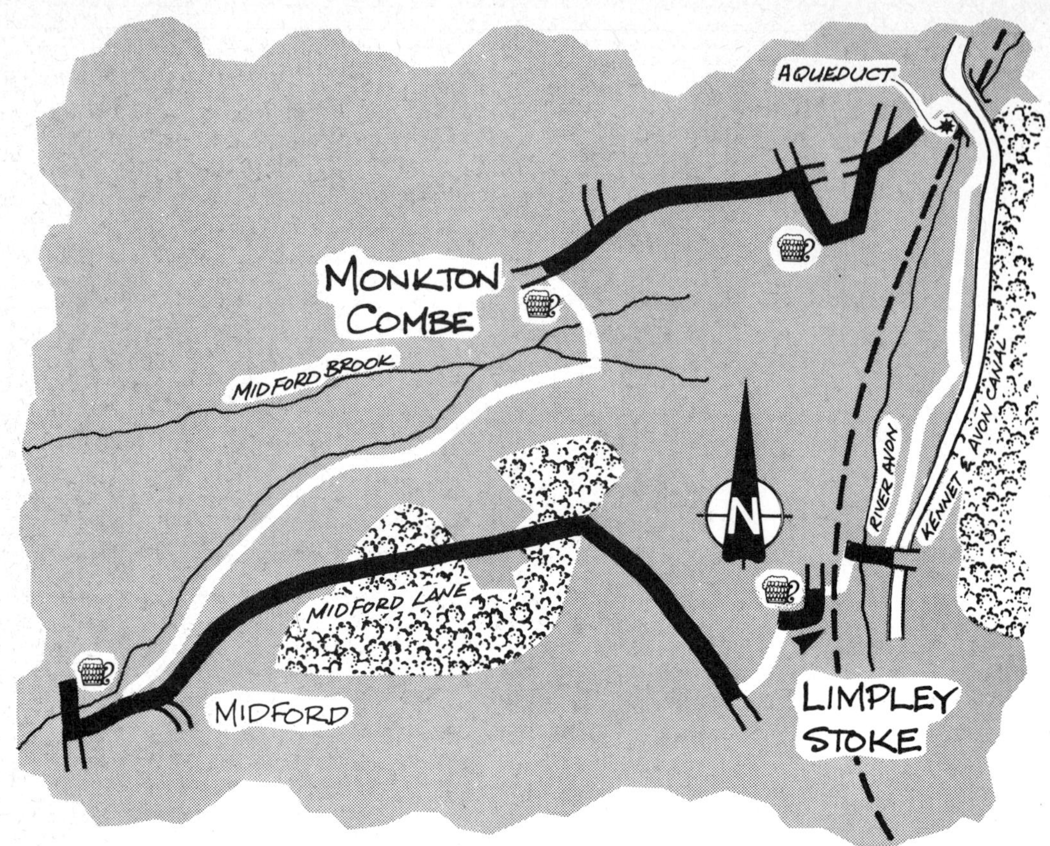

31 Limpley Stoke

APPROXIMATELY 5½ Miles

The District

Highly radioactive water, containing metallic sulphates, chlorides and other salts, is, believe it or not, the source of Bath's importance and fame. Legend has it that King Bladud, a leper and father of King Lear, was expelled from court, became a swineherd, and regained his health by rolling with his also leprous pigs in the curative mud from the hot springs here. These springs gush ½ million gallons a day at about 49°C, so there was no shortage of warm mud.

One thing that gave the Romans an aura of civilization, was their obsessive cleanliness and love of bathing. And so, they came in droves to Bath to wash away the grime and ill-health incurred keeping occupied Britain under control. It became a resort and has remained so ever since. Oddly enough it wasn't until 1775 when they were pulling down the old priory, that they discovered Saxon coffins and, below them, some Roman masonry. Even more oddly, at least to our more 'museumistic' eyes, no further excavation was done until a century later, when the site of the Roman Baths was slowly uncovered, revealing, within the best Roman spa outside Italy, a wealth of Roman sculpture, masonry, jewels and ceramics. It was only then that it was realised how important Aquae Sulis was, and that for 400 years these large baths had been the centre of a settlement of large villas with a temple and forum; to quote another writer – "a Rome from Rome".

At the end of the 6th century, Aquae Sulis

was overthrown by the Saxons and a college of secular canons, whoever they might have been, was established in 755, to metamorphose into a Benedictine monastery in 970. The Norman Abbey which developed later, became neglected and ruined, and Bath then entered an uneventful, even blank, period of its history.

Bishop Oliver King had a dream, which started the Bath revival. He saw angels ascending and descending ladders and heard a voice saying, "Let an Olive establish the crown and let a King restore the church". So Bishop Olive(r) King set to work rebuilding the abbey. You can see the angels and ladders on the West Front.

Ruin loomed again in the form of grand dissolver Thomas Cromwell who stripped the glass and lead from the building to add to Henry VIII's coffers. Later, however, another building Bishop – Montagu – sheltered from a rainstorm in the Abbey, only to find it raining just as much inside as out. He promptly restored the building. And we should be thankful to these two Bishops, for it was in Bath Abbey nearly 1,000 years ago that Archbishops Dunstan of Canterbury and Oswald of York jointly crowned Edgar King of all England, uniting, for the first time, it and its people under one leader. A fairly important event in any nation's history.

The next important man in the city's history was Ralph Allen, a Cornishman and the model for Squire Allworthy in Fielding's *Tom Jones.* He quarried himself a fortune from Bath stone and spent it building 18th century Bath. He employed two John Woods, senior and junior, as architects and town-planners. Together they created much of Bath as we know it, though specifically it was father who gave us the Circus and son the Crescent. Musicians, writers, artists, scientists, royalty and the court – in fact everybody who was anybody – flocked to

The Hop Pole, Limpley Stoke

A lovely 14th century building, it was originally a monk's wine lodge, where monks from the priory at Norton St Philip could stop for a home-made drink or several (after all, what other fun were monks allowed to have?) on their way to Bradford-on-Avon, which was a cloth centre. Built of Bath stone, it has a clematis over the porch and one cultivated and one wild hop climbing its walls. Inside it's a cosy and friendly two-bar pub with oak panelling, open fires, a children's room and garden and, amongst other things, old bottles, hunting horns, clockwork roasting spits, two English sabres and assegais, yes assegais, somehow add to the cosy atmosphere.

It's a Courage pub and there's Director's, BA and Best Bitters on handpump with Guinness, JC, two lagers and Blackthorn Cider on draught. To spoil you for choice, there are six malt whiskies and a good selection of wines. The bar food is good and ranges from sandwiches up to chicken and cider curry and a daily Hop Pole Surprise.

The Wheelwright's Arms, Monkton Combe

This Bath stone, Georgian pub was built round its courtyard around 1700. It became a pub in 1871, but there was a fully function-

Bath. And with Beau Nash as Master of Ceremonies, it flourished as a fashionable centre and spa and, in many ways, has done ever since.

For the visitor there are innumerable sights to see, things to do, and places to wander. Good guide books are available. It has also some good and interesting shops. It goes without saying that time should be set aside to investigate this small city if you don't know it, and even if you do.

The walk is however, in Limpley Stoke, upriver or over the hill from Bath. This village has a lovely church, which was built in 1,001 to commemorate a Boundary Pear Tree planted here by the Abbess of Shaftesbury for Ethelred. He had murdered his step-brother Edward (the Martyr) and tried to expiate his guilt by planting seven pear trees. This church is the only Pear Tree church remaining. Used at various times as a stopping-off point for Glastonbury-bound pilgrims and by villagers when attacked by the heathen Danes, this church amply rewards any more peaceable visitor.

How to Get There

By road take the A36 south-east from Bath, Limpley Stoke is on this road (approx $5\frac{1}{2}$ miles). *By rail* to Bristol, on the regular 125. *By bus* the 253 runs regularly from Bristol.

The walk follows the Kennet and Avon Canal along to and over the aqueduct, climbs to Monkton Combe, follows Midford Brook to Midford and returns, over the hill, to Limpley Stoke.

The Limpley Stoke Walk

Hop out of **The Hop Pole** and cross the railway line (still used – so be careful) through the pub's bottom car park. Turn left down between the railway and the River Avon. 'Avon' means, would you believe it, 'river', so at the main road, turn left over the bridge over the River River. The view up and downstream from the bridge is worth musing over, with the two weirs and the river-bank trees hanging over the water, but five minutes musing is all you're allowed – there's plenty more to see yet. Walk on to the next bridge and go left just before it and take the gate on your right to get on to the canal towpath.

This part of the Kennet and Avon canal seems to have attracted more than its fair share of bureaucratic and plain short-sighted blunders. Let me explain. The section on the other side of the bridge had been leaking a little. The Canal Trust, in their wisdom, decided not to repair these leaks with the usual fresh clay-lining; instead they removed all the clay and replaced it with concrete and small walls for the banks. £1m later, the section still leaks and the walls make it much more difficult for a child or animal to get out if they fall in, which seems to regularly happen. In addition, the Trust decided to dredge the part of the canal you'll be walking along. Previously it had been navigable for canoes, small boats, swans and ducks and had healthy, though not overwhelming, growths of water-lilies and rushes. The dredging unfortunately acted just like pruning, making the rushes grow uncontrollably and sadly the canal looks more neglected now than it did before.

Nevertheless, as you turn left along the towpath, you may be lucky to spot a dipping kingfisher or a darting flycatcher and there's still the odd swan haughtily drifting on the shallow black water. Conkwell Wood covers the hill on your right and to your left, in places, you can see the river, the railway and the main trunk road, as you walk along the canal – the valley is indeed rich in transport systems. After the old lock, now with no gates, you can look back at Limpley Stoke climbing the far side of the busy valley.

Walk on past the lock-keeper's cottage and follow the canal as it curves to the left and over the fine, ballustraded aqueduct. It's perhaps not as impressive as the Roman aqueduct at Nîmes, but that wouldn't fit into this valley and this aqueduct does, like a hand in a glove. It's one of those spots ideally suited to watching the sun go down on a warm summer evening, as the views up and down this once heavily-trafficked valley are wonderful and, yes, you may muse here.

Beyond, at the canal basin with its old crane, look to your right, past the white bridge, along the higher level of canal which the Canal Trust has mercifully spared. At the basin, take the little access road to the left which leads up behind Dundas to the main A36, where you turn left downhill. Walk down to The Viaduct Hotel by an astonishing array of bridges. There's the viaduct and two bridges over disused railway lines (one the old Somerset and Dorset railway, the other now a road). The viaduct takes the main road over Midford Brook's valley with the playing-fields of Monkton Combe School below. In fact it's because the school bought the old railway line and made it into a road, that it's necessary for the walker to turn uphill at the hotel towards Monkton Combe and Claverton Down. The road ascends Brassknocker Hill – is there a joke here? – and there are lovely views along the sleepy valley to your left.

At the crossroads, turn left for a leisurely saunter down into Monkton Combe. School pitches stretch out across the valley bottom as the lane takes you through and then round the back of Monkton Combe School, where every pupil seems to be running (to or from something?) Just after the school, you arrive at **The Wheelwright's Arms.**

Having chatted with off-duty teachers escaping the clutches of their young charges, go down Mill Lane which is between the school and the pub. You pass the old 16th century lock-up, incidentally one of the first jails to segregate men from women. Really though, it seems only big enough for one man and one woman or perhaps two schoolboys and two schoolgirls, as a sadistic history teacher hinted to me.

Walk down the path to the right of the sign for the Manor House and the Old Mill, past the Mill (now a carpet factory), over a footbridge, over a now forgotten backwater, along the fenced path and then over Midford Brook, which is, in fact, somewhat larger than a brook. Just after this second footbridge, turn right over the stile along the public path.

This path runs alongside Midford Brook, over a stile, past the waterfall and sluice and past riverside beeches and willows. Follow upstream, until the path is forced away from the bank by an encroaching railway embankment; here, follow the fence on your right as far as the gap in the embankment; through which you pass, to where you can follow the meandering Brook again. When it becomes impossible to follow the bank without falling in, cross the broken stile to your left and continue along the slightly difficult path through the trees. A wooden railing has helpfully been provided for you to grab at the last moment when you thought

►

ing wheelwright's workshop (and wheelwright!) here until 1935. He would usually have worked in collaboration with a blacksmith and a farmer and parts of the courtyard buildings were probably used as a hayloft and for stabling and, to come right up to date, will be converted to B&B accommodation by summer 1981.

The pub's interior consists of one cosy bar with old elm tables, exposed stonework and a large log fire and a small stove. Mr Gillespie, the landlord, has a collection of 'oversize tableware' and old bottles.

Amongst the beers on offer are West Country PA and Wadworth's 6X, both on handpump and Whitbread's Best Bitter on gravity. There's a full range of bar food with home-made pies in winter and home-cooked hams etc. in summer and there are good grills of the steak/scampi/gammon/chicken variety in the evenings.

The Hope and Anchor, Midford

Part of the pub, which was probably built as such, is 300 years old, thereby predating the now disused and filled-in canal which it served and indeed changed its name for. The canal sadly fell into disuse after the arrival of the railways which have in their turn sadly fallen into disuse. And, while the pub was once the haunt of bargees and railway workmen, it's now been left for the villagers and personnel from an MOD establishment close by.

Built of Bath stone, the pub has one long bar with original beams, exposed stone walls and a flagstone floor with a large fireplace at one end and a wood-burning stove at the other. It's warm, welcoming and urbane, yet retains its rural atmosphere.

The assets of this pub aren't only limited to the atmosphere – there's an excellent selection of good beers from all over the country. Draught Bass, Badger Bitter, Eldridge Pope Dorset Bitter, Marston's Pedigree and Marston's Old Roger, from Burton-On-Trent and possibly the strongest commercial beer in the land, are all on hand-engines. Lunchtime bar food is no less impressive, ranging from ploughman's with cheddar or stilton through smoked

►

you were a goner. Anyway try to get back to the bank dry and in one piece. You now walk along the bank for, virtually, a full circle (sometime in the future this will be an ox-bow lake) and again the bank becomes a bit dodgy, so it's best if you climb to the top of the railway embankment and walk along there. When you emerge from the trees, you can see Midford Castle – an inhabited Victorian folly – to your right at the top of the slope. Go on past pig-fields and through young beeches, down a dip where the embankment mysteriously disappears and on. Just before the end where the bridge has been removed, descend a steep little path to the visible garages below. At the main road, turn right, over the Midford Brook bridge to **The Hope and Anchor**, sheltering in the lea of the beautiful Victorian-engineered, and therefore listed, disused railway bridge.

Refreshed and revived, walk back over the Midford Brook bridge, past the removed railway bridge and then immediately turn left up Midford Lane, which leads you for a mile up and down the hill which separates Midford and Limpley Stoke. It's a pleasant, quiet country lane with good views across Midford Valley to Midford Castle which is above and to the left of Tucking Mill and the village of Monkton Combe. It winds on up through woods to the top of the hill and then gradually down past the modern bungalows and houses of upper Upper Limpley Stoke.

Watch out for a gap to your left by a telegraph pole with a street light attached, where there's a public footpath to the village proper. Go up the steps, along the narrow walled path and then down the steps to the main road. Cross the road (carefully) and, slightly to your left, go down the steps on to the lane below. Turn right here and then, by a telegraph pole turn left through the gateway. Follow the path which curves round to the left, goes over a broken wall and into a grassy recreation area. Leave by the gate in the bottom left-hand corner and go straight over the road down a very steep hill. This joins Woods Hill, so if you go on down, you can't miss The Hop Pole. Here, give in guiltlessly to its liquid temptation and friendly warmth.

mackerel pâté, whitebait and scallops to a daily speciality. And there's an à la carte menu in the evening. Enough?

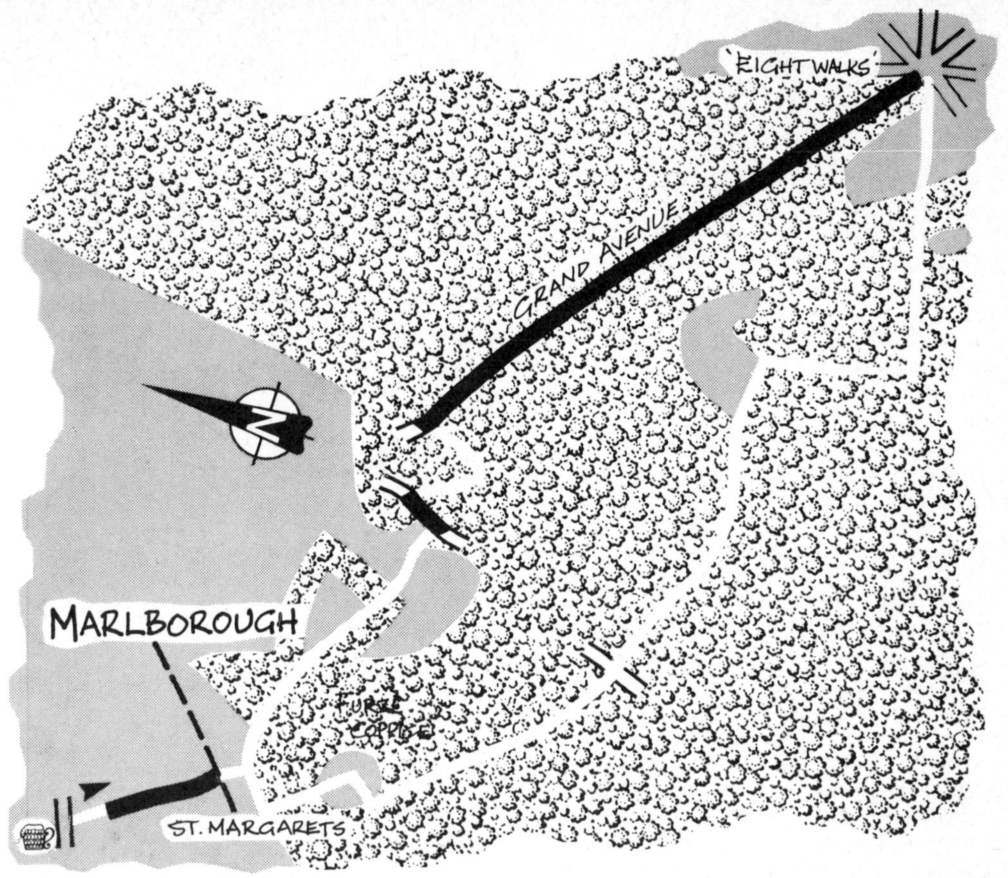

32 Marlborough

APPROXIMATELY 5½ Miles

The District

It seems that the advertisers were about five millenia too late with their slogan 'Come to Marlborough Country', for this area has been inhabited since the old Stone Age and since then, was one of the most populated regions in Great Britain in prehistoric times. Due to its unforested open chalk downlands, ideal for arable and livestock farming, it attracted Stone Age man and a little later continental Beaker Folk, who brought with them their knowledge of metals and metal-working. An area of stone-circles, 'causewayed' camps and henges, it does seem however to be a vast graveyard of former incarnations of the human race. It's littered with long and bowl-shaped barrows both earthen and chambered, all evidence of the elaborate funeral arrangements of these unsophisticated yet relatively civilized peoples.

Elegant Marlborough with its wide and long High Street sweeping through the centre of town, was important in coaching days and earlier, as a stopping place for travellers between London and Bristol. The River Kennet was fordable here and this avoided the bog where the Og met the Kennet (wid ye ken it?). In 1635 the Great Fire destroyed much of the town. This was repeated in 1679 and yet again in 1690 – three times in 37 years seems a fairly poor fire record, though, I suppose it kept the builders happy.

Savernake Forest's 2300 acres date from before the Norman Conquest and contain

thousands of tall and noble beech, elm and oak. Avenues of beech dissecting the forest were driven through by that landscape gardener par excellence. 'Capability' Brown, proving if nothing else that he was capable of using a ruler and compass. In the centre of the forest, Eight Walks is the crossing of eight walks(!), that run N-S, W-E, NW-SE and NE-SW.

How to Get There

By road from the M4 (junction 15) go south onto the A345. Marlborough is at the junction with the A4 (approx 8 miles). *By rail* to Pewsey. *By bus* the 205, 206, 215 and 219 all run between Pewsey and Marlborough.

The walk starts from the St Margaret's end of Marlborough, so named because of Maerl's Barrow to the west, possibly the burial place of Merlin – an old conjuror with stars and moons on his pointed hat. It ascends into Savernake Forest, goes along Grand Avenue to Eight walks and thence to Postern Hill and back down into town.

Forest walks are, by their very nature, difficult to describe – there are very few points of orientation, there are many seemingly identical paths and, due to the fact that you are surrounded by trees, you can get no overview and can easily and often lose your sense of direction (if you have one). Therefore the walk below sticks to paths and tracks marked on the O/S map and consequently may not be as adventurous as you'd wish. In which case, follow the instructions up the hill out of St Margaret's and then roam as and where you please.

The Marlborough Walk

Turn left out of **The Roebuck** along the A4 and turn right up the tarmac path on the far side of Prout's Garage. Passing fancifully named Kainga Tupu, go straight on up Queen's Way. At Five Stiles Road, continue in the same direction up between the houses, to where the path goes off leftish. You cross the wooden bridge and on the far side, fork right and continue uphill with a field on your right. At the line of beeches, which form the perimeter of the forest, the intrepid can put their books in their pockets and pioneering spirit in their hearts and head off to adventures uncharted. Be sure to remember this spot where you descend back down to the pub. For those non-Chindits among you, come with me . . .

At this line of beeches, turn left and follow the track through the trees (!) – some of them have yellow daubs – up to a pavilion and its pitches. Just by the metal garage/shed, fork right and follow the path with a field on your left. The path runs between baby oaks. This is Furze Coppice and coppicing is an old-age method of husbanding woodland. In bygone days, woods were crucial to the economic well-being of the rural community – timber was needed for houses and wood was needed for fuel and things like fences. Coppicing catered to these requirements. A coppice consisted of widely-spaced tall trees (for the timber), with the ground in between covered with smaller trees, regularly cut back to produce long straight shoots (for the wood). A young tree is allowed to replace a felled tall tree. OK, Social History lesson over.

At the picnic-tabled clearing, surrounded by beech, go very slightly to the left of straight across and, at the stony track, go left. You pass a barrier and just after it, turn left, along what is White Road (you'll see no sign – you'll have to take my word for it). This broad track curves left and runs alongside railings and a plantation of pines to its left. You soon begin to hear the roar of the A4 traffic which means you're coming to your next instruction, which is . . . turn right along another stony track, which becomes metalled and curves right and then left to meet Grand Avenue, where you turn right. It's another broad stony track which also becomes metalled and runs dead straight between the two ranks of beech trees, drilled and stood to attention by 'Capability' Brown. One thing you may not notice as you trundle along – it's invisible unless you venture into the forest and look for it – is that you cross the Wansdyke, a great earth wall stretching from near Bristol to the Salisbury Plain and probably used by the Romano-British for defence against the invading West-Saxons.

After about a mile of the singlemindedly straight Grand Avenue, you come to Eight Walks – the eye of 'Capability' Brown's compass. Here you go west, or, treating it as a road roundabout, you take the last exit. This similarly straight track runs between two fields and passes Thornhill Nursery with its Nissen huts on your right. You pass a wooden pole-barrier on your right and then descend slightly. Just before the bottom of this dip you turn right along another pole-barriered, red-arrowed grassy path through hawthorn, silver birch and oak. Just before you reach another pole-barrier, turn left, and at the crossing of tracks and paths go straight ahead, with open ground on your right. This path leads you through more oak saplings to a pole-barrier. Here you go straight across the track – it's White Road again, folks – and on. After a while, at another pole-barrier (where there are barely concealed toilets ahead), you go right and into a clearing.

Turning left, you head across the clearing and take any one of many paths through the trees to the perimeter fence and line of beeches. If you don't meet a fence, then turn left until you come to the corner of the fence, turn right and then at its corner, go downhill. Walk back down the path, over the wooden bridge, through St Margaret's and back to The Roebuck. If, after all this forest walking, you're feeling more like Robin Hood or Maid Marion than yourself, then enter this fair tavern and demand of thine host a hogshead of Strongbow to quaff heartily as ye play a game of 'arrows'. Bullseye!

The Roebuck, Marlborough

You find The Roebuck as you leave Marlborough on the A4 and it stands between the town centre and Savernake Forest. As with many of the pubs in town, The Roebuck was a coaching inn when almost every London to Bristol, and of course, Bristol to London, traveller would have stopped in Marlborough for rest, refreshment and a change of horses. 400 years old, the pub is a rendered building with window canopies. It has two bars with exposed brick walls, open fires and, in the public, original beams.

The landlord, Welsh Michael Carroll used to play cricket for Glamorgan and rugby for Maesteg and Penarth – quite an all-rounder in fact. The decorations in the lounge reflect his sporting interests. Now that he has become a landlord, he'll have to learn another skill. A tradition of the pub is that on New Year's Eve and other high days and holidays, the landlord must climb up to the pub sign outside and kiss the Roebuck's hind-quarters (if that hasn't mixed genders too much).

It's a Watneys/Ushers house and so stocks Ushers Best, IPA, Ben Truman, Watneys Special and Starlight. There's also Guinness, Strongbow Cider and Carlsberg on keg.

The menu is good and includes cottage pie, other pies, pasties and chicken and chips in winter, and salads, gammon and fresh trout in summer. Sandwiches and ploughman's are available throughout the year. There's a fine garden where you can take everything (food, drink, children, dogs etc.).

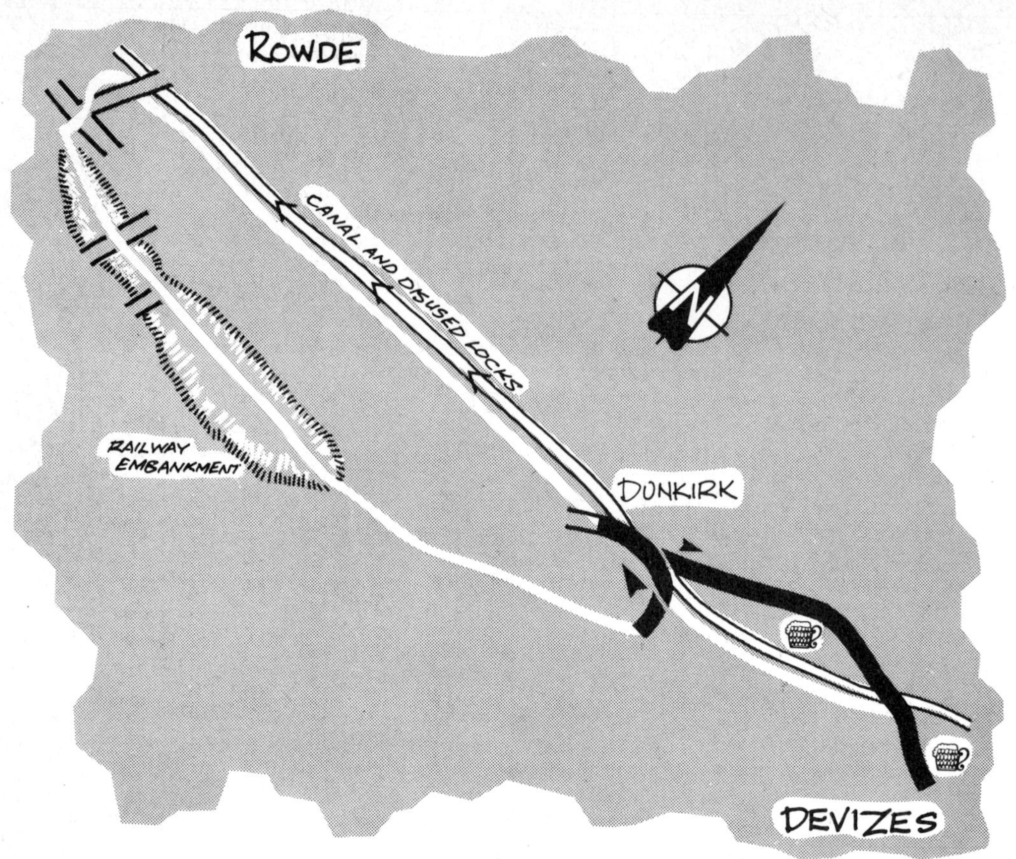

33 Devizes

APPROXIMATELY 3¾ Miles

The District

Osmund, the oldtime Bishop of Salisbury, didn't know what he was starting when, in 1080 AD, he built a castle on the old Roman site of 'Ad Divisas' – or 'on the border'. What he was starting was a settlement which grew up round the castle, came to be known as Devizes and soon became one of the most important centres of Wiltshire, belying its former marginal status.

Devizes has been in the wars a bit since then, notably in 1643 and 1654 during the Civil War, yet remains rich in fine buildings, particularly of the 16th, 17th and 18th centuries. Fortunately, the walk itself is short enough to leave you time to your own Devizes, things you should see include: The Devizes Museum, run by the Wiltshire Agricultural and Natural History Society, which has on show the best collection of fossils and Bronze Age, Neolithic and Iron Age relics in Britain – open Tuesday – Saturday 11.00-17.00; the three beautiful churches of St John's, Mary's and James's; the town hall, the Corn Exchange, the Bear Hotel, the Assize Courts and St John's Alley; the Market place, where in 1753 a trader called Ruth Pearce, while haggling with a customer, chose the wrong marketing ploy in declaring "The Lord Strike me down if I tell a lie!" Whether she had or not, she dropped dead on the spot, an incident which is commemorated by the Market Cross of 1814.

Another local story explains the origin of the term 'moonraker'. As with the Irish, there is a misplaced notion that the people of Wiltshire are stupid. The story goes that during the days of smuggling, a keg of brandy was hidden in the waters of the Crammer, the pond beside St James's church. One night, an excise man came riding by, just as the smugglers were in the act of retrieving it. The smugglers were not slow to react and, no doubt unctuous to please, pointed to the reflection of the moon on the water explaining that they were raking the water for the large cheese. Exit the excise man chuckling – moral; never underestimate the people of Wiltshire.

How to Get There

By road from the M4 (junction 17) go south on to the A429 for Chippenham and then turn east onto the A4 and then right onto the A342 for Devizes (approx 9 miles). *By rail* to Chippenham or Trowbridge. *By bus* from Chippenham catch the 278, 279, 280 or 281 to Devizes (not Sundays) and from Trowbridge take the 276 or the 277 (not Sundays).

The walk takes you from Devizes along the towpath of the Kennet and Avon canal at its nearest point to Rowde. The second half brings you back to Devizes along the old railway embankment. It is a delightful walk but Wellingtons should be worn for the inward stretch.

The Devizes Walk

Top up your own inland waterways with a pint at **The White Lion** where wry Dundonian, Mr Donald, will be delighted to serve you with what he calls, 'the best pint in town'. Turn right out of the pub and walk 100 yards up the road, Northgate Street, to the canal bridge. Cross the road here and locate the steps down to the towpath. At the foot of the steps, turn right and head along the gravelly path with the canal water on your right.

The White Lion, Devizes

This is a pub where it hardly matters whether the beer has travelled well or not, since Wadworths brewery is just round the corner. In any case, Wadworths make all local deliveries by horse and cart and can thus apply close supervision over transportation.

The White Lion was first granted a license in 1568 and operated as a coaching inn for years. Nowadays it is a plain and homely pub with a friendly, open atmosphere. The collection of horse brasses in the bar is 300 years old and one of the largest in the county. There's an aviary in the beer garden out the back and in the bar there's a cockatiel which doesn't speak but makes up for this social failing by being a good listener.

Snacks, sadly unavailable on Sundays, are OK, and you can pit your wits against hand-drawn Wadworths Old Timer, 6X, 10.53 and IPA any day of the week and specially on Thursday, with its extended 'market day' hours. These beers are truly excellent!

The Black Horse, Devizes

The Black Horse stands on the banks of the Kennet and Avon canal. The building is more than 150 years old and was built (for canal workers) only 200 yards away from the old prison. One of the beams in the pub used to actively support hanging, once

You are now beside the Kennet and Avon canal. Walk under a bridge which carries fairly heavy road traffic and head out of town. You are entering a placid landscape where graceful swans float gently past lock-keepers' houses and raucous-voiced ducks sound like klaxons in the peace and quiet.

The Kennet and Avon canal was inspired by the 'canal mania' of 1792, authorised in 1794 and completed in 1810. In its prime, it moved 341,000 tons of goods a year and now it is slowly being restored – from Newbury to Bath there are 57 miles of waterway including this stretch at Devizes. The downfall of the canal came about largely because of the excesses of 19th century private enterprise, when the rival railway operating the same route became too strong for the canal and forced it out of business. Had transport been nationalised, as in other European countries, it could perhaps have survived in a more sensible union of resources. Canals are very practical!

Anyway as you can clearly see, the canal is a triumph of architecture and, as you can't, an engineering disaster, with constant leakage from its porous rockbed. Devizes is the canal's highspot with its marvellous straight flight of twenty-nine locks, 'the most spectacular in England'.

It *is* very beautiful, specially as it abounds with mistle thrushes, swallows, kingfishers and all manner of birds. Dragonflies hover fitfully above the water which is home to frogs, newts, perch, tench, carp (up to 10lbs) and the odd pike to keep them all on their toes. The watery pounds range alongside the series of disused locks (in the process of being restored) and used to stop the water running to waste. Someone told me it used to take a whole day to negotiate the twenty-nine locks at Devizes when the barges used to carry 50-70 tons of goods at prices ranging from 1d a mile for dung and straw, to 3d for corn and flour, the daintier end of the market.

Walk along by the canal till you reach the end of the flight of locks, marked by a tiny hut with an oversize chimney across the water; the hut is about the size of a large fireplace. You can see the village of Rowde

to your right, just before you pass under a broad bridge and turn immediately left to go up the path and a short distance to the road.

At the road, turn right and go to the junction ahead, signposted Devizes and Trowbridge etc. Opposite and across the road is a path up the old railway embankment going to Devizes. Take it.

The railway, once such fierce opposition for the canal, has done even worse in the long run.

Now it is a one track line, a dirt track, with a view to the left of a scrapyard and to the right of agricultural riches. At times, as you proceed, you must leave the embankment where a bridge has been destroyed and removed, to spare British Rail the cost of upkeep, but do climb up the other side of the embankment again. There are a couple of fences to be climbed, too.

Eventually you come to an old footbridge with a fence below it. Cross the fence below where you will find that the mud is deep and strength sapping. Puffing like a train (in the absence of the real thing), chuff along till you go through a metal gate and meet a track. Continue past a second scrapyard which reveals a cross-section of recent and rusting British cars. Lurking discreetly below to the right is a sewage works and a charming valley.

At the end of the track turn left up Webb Lane with the scrapyard fence on your left. Follow the lane to the main road and turn right across the bridge into town. Soon you encounter **The Black Horse** on your right and, if you follow the road which curves right, you will find yourself back at The White Lion. This gives you a chance to decide which *is* the best beer in town!

being part of the old gallows.

Uncluttered, plain and pleasant, there are two bars which are decorated with old photos of barges and barging, a collection of army badges and an ice-axe going up the wall with inactivity.

There are good snacks to be had, but not on Sunday and the beer is good, too. Make the mistake of asking if the beer is good and you provoke complacent mirth among the locals, who bring in huge gallon flasks to be filled with Wadworths Old Timer, 6X and IPA. This is beer engine beer and you can enjoy it by the canal, even if you have to share the garden with a motley assortment of ducks.

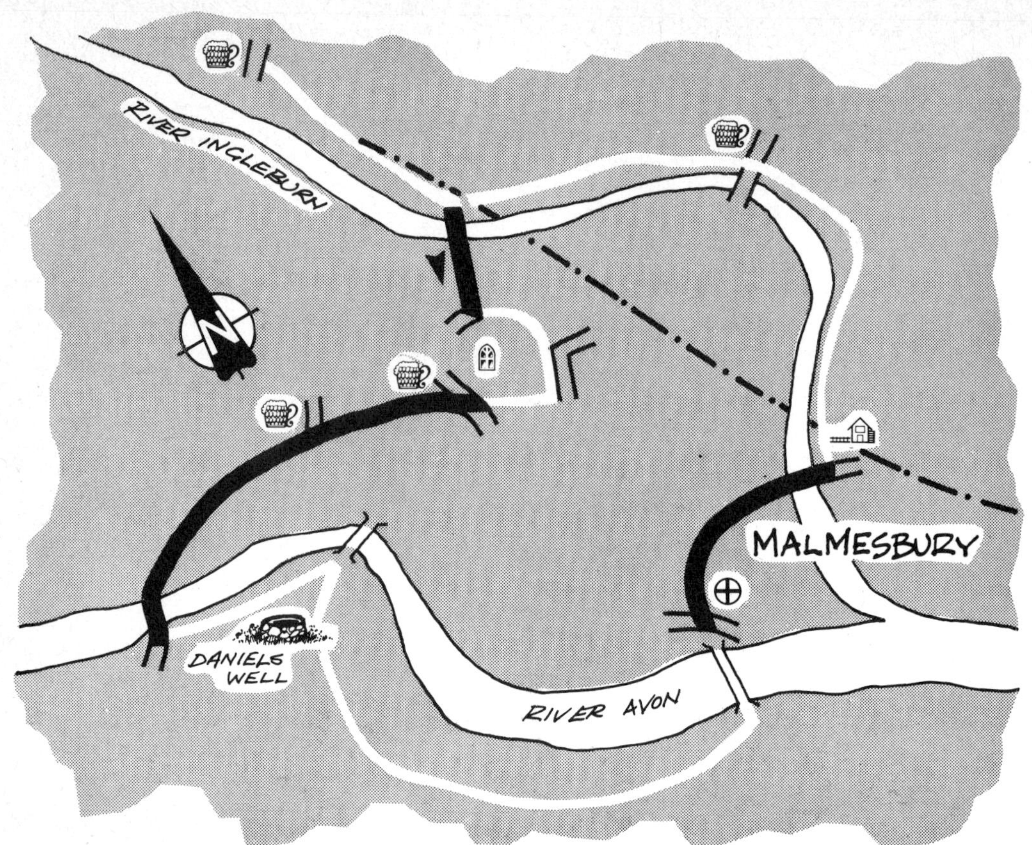

34 Malmesbury

APPROXIMATELY 3 Miles

The District

"The toune of Malmesbyri stondeth on the very toppe of a greate slaty rok, and ys wonderfuly defended by nature . . ."

Whether you're only here for the beer or merely here for the atmosphere, you won't be disappointed by well preserved Malmesbury. Arguably the oldest borough in England (and Malmesburians would argue this to the death), it is a beautiful place whose Royal Charter dates from 880 which we all know was almost 200 years before the Norman Conquest.

Clearly, the warm and winning citizens of Malmesbury are no novices at civic organisation and so it comes as less of a surprise than it might otherwise have done, to discover that this close-knit community, surrounded on three sides by river, has two quite distinct corporations. Unastonishingly these are known as the Old and the New, but before you start pitying the local ratepayers, a little explanation should perhaps be offered.

The first (the Old) corporation goes back to 916 and its powers now largely concern the administration of the King's Heath or common land. The King's Heath is the title of five hides of land granted in 939 to the men of Malmesbury by King Athelstan, first King of England, following their doughty performance in helping to defeat the Danes at the Battle of Badon. This was no short-term gift and the land still belongs to the Freemen of Malmesbury (and will 'in perpetuity'), descendants of the original combatants. However, if you are male and can entice a local maiden into marriage you could become a Freeman, too, as the right may also be handed down through the female line. The history of the corporation is fascinating and well worth investigating.

The second (and New) corporation had a more mundane birth three years after the local Government Act of 1883 which removed fiscal and civic powers from the Old Corporation, yet allowed it to retain its land and properties.

There's not enough space to discuss half the interesting aspects of Malmesbury and its history but let me, instead, tell you the tale of the 'flying monk'. 'The first man to fly' . . . heard it before? . . . well, naturally he came from Malmesbury and was a monk called Elmer (or, some say, Oliver) who had the strange idea that if birds could fly there was no reason why people/monks could not. Ridiculed by his less imaginative comrades and contemporaries – he refused to give up his glorious obsession. Despite a course of psychiatric treatment at Daniel's Well (see below) and the taunts of those who thought he was crazy, he built himself some wings and one day launched himself on a graceful furlong of flight from the abbey tower . . . which ended in his breaking both his legs and being maimed for life. However, Elmer was not to be discouraged and, despite being refused permission for further take offs by his abbot, continued trying to unravel the mysteries of flight till his dying words . . . "if only I'd added a tail". Well, he did . . . to the history of Malmesbury and, no doubt, St Peter has been gracious enough to award him his wings at the great passing out parade in the sky.

How to Get There

By road from the M4 (junction 17) go north on the A429 and then left onto the B4040 for Malmesbury (approx $5\frac{1}{2}$ miles). *By rail* to Chippenham. *By bus* the 291 and the 292 ➤

The Old Bell Hotel – Castle Bar, Malmesbury

Right next to the abbey, with a view of the graveyard, The Old Bell is a fine old building. Wisteria grows cosily on its outside walls and inside you should find the atmosphere warming. Built on the site of a 12th Century castle, it features a number of charming architectural quirks including a gazebo in the back garden. A gazebo is a kind of minor folly, usually 18th century, built for the view it offers.

The Castle Bar itself has leaded windows and a plain unpretentious interior. A coal fire keeps it warm as toast in winter and it is a gathering place for locals and local darts players.

Beers include Wadworths 6X from the wood and hand-drawn Ushers PA. There's also keg McEwans and Ben Truman as well as two lagers. Snacks are extensive and out the back there's a rose garden, where you can take the kids.

The Three Cups, Malmesbury

The Three Cups is an excellent pub by any standards. It is supposedly named after the three earthenware cups once found in the chimney breast although publican Theo Shipway thinks the name may have more to do with the chalices on heraldic shields. The building itself contains the entrance to an underground passageway which leads ➤

run regularly between Chippenham and Malmesbury.

The walk is a simple affair which is designed for all but the bedbound as it follows the lovely course of the rivers Avon and the Ingleburn around the ancient town of Malmesbury. It also takes in four pubs so have some loose change on you. It is a short walk and this leaves you plenty of time to inspect the town.

The Malmesbury Walk

Turn right out of the Castle Bar which belongs to **The Old Bell Hotel.** The Old Bell is built on the former site of Malmesbury Castle and stands right next to the abbey. Whatever your spirits, proceed soberly along Abbey Row till you have passed The Strict Baptist Chapel on your right. You can relax when you get to 'The Triangle' and its war memorial, where you will find **The Three Cups**, a pub I can warmly recommend. However, if you're still feeling the cold stare of the Strict Baptist Chapel on the back of your neck, turn left immediately down Bristol Street.

At the first road junction, turn down left towards Foxley and Norton. The lane here takes you across the Avon on a low bridge, called Turtle or Truckle bridge, after which you branch left as the road swings right. Almost immediately there is a footpath to your left which you attain by climbing a hybrid-style stile. The path follows along the River Avon – ahead is Malmesbury and on your right, up the hill, is the King's Heath – a present from England's King Stan to Malmesbury. (Athelstan to you.)

Lots of geese and ducks quack and waddle around here and you must keep dogs strictly under control – if you meet a duck called Euclid then please return him to the house in town of the same name.

Not far along, just before the old stone bridge on the left, you'll find Daniel's Well 20 yards to the right of the path. This is where 'the flying monk' was placed up to his neck in water by his confrères in an effort to bring him to his senses . . . however this treatment couldn't quench his pioneering spirit. (See above). Notice that water still flows

from the cellar to the abbey and upstairs there is a Dominican priest hole, from which the priests could go quickly into the stables and ride away from pursuers.

Parts of the pub go back to the 13th century and there are two bars, one of which serves excellent, reasonably priced food. The main bar's timbers come from old ships and there is a splendid collection of old farm implements on the wall, including a horse tail-docker, a contraption for making ropes out of corn, cruel horse bits, yokes and a selection of rat and mole traps. At first you think they are tools for torture and on reflection you realise many of them were. The lay-out is spacious and only the surrealist painting by the pool table is out of place.

The beer is Whitbreads. Mr Shipway does not believe in 'real ale', still it's not a bad pint. You can also buy Guinness. There are good snacks on sale, too, and the meals in the lounge bar are highly recommended both for value and taste. Sometimes you must book for an evening meal. In summer there are tables in the car park and if the lounge is not being used children can be left there.

The Duke of York, Malmesbury

The Duke Of York is situated beside the River Ingleburn. It is a wooden building of recent design. There are two bars and a skittle alley.

Keg Whitbread beers including Trophy are available (and Tankard, too). In summer you can sit on the lawn by the river. There is always food available and the specialité de la maison is 'chip butties'.

Three darts teams and seven skittle teams operate from this pub and they're open to challenge any time.

between the stones of the well wall – you have to peer through the rather unmedieval concrete lid. After the bridge you can see the pool, which the water flows to, which once served as the community washing place and is now frequented by squabbling seagulls – and ducks, of course.

Follow the path alongside the River Avon; over one stile, then another and a footbridge just after that. As you wend your way you gain more and more insight into the structure of the town. Another stile and you come to the road – if you move as slowly as the river you'll have plenty of time to admire the view; it may take time, but eventually you'll reach the road.

After squeezing yourself back to normal shape following the severely angled gate by the road, turn left across the pedestrian bridge. The building opposite, marked 'Antiquities and Works of Art', was once a silk mill till it discovered what is, judging by the size of the building, a modern growth industry.

After the bridge turn along quaint old St John Street, the building on the corner is where the Old Corporation meets and again is very interesting to visit.

At the end of St John Street cross the river (now 'the Ingleburn', a tributary of the Avon and only 50 yards from meeting its 'mater') by the Old Goosebridge across which herds of geese were once driven on their way to the water meadows. Just before Wynyard Mill turn left after the bowling green down a path which begins with the bowling hedge on its left. The mill is one of eight or so which once operated with local river power; Malmesbury's wealth grew from its once prosperous weaving trade.

The path carries you over a sluice gate and a stile through lovely country where in summer you can see kingfishers skimming the water. Soon you cross another stile, just before which you can see the start of the old railway bridge on your left. Suddenly the river (or part of it) is on your left and the path takes you to **The Duke Of York**, named after that grand old disciplinarian drill master.

From the pub go to the river which runs past, turn right and head along the bank continuing your previous direction. Notice how the river is incorrectly signposted 'The

The Flying Monk, Malmesbury

The Flying Monk used to be The Railway Hotel till the cuts of 1962 saw the closure of the line between Somerford and Swindon. You couldn't keep calling it The Railway Hotel in such unsuitable circumstances so a poll was held and the name The Flying Monk chosen. It's snappier than The Railway, Commercial and Farming Hotel and Posting House, which was its name when it offered 'Accommodation for Hunters' and carriages were kept out the back.

Nowadays, it's a plain old-fashioned country pub with a long bar, a gas fire and a footrail to lean those aching feet against.

It supplies hand-drawn Whitbreads Bitter Best and Pale to the nearby countryside – if you want the Best, you have to ask for 'Druid's Fluid' and a potent brew it is to be sure. There's also Guinness, Trophy and Mild. Sandwiches are available as are beefburgers, chips, soup etc. In summer there are tables out front and you can play skittles and pool inside. The atmosphere is always friendly and John and Marilyn Somers are welcoming hosts.

Avon' – it's the Ingleburn. The river bank pulsates with life of the chirping and fluttering variety; follow it over a stile, to the right a little and out near a car park. At this point, you can turn left into town but I suggest you go to visit **The Flying Monk**.

Detour: Go straight across the car park and follow the road beyond it to the main road. You pass the forlorn old train shed, a pre-Beeching structure, and a fire station at the end of the road (unfortunately the lads were not around with a tarpaulin in the days of the flying monk). At the junction, cross the road, order a pint of 'Druid's Fluid' and make with the 'readies'. When ready retrace your steps to where you left the path, turn to face in your original direction and await your next instruction. *End of detour.*

Turn left and up the steps in the direction of the abbey. You pass the back of the abbey on your right with its bad case of fallen arches and come out on to the street by the Market Cross dating from 1490. The purpose of the octagonal Market Cross was for 'poore folkes to stand dry when rain cummith' and to judge by the deep imprints made by centuries of bottoms, most of the poor have chosen to sit and a lot of rain has fallen since then.

Turn right from the Market Cross into the abbey yard. Look around the grounds before going into the building. watch out for the gravestone of Hannah Twynnoy who, in 1703, was eaten by a tiger which escaped from a travelling circus; this is not believed to be a common cause of death around Malmesbury. The abbey dates from the 12th century although the original building was established in 640 AD. This later place of worship contains the tomb of Athelstan (though not his body) and much else besides. On the slopes below, the monks had vineyards . . . no wonder Elmer felt he could float. After seeing around the abbey, return to the Old Bell by the gate on your right as you leave the ornate front door.

You won't be the first customers here either, since the building has sections dating from the 12th century. As monks will know, there's a foolproof way of getting rid of surplice cash, an old abbey habit, go to it at The Old Bell.

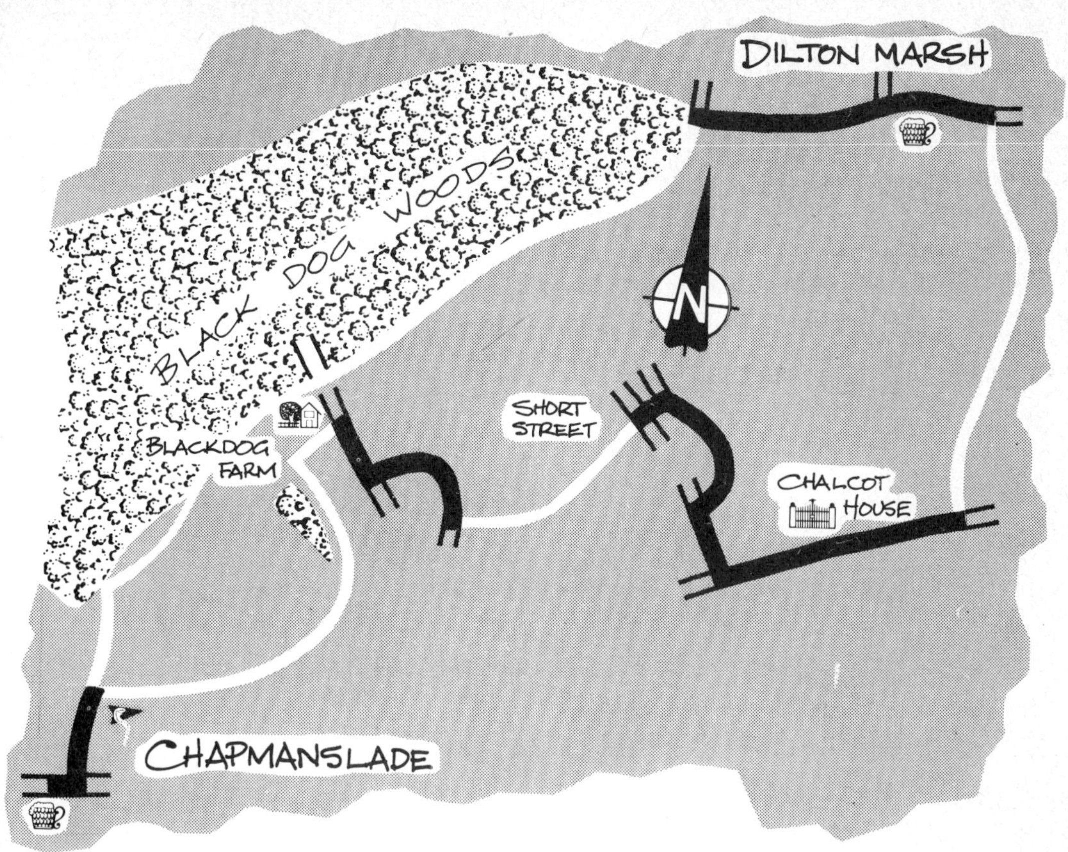

35 Chapmanslade

APPROXIMATELY 4¾ Miles

The District

£53 is what Sir John Thynne paid for the Augustinian priory out of which the first Longleat was built. Fire destroyed this edition in 1567. After a rethink he employed master-mason Robert Smythson to create the Longleat we now see – an Italianate, staggeringly big and consequently revolutionary building. Completed in 1580 at a total cost of £8,086 13s 8¼d, it has been described as a 'work of art, noble, delicate and intelligent.'

The 19th century saw the rebuilding of the North Front by Wyatville, the landscaping of the park and gardens by Capability Brown, the addition of the stables and Orangery and the redecoration of the interior. Italian workers were brought over to Italianise many staterooms with, amongst other things, marble fireplaces and doorcases and marquetry doors. The house contains many works of art – paintings, furniture, velvet from Genoa, leather from Spain, tapestries from the 16th century and wallpapers from China and more.

But perhaps the most interesting, if plainer, part of the house is Bishop Ken's Library dating from the 1690s and remaining largely as it was built. He had achieved notoriety when he was Bishop of Winchester by refusing to let Nell Gwynn stay in that city's Cathedral Close as her relationship with the King was to a man of God, sacrilege. Charles II, however, forgave him and even installed him as Bishop of Bath and Wells. When this principled cleric refused to

swear allegiance to William and Mary he was offered a home here.

However, very often when people think of Longleat, they think of lions. It's justifiably renowned for its Safari Park which contains much more than just lions. The house and estate reward a vast variety of tastes – spend some time here.

But also allow yourself time to look round Warminster and Westbury, both lovely towns, espcially the latter. Both contain good Georgian houses and it's thought that the palace of the Kings of Wessex stood on the moated site of Palace Green in Westbury. If so, that accounts for the White Horse on the hill which commemorates King Alfred's victory over the Danes in 878. Also worth investigation is Cley Hill, an 800ft hill rising impregnably from the surrounding land and not unexpectedly topped with an Iron Age hillfort.

How to Get There

By road take the A36 north-west from Warminster and then right onto the A3098, Chapmanslade is on this road (approx 4 miles). *By rail* to Frome. *By bus* there is an irregular bus service, the 256 on Saturdays and the 247 on Wednesdays, both from Frome.

The walk crosses fields and the A36 to get to Short Street, when it skirts Chalcot House and descends to Dilton Marsh. From here back to Chapmanslade is along the edge of Black Dog Wood.

The Chapmanslade Walk

From **The Three Horseshoes**, turn right down the A3098 and then turn left, just after the Post Office Stores, up Wood Lane, a No Through Road. You walk past pretty ancient and modern houses and cottages. After the last cottage on your right, a white one with no name, turn right through a gate and walk straight along the track that's soon bordered on the right by a line of cypresses. This public footpath takes you through the nursery and from it to your left you have good views over Black Dog Wood to the village of Standerwick and on to larger Beckington on the horizon.

Where the track bends to the left and descends, turn right up to a stile into a field. Here walk along its left-hand edge aiming to the left of the buildings at Dead Maids. Uninterestingly, this name refers to trees not people. But if you squint hard enough, you may be able to see Westbury's 180ft x 107ft White Horse. Good King Alfred had thrashed the bad Danes at Ethandun in 878 and at some unknown date afterwards, the horse was cut to commemorate the victory. Apparently it was cut very crudely because in 1778 the steward to Lord Abington – a man half-appropriately named Gee – re-cut the horse to make it more refined. At one of the gaps in the hedge/fence to your left, descend to the lower field, but continue in the same direction, so that the hedge/fence is now on your right. At the gate in the top corner of the field, go through, back up to your original level and continue again in the same direction (hedge/fence now on left). You walk through the line of tree-stumps and go through the gate beyond the holly bush at the foot of a clutch of four 'dead maids'. Keeping to the top edge of the field, you go through the gateway and at the corner, carefully climb the fence.

Now walk left, down the edge of the trees. At the end of this strip of trees, follow the fence that leads off to the right and, passing through the gap in it, drop down below the bramble bushes and follow the path round the contours of the hill. When you see Black Dog Farm below, walk down the hill, aiming for the metal gate to the right of the buildings. Go through this gate and, having crossed the A36, walk up the verge for 200 yards or so until you see a small, now disused No Through Lane up to your left.

Depending on the complaints of local residents and the persecuting tendencies the local council might have, you will pass a gypsy settlement on this overhung lane. It curves round to the right and just before a concrete wall on your left, take the sunken muddy track up to the left. Follow this, not veering off into fields to right or left. You can see Cley Hill, which has a fort and ramparts, standing high about 4 miles to your right, beyond which lies Longleat and its Safari Park.

Just before the first house of Short Street, there may be a few dappled sheep in the field – their wool is obviously for patterned carpets. You walk through the cluster of houses of this by-passed and grateful-for-it hamlet and straight over the little crossing, where the lane drops downhill. At the junction, turn right and walking along here, you get good views down over Dilton Marsh. The lane curves round under a pink house and then climbs and you can now see red-brick Georgian mansion Chalcot House, which is open to the public one day a year.

At the A3098 you turn left and walk for about half a mile along it. It can be busyish. It's worth climbing the steep bank to get a frontal view of Chalcot House. Turn left down the drive to the House which is marked from the other side of the road as a public footpath to Dilton Marsh. Just before the first fenced cedar tree, turn right over the stile and then walk down the valley floor dotted with oaks, to and over a stile; you pass two old and completely redundant stiles (no fences) to a stile by a gateway. Here strike out diagonally left towards a copse to the left of the council houses. Go over the stile by the gateway into the copse and follow the track, past a row of broken garages to the road. Turn left along it and walk through mostly modern Dilton Marsh to **The Prince Of Wales** and self-congratulation, in liquid form of course, on completing more than half the walk.

Turn left out of the pub and then left along Stormore with its modern and tastefully restored old cottages. Just after the wee bridge where the road bends to the right, go left along the metalled and marked public footpath to Black Dog Farm. The path runs along the edge of Black Dog Wood, so called because it was once the territory of a great, black and devilish dog. More comfortingly to your left, you can see lawns sloping to the little brook with stepping stones.

At white-painted Stormore Cottage, continue in the same direction over the stile by the gate and on to a second stile by a sec-

➤

The Three Horseshoes, Chapmanslade

Built within a mile of a forge (where, I'm reliably told, you got the fourth shoe) and in the centre of this long village on the Westbury to Frome road, this pub almost shouts 'Welcome' as soon as you can see it. One of the prettiest pubs I've seen, it has justifiably won 'Pub Front Of The Year' awards. It's built of partially rendered and Virginia Creeper covered stone, roofed with very old tiles and decorated with window boxes and hanging baskets.

Inside is no less attractive. The bars have open fires in old fireplaces, an old dresser with many plates, a piano, antique-looking tables, pewter mugs and measures and railway prints. It's a warm, snug and very friendly pub.

Paul Halligan stocks Ushers Best and Ushers PA, both drawn by handpump along with Watney's Special, Carlsberg, Holsten and Guinness, all on keg. He also stocks a good selection of wines and eight malt whiskies which would go down well after a winter walk.

Thanks to Mrs Halligan, the pub features in guides for good eating. Her menu, some of which changes daily, includes three starters, salads, grills, casseroles, hot snacks, sweets, seven or eight cheeses and coffee. Everything that can be home-made, is home-made.

A whole-heartedly recommended pub.

➤

ond gate. Walk along the edge of the wood to a gate in the hedge, which you go to and through. You cross another field to another gate, again staying close to the wood. Black Dog Farm is ahead and you aim for it along a muddy farm-track. Go through the metal gate and out on to the A36 where you turn right.

Just after the farmhouse on the far side, turn left across the road and down the track, still (I'm sorry, you superstitious ones) along the edge of Black Dog Wood, though now there are a few of its trees to your left as well. Follow the track along to a fork, where you go left, away from the white house surrounded by trees. The track runs down between fences and takes you to a gate by a small cowshed and yard. Once through the gate, go rightish down the track that goes under and in front of the house. The track dips, then rises and almost meets the wood again, but by now is sick of it and veers away, disgusted, uphill more steeply now. It passes a small reservoir with its floating, waddling and strutting birds, mainly ducks and geese. Go on up the muddy track as it cuts into the hillside. This is the only tough bit of the walk and it's short. You arrive at a gate at the top and climb the stile by it. Go straight on along Wood Lane back the way you came to return to your car and the pub, though not necessarily in that order.

The Prince Of Wales, Dilton Marsh

The county records started 307 years ago and The Prince Of Wales was alive and well then; in fact it was only 40 years ago that it stopped brewing its own beer. Since then it's belonged to many different breweries and this is reflected in the large bar's somewhat contrasting styles of decoration. It was named after Edward II and its bar has a stone fireplace, newish beams and a separate area if you fancy a game of darts.

There's Bass, Worthington E and Best, Toby and Carling lager on keg.

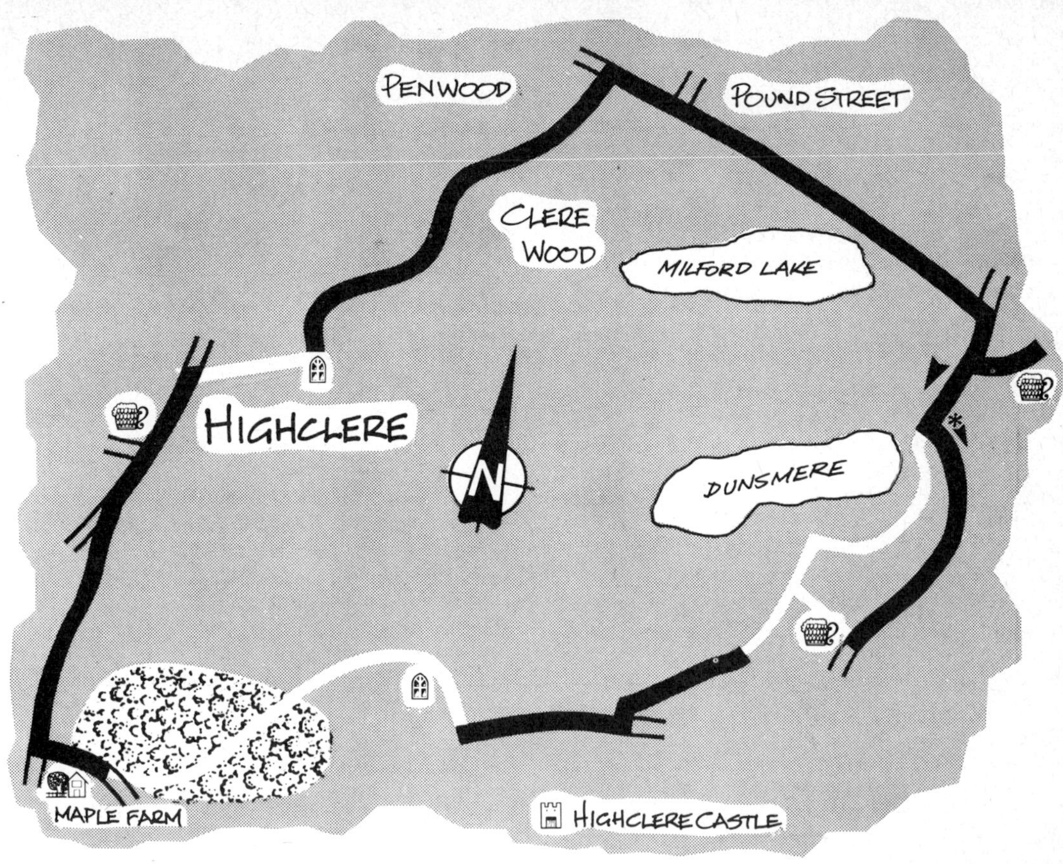

36 Burghclere

APPROXIMATELY 6 or 5¼ Miles

The District

"I came from Burghclere this morning through the park of Lord Caernarvon at Highclere . . . This is, according to my fancy, the prettiest park that I have ever seen. A great variety of hill and dell . . . a good deal of water. I like this place better than Fonthill, Blenheim, Stowe or any other gentleman's grounds that I have seen!"

(William Cobbet, 1821)

The A34 (trunk) from Newbury takes you South along the route of the old Salt road – from the days when salt was essential for storing meat – to Burghclere, a pleasant village which houses the Sandham Memorial Chapel and its collection of nineteen Stanley Spencer paintings.

From Burghclere the walk goes by public footpath from the back of **The Carnarvon Arms** through Highclere Park to Highclere village. The park used to be the site of the palace of the Bishops of Winchester and is now the seat of the Earl of Caernarvon.

Nearby Beacon Hill is part of a ridge of chalk stone which runs to Kent. It is 858 feet high and offers a fantastic view over the downs as you stand on the summit by the Iron Age ramparts which were constructed when all below was forest. Also on the hill is the grave of the 5th Earl of Caernarvon who died mysteriously after leading the excavations of the tomb of Tutenkhamen. Was he a victim of the mummy's curse?

How to Get There

By road take the A34 (trunck) south from Newbury, Burghclere is off this road (approx 5 miles). *By rail* to Newbury. *By bus* the Hants and Dorset 335 bus runs regularly to Burghclere from Newbury but not on Sundays.

The walk takes you from Burghclere to Highclere via Highclere Park and then back along twisty country lanes. It is a fairly long walk but is easy-paced.

The Burghclere Walk

Start at **The Carpenters Arms** in Burghclere; this is just up the road from the Sandham Memorial Chapel where you'll find a collection of Stanley Spencer's paintings, a permanent exhibition you should not miss.

Turn left out of the pub, motto 'united we stand, divided we fall' and walk up to the main road, the A34. At the junction, turn left and walk along the pavement. Ahead of you is a massive gateway decorated with a grotesque, guardian head, as the road twists left. Although marked 'strictly private', I was told that the locals use the gate and you could go through it to get to the Ionic Temple, a Victorian folly overlooking glassy Duns Mere and situated among magnificent yews and woodland. If you do go through, keep strictly to the track. Sadly, it's round about here that the re-routed A34 will go, the Winchester-Preston trunk road, a new prospect for the folly which was remodelled by Sir Charles Berry for the 3rd Earl of Caernarvon in 1838. Follow the track 200 yards past the temple and there's a grassy track up to the left which takes you over a stile to **The Carnarvon Arms** – This is a public footpath which goes right across the sumptuous parkland to Highclere. There's a lot to see at The Carnarvon Arms with its 'De Havilland' connections and the old courthouse beside it, once the smallest in Britain.

(If you don't want to go through the large gate, then you must follow the busy A34 right round to The Carnarvon Arms.)

Take the stile at the back of The Carnarvon Arms and follow (retrace?) the path into Highclere Park with its subtly landscaped grace, it's discreetly placed junipers, yews, cedars oaks and cypresses. At the track, turn left and head away from the Victorian folly. The track takes you by bridge over the lovely mere and then through a gate and over a cattle grid. Follow to the right when you join a well-surfaced road. Up to the left is Highclere Castle, which has a few less windows than Buckingham Palace and was designed by Sir Charles Barry, who did the same job for the Houses of Parliament. This area has been a park since 1320 when it was owned by the Bishop of Winchester; the present lay-out was first worked on by Capability Brown and translated into the present estate by Henry Herbert. These are grasslands with that stately home sweep to them and nowadays there are more pheasants than peasants in the grounds, a massive expanse of park owned by the present Earl of Caernarvon, now aged 82, a popular man in the area. There are plans to open the park to the public, not just the part where the public footpath is.

The track takes you to the estate village, a relic of past feudalism. Turn right at the houses here and walk past the old farm buildings. As the road turns right out of the village, go straight into the cemetery past the delightful old chapel on the left with its family crests. Go down the steps (careful – they're slippery after rain) and when you come to the boundary fence, go left till you come to the gate secluded under trees. Through this, follow the track towards the left-hand corner of the field.

However, as you go, you'll see a gate on your left-hand side – go through this and follow the track uphill into delightful forest land. Soon, just where you have a fine view of the farm's walled garden to the left, there's a choice of three tracks. Take the track to the right and in next to no time there's a plantation on the left – keep following the main track disregarding any imposters which cross it. Watch out for green woodpeckers, hopping jerkily in search of ants and making their 'tew-tew-tewk' noise.

At the first choice of tracks, keep left by the trees, with the ratholes on your right. 100 yards on, fork right and soon you come to a junction of tracks by open fields. Turn right with the ploughed fields on your left; this lane takes you to Maple Farm, which is on your left as you turn right to walk along past woodburning cottages to Highclere Farm and the A34 – this time not the trunk A34 as at Burghclere. At the road, turn right and walk past the sign for Flaxford House School and to The Red House on your left in Highclere's main street.

Turn left out of the pub, then turn right on the other side of the street just after a house called 'Springfield', with a flurry of chains outside it. This was once an old coach road, a fact which is almost impossible to believe since it is so narrow and takes you through a rickety kissing-gate to the church, which you get to by another kissing-gate. Momentarily the landscape seems Norwegian here. The church dedicated to St Michael and All Angels, is lovely. From the front gate of the church, go left past the War Memorial and swing right with the road.

At the triangular junction by the bridge, turn right and walk up the lane past a beautiful farm on the left and along Rhododendron Walk with Clere Wood to the right. Now it's a fair way along the lane to the road junction, where you turn right and walk up to the A34 (trunk). Turn right here, then first left and you're back at The Carpenters Arms on the outskirts of Burghclere, where the walk began.

The Carpenters Arms, Burghclere

The Carpenters Arms stands on Hearts Lane near the old railway bridge and therefore near the chapel which houses the magnificent Stanley Spencer exhibition on the outskirts of Burghclere (which you pronounce 'Berclere' with a Hampshire burr!).

Many dubious tales are told here of the old landlord, Fred Ball, who drove the horse-drawn mail cart from Newbury to Micheldever, ran the village shop (where the present bar is), played host at The Carpenters Arms and still found time to run off with customers' wives. It's possible (but unlikely) that his ghost still haunts the place; certainly his memory does.

There's one bar with a log fire and a plain interior. Over years of evolution, several small rooms have become one big one. The beers are all keg Watneys and Ushers, draught Guinness is also available. Try the home-made cottage pie for good value.

The Carnarvon Arms, Burghclere

There's lots to fascinate you at The Carnarvon Arms. Originally it was a coaching inn, the last stop on the Southampton to Newbury route, and now it refreshes modern travellers along the A34, as well as its regular clientele.

This attractive building has strong connections with the old De Havilland aircraft company, whose history you can glean from the extensive illustrations on the walls. Just beside it is a small building which used to be the smallest courthouse in the country – one of the older regulars used to come to The Arms for a drink as solace after each punitive poaching sentence. What's his excuse now, I wonder?

The two bars are comfortable and there's a good range of hot food. You can get hand-drawn Courages Best and other Courages beers on keg. Out the back, there's a lovely garden with 50 seats (maybe a 100 soon) set amongst apple, plum and damson trees.

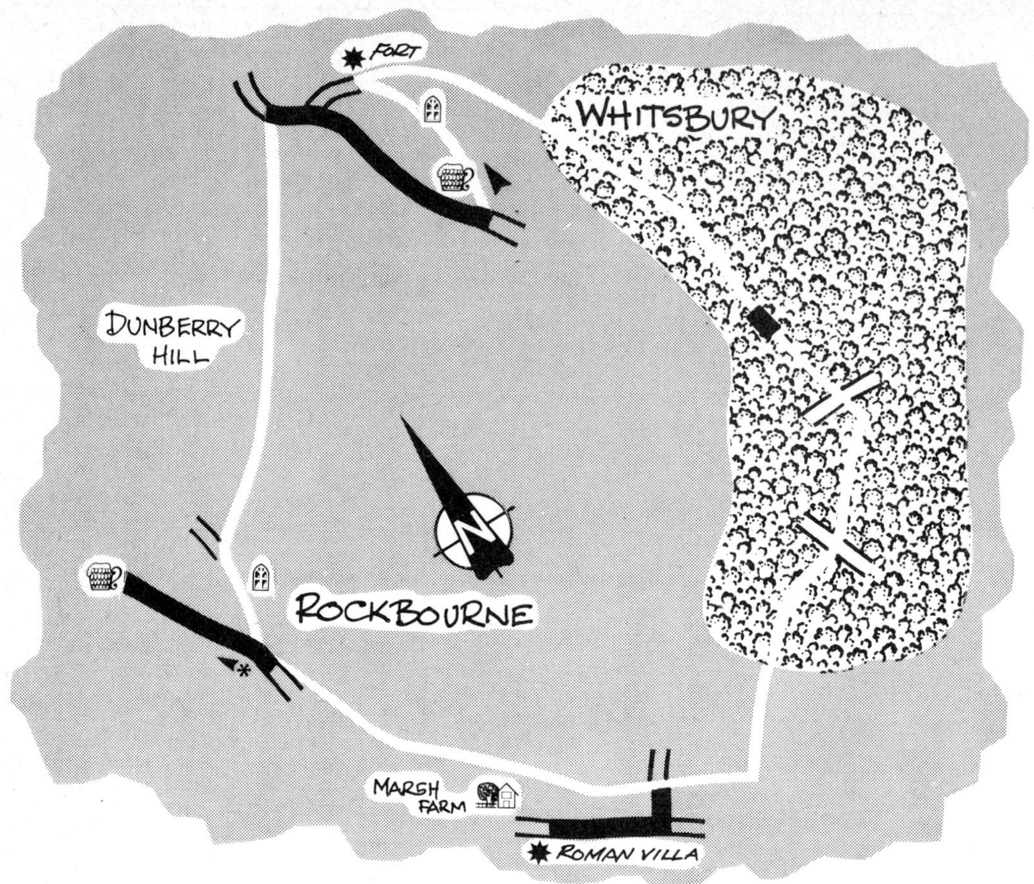

37 Whitsbury

APPROXIMATELY 4¾ Miles

The District

It is written (admittedly, mostly in the guide books) that Salisbury Cathedral's site was chosen almost completely at random by firing an arrow into the air and waiting to see where it fell . . . building commenced on the spot. The background to this event was the years of squabbling between the clergymen and the soldiery of Old Sarum who found their mutual proximity too much and the water supply on the hilltop where they lived too little. Eventually it was agreed that the ecclesiasts should go down to the plains and the foundations for the cathedral were laid in 1220.

Streams were re-routed, roads, re-directed, bridges built and before long the new cathedral was erected at the confluence of four river valleys – the Avon, Bourne Wylye and Nadder. Salisbury became a thriving city, dominated by the power of the church, and in particular by the 404 foot spire (the highest in England) which was added to the building in 1334.

Since then Salisbury has been largely unaffected by the worst horrors of history and has grown graciously in peace. In this city which epitomises 'Englishness', you should manage a visit to Mompesson House, the Cathedral and its cloisters and Close (including pages of the Magna Carta) and the Salisbury and South Wiltshire Museum where you'll find what others found on the sites of Old Sarum and Stonehenge.

Whitsbury is a lovely village in racing

country not far from Salisbury and close to the famous Grimm's ditch. Rockbourne is arguably the prettiest village in southern England and is where, in 1942, a farmer searching for a ferret gone to ground under the village cricket pitch discovered a pile of non-indigenous oyster shells – excavations followed good deductions and revealed a huge Roman villa

How to Get There

By road take the A354 south-west from Salisbury and turn off right onto an unclassified road after 4 miles. *By rail* to Salisbury, then take either X38 or 238 bus to Fordingbridge. *By bus* there is a bus, the 242 that runs between Fordingbridge and Rockbourne, but you will have to walk (approx 2 miles) from here to start. Alternatively try the private bus company, A Herrington coach hire, in Rockbourne.

The walk goes by way of forest tracks to Radnall Wood, then across farmland to the Roman villa at Rockbourne. From here there's a visit to Rockbourne itself and a return journey to Whitsbury by the bridlepath which leads to Manor Farm. It is a delightful and untiring walk for all but dendrophobics, namely those who suffer from fear of trees.

The Whitsbury Walk

Turn left out of **The Cartwheel** in Whitsbury and left again up the grassy track across the road from the nearby telephone box. Rapidly you reach a stile which you must cross to reach the old church by the piously well-worn track running across the field, the old monk's walk. Once through a kissing-gate, you're in the peaceful churchyard of St Leonard's and it's well worth a look at the building before you leave by the gate to the right of where you came in.

The Cartwheel, Whitsbury

Whitsbury, set amongst the chalk downs is a village which has altered. It used to nestle round the old church till a landslide slid and precipitated rapid removals; there used to be a monastery where there are now lots of stables (in fact now there are twice as many horses as people in the village) and there used to be a river where the road now runs. Thankfully the gallows have also gone from the nearby hill.

The pub itself is half old, half new with a lovely old coal fire and sloping beams. There are pictures of locals on the wall, that is the four-legged majority, and the atmosphere is as easy to settle into as the old fireside bench.

You can drink hand-drawn Burtons and Harvest and keg Ind Coope, Double Diamond and Tartan. There's a hidden entrance from the bar to the restaurant where a full à la carte menu is available. The speciality is lasagna, a daily reminder of home for Mr Tegoni, the landlord.

From this gate turn left along the track with paddocks to the right. This is horsey country and you can see why as the countryside slopes gently away into the distance – just the place for riding! When you come to the road, fork right. On your left now are the ancient castle ditches whose origins are shrouded in prehistoric mist. These days they protect a stud farm from prying eyes – no excavations have been carried out here where the thoroughbreds graze.

Swing round to the right with the road ignoring the road for 'Barren and Maiden Mares'. Take the track next right on the far side of the trees, opposite the start of an evergreen hedge. Follow the track along the edge of the trees – on your left is a view over the paddocks and more paddocks which stretch across rich and undulating farmland. When a path joins you from Lower Farm to the left, turn right and go to the far side of this thin strip of wood here you turn left by the paddocks to follow the other edge of the wood (in the same direction as before). The silence here is only broken by the snorting of horses and the tapping of woodpeckers in the trees as the track goes into the wood (it's a lovely neck of them, too!). You must keep right, that's almost straight on, at a junction of tracks. Keep on the public track, here, across Whitsbury Common and keep dogs on leads!

You're walking on the site of Iron Age earthworks. Soon you come to a road, down which you mark 20 strides left before disappearing left on another track under cover of more trees. You pass 'Brides Cottage' and at the end of the track on the right there's a duck pond by a lovely country crossroads. Go straight across the road past the post box to find the 'Donkey Path' through the trees which make up the beginnings of Radnall Wood. This passes laurel bushes and peoples' large back gardens before you have to bend right with the main body of the path. In this delightful setting you may see greater spotted woodpeckers criss-crossing through the undergrowth.

At the road, take the path to the right of the house opposite. This path starts by the power line and is difficult to see at first, but continues into the trees as you keep the fence and the fields just to your right. Near the end of the wood climb the fence to your right and continue in the same direction with the wood to your left till you reach a farm track. From the edge of the wood, turn right and continue for 25 yards, where you'll find an opening on your left into a field, marked with a yellow arrow. Cross straight through the field following a track which goes to the left of a jutting outcrop of trees and then to a stile in the right-hand corner. After a steep and muddy descent from the stile, turn right along the (higher) track which takes you past swaying wheat fields to the road. To your left on the hill is the tall monument to Eyre Coote who fought with Clive in India.

At the road there's another public footpath signposted straight across – but first, for a visit to the Roman villa which is possibly the largest uncovered in Britain with over 70 rooms and a series of mosaic floors – turn left, then right at the main road and then left again and you're there. It's a very interesting site and not at all far from your path.

Anyway, back at the road (where the footpath is signposted), go straight over the stile in the direction of Rockbourne, aiming just to the right of Marsh Farm ahead. Keep off the crops if you can, going to the right of the swimming pool and the white house, to find the next stile across the lane to the left of the bulky hedge. Once over, follow the fence on your right in a pleasant meadow with a stream on your left. The path leads you to a stile on the right, jump it and continue towards Rockbourne past a series of inventive scarecrows flapping warningly in the breeze. Go just right of the electricity sub-station and there's a stile in the corner of the field by the houses. Over this, you soon reach another and then you must follow the road down left into Rockbourne's main street.

At the street turn right and you're in a lovely village set in a hollow in the Hampshire downs with a view over to the Wiltshire hills. At one point nearby Fordingbridge's station was in three counties, Dorset Hampshire and Wiltshire. Many of the cottages are thatched and a clear chalk stream runs like a moat between the cottages and the road on its way to the Avon. Continue to the end of the street for The Rose and Thistle. Opposite the village hall, on the left of the street, there's a path which runs to the church, follow it to find a fine old building which stands on a grassy knoll secluded under yews and above a yard with a view. This site has been a place of worship for 900 years, in fact, since Rockbourne was a royal manor held by King Edward.

From the church go back down the steps across the yard, admiring a remarkable shoe cleaning device on your way, and then straight along the lane passing the wooden house on your left. Turn right at the end of the lane and go past the old Manor Farm with its great barn which is almost 600 years old. The farmyard is stunning. 40 yards on, go up the track between the roads for the bridleway to Manor Farm and Whitsbury. Once through the gate, with pheasant coops on your left, follow the valley bottom straight up the field to go through a metal gate and then another by the thin line of trees. You may see hawks and rabbits playing cat and mouse here or even deer which bound across these gentle hills like racehorses.

Walk up a sylvan avenue, zig-zagging between thick tree trunks and you find another metal gate which you go through. You then come to a wooden gate and finally another metal one where you turn left alongside a paddock on a grassy stretch which takes you past stables and through a white gate, which you must close with dexterity. At the road turn right to walk back to The Cartwheel in the centre of Whitsbury, where you can turn your thirst into fluid movements by the bar.

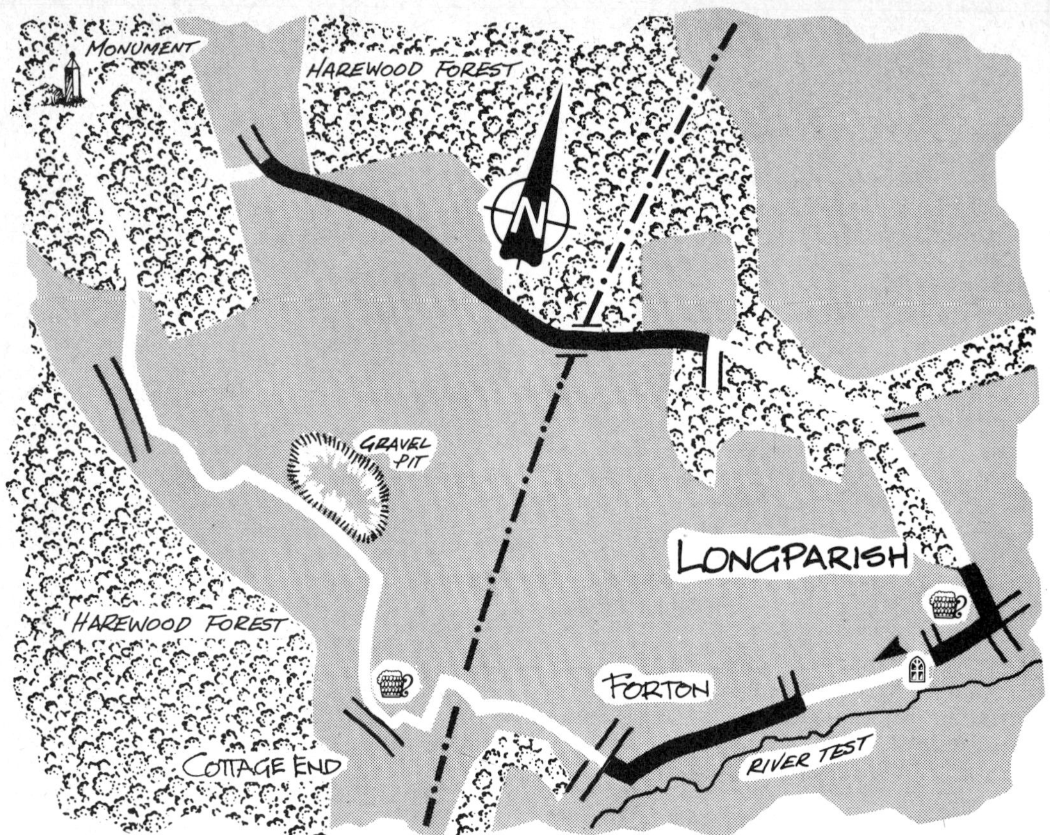

38 Longparish

APPROXIMATELY 4¾ Miles

The District

A story of animal passion that *Ye News Of Ye Worlde* must have carried in the 10th century was the grim tale of Athelwold, Earl of the Forest near Longparish. Yes, not far from Andover, and near a quiet stretch of the River Test, where today local swans swan happily and the neighbourhood's geese and ducks lazily lark at their leisure, a heinous act of regal retribution made the headlines. Hard to believe it now.

Once upon a time in the lovely village of Longparish lived Elfrida, an early Anglo-Saxon Brigitte Bardot, famed throughout the land for her pert good looks. King Edgar the Peaceful came to hear of her appealing exterior and decided to send Athelwold as his emissary to 'check her out'. This was a mission he carried out enthusiastically to say the least . . . to the extent in fact, of marrying her himself and misinforming the King about her and her about the King.

Unfortunately, the King decided to come to Longparish to see comely Elfrida for himself. Hearing of this impending visit, Athelwold ordered Elfrida to look her worst . . . a headstrong lass, she did the opposite, since, she was hardly adverse to the idea of becoming Queen and ruling the royal roost. To cut a long story short, Edgar (the Peaceful?) cut Athelwold short with a javelin in his own neck of the woods and then took the delightful Elfrida in wedlock. All this happened around 963.

A sequel to this sordid tale of lust and intrigue is that when Edgar died in 975,

Elfrida murdered her stepson (his son) in Corfe Castle and set her own child on the throne . . . if only Edgar had known that beauty is only skin deep.

Longparish itself was called Middletune in the Domesday Book when it was a manor owned by the Benedictine nunnery of Wherwell, financed by the beautiful, wealthy and powerful Elfrida in 986. The church here is 500 years old and the main street is one of the longest in England with cottages straggling on either side – perhaps where the name comes from.

There's a public grindstone for local knives and noses and a wishing well for the hopeful. Half a set of stocks by the church's lych-gate reveal a traditional form of justice, and if you're in Longparish at midnight (certain times of the year only) you may see the ghost of the 'the bad monk' who prowls the parish in the form of a black dog with a tom-cat's late night existence,

How to Get There

By road take the A303 east from Andover and go left onto the B3048 through Middleton for Longparish (approx 4 miles), *By rail* to Andover. *By bus* from Andover the X12, 68 and 275 buses operate regularly.

The walk follows the River Test out of Longparish and cuts across fields to The George Inn on A303. It skirts a gravel-pit, briefly follows the main road and then plunges into the northern half of Harewood Forest. Quiet Middleton Lane takes you along the ridge and Sugar Lane brings you back to the start.

The Longparish Walk

Turn right out of **The Plough Inn** and walk along the road. You pass between school pitches and old cottages and it was on this road that the villagers rioted in the Boer War. A Wesleyan cobbler sparked off the incident by delivering an anti-British speech and the disgusted villagers staged a counter-demonstration in the form of a 'skimmity-ride'. Stuffed effigies of Mr and Mrs Kruger were towed round the village at night and held up to public ridicule and scorn, as happened to Henchard in Thomas Hardy's *The Mayor of Casterbridge,*

The road bends to the right and here you go straight on to St Nicholas' Church, passing the stocks, and you enter the churchyard. The church was built in the late 12th ➤

The Plough Inn, Longparish

The Plough has gradually and fittingly developed from the 18th century beerhouse it once was (its first licensed landlord was a farmer in 1838) and is a brick and tile house with a front porch and bay windows. The one bar and the dining room are in keeping with the building's style and date the bar counter has a thatched canopy and is tastefully festooned with Kentish hops. Beyond the car park is a large garden with a lawn, a rose pergola and a herbaceous border as well as a Wendy house that Mrs Colgate, the landlord's wife, played in as a child.

Mr Colgate stocks Pompey Royal and Strong Country Bitters on handpump and Tankard, Trophy, two lagers and Guinness on keg. There's also a good selection of liqueurs, malt whiskies and wines. In the dining room, there's an à la carte menu and in the bar, food ranges from ploughman's and sandwiches to home-made soups and pâtés, salads and a plat du jour. There is no food on Mondays.

The George Inn, on the A303 near Longparish

This pub was quite obviously on old coaching inn in days when the A303 was called the Exeter to London road. Unfortunately the width of the road and the volume of ➤

century and interestingly, St Nicholas 'has more churches dedicated to him than any other Saint not mentioned in the Bible'. The guidebook in the church gives full information on the church but if you are pushed for time, just have a look at the tower clock, and the lovely rush-matting kneelers.

Leave the churchyard through the other lych-gate (opposite the porch) and turning right, walk along between the old barn of Church Farm and the unmoving Test tributary. Pass through the wooden gap in the fence, just wide enough for slim humans – horses, cows and fatties must jump or climb. While you walk along the left-hand edge of the field, Georgian Middleton House is to your right and the River Test to your left. As you near the kissing-gate in the corner of the field you get a better view of the river with its built-up banks almost like a canal. A chalk stream, it is consequently crystal clear. Ducks, geese and moorhen cruise above trout, eel and grayling, descendants of grayling brought here from Italy by a monk. Go through the kissing-gate and walk in the same direction along the lane between hedges of yew and beech. Where the road opens out, you pass an old mill or fishery (I'm not sure which) with its 'Private – Poisonous Adders' notice and the peculiar wooden house with mullion windows and a tall brick chimney.

You now follow the lane through very English Forton. Its brick cottages look a little more robust than its wonky and distorted, black and white timbered ones. Almost every cottage is thatched; in fact, there's even a thatched dovecot on your left. Soon the road swings right and you can hear the roar of the A303 in the distance. You now head towards that roar.

At the junction, go straight across and, aiming for the gap in the treeline on the ridge, head half left on the strip that runs through the middle of the field. At the track at the top, go right and just after the wooded disused railway-line, turn left down the edge of the trees. You then turn left along the line of telegraph-poles and climb over the stile into **The George's** garden. When you leave the pub, turn right along the A303 and then right into the Little Chef's car park. Climb the stile to your left and walk up the track on the left of a line of trees and bushes.

Just before the gravel-pit, turn left leaving its grassed heaps and ridges on your right. Walk round to the far end and a few yards after you begin to climb to the crest of the ridge, turn left across the field towards the gap in the trees, bushes and fence. Go through this gap and then follow the edge of the wood ahead round to the left i.e. towards the A303. Keep to the edge of the field and follow it round under the edge of the wood. When you reach a broken stile leading into the wood, turn left across the field down towards a gate by the A303. On the far side of the dual carriageway is the bulk of Harewood Forest, but we don't enter that section. Instead turn right along the verge for 200 yards or so and then turn right down the marked public footpath and along the avenue of beech trees, the haunt of squirrels. The track becomes concreted and, on the right, you may notice Wilma's personalised seat, hand-carved with a chain-saw in 1980. The track continues through oaks, silver birches and a few beeches. At the fork, go left and at the next fork (these are main tracks), go right. Look out for a tall cross in the trees on your right. When you see it, go for it. This monument was erected in 1826 in Dead Man's Plack Copse to mark the scene of King Edgar's crime, the murder of Athelwold.

When you've deciphered the inscription, continue along the path behind the monument and follow it as it wiggles and winds through the trees to meet a track, where you turn right. Where a track forks right, go straight on to a crossing of tracks. Here, go left. Go straight over the next crossing and follow the now gravelly track downhill. In the valley, it meets what is Middleton Lane, though you don't know that. Turn left along it and follow it for some way as it initially climbs and then runs along the ridge with an almost solid wall of silver birch across the field to your left. As you look down the valley to your right you can't quite see Forton but on winter evenings you can see its cottages' chimney-smoke.

After a while the lane dips by a pig-field and then rises to cross the disused railway-line. Walk on past the efficient-looking buildings of Middleton Park Pig Farm and where the road bends to the right, go straight on along a broad track. Through the trees to the right, you can see a field like an army camp for pigs with hundreds of pig-size Nissen huts. If *Animal Farm* were to really happen, this is where. At any rate, if you walk by when the farmer is doling out the evening bales, your ears are assaulted by the frantic and incessant squealing of hundreds of pigs – quite a sound. It was near here, though I think in pre-pig days, that Longparish's very own hermit lived. Old Dick Brackstone lived in two caves with only an owl for company. He tamed snakes.

The track dips and to your left, there's a beautifully contoured field. At the bottom, you turn right on the far side of a strip of trees along a muddy track, known as Sugar Lane. This was due to sugar smugglers who turned off the road through Longparish and came up this lane to hide in the woods and thereby avoid the clutches of the law. However, in their haste, they spilled most of their contraband and the lane's had a name ever since. Follow it down to where it meets the road through Longparish. The little brook here couldn't be clearer as it disappears under the road on its way to the Test. Turn left along the road back to The Plough and refreshment.

traffic has increased as a wartime photo in the bar shows. There were two little cottages next door, where the execrable but, I suppose, convenient Little Chef now stands. The pub is painted bright orange – breweries have very odd ideas about the pastel colours they use – but despite the drawbacks, it's a very friendly, if plain, pub run by optimistic Steve and Maxine Allen. They say that there is a youngish ghost who walks about the back of the pub wearing a top hat and crumpled clothes.

There's Strong Country Bitter on handpump with Tankard, Trophy, Heineken and Mild on keg. There's also a goodish range of liqueurs, Maxine's favourites. She produces a good menu which includes pâté, steak, gammon, scampi, plaice, a seafood platter, pizza, pies, salads, curries and various sausages, burgers and eggs.